Winner of the Jules and Frances Landry Award for 2017

NEW ORLEANS CARNIVAL BALLS

THE SECRET SIDE OF MARDI GRAS 1870-1920

JENNIFER ATKINS

LOUISIANA STATE UNIVERSITY PRESS BATON ROUGE

Published by Louisiana State University Press
Manufactured in the United States of America
FIRST PRINTING

Designer: Barbara Neely Bourgoyne
Typeface: Adobe Garamond Pro
Printer and binder: Sheridan Books

Portions of this book first appeared in "'Using the Bow and the Smile': New Orleans Mardi Gras Balls, Grand Marches, and Krewe Court Femininity, 1870–1920," *Louisiana History* 54 (2013): 5–46, and are used with permission of the editor.

LIBRARY OF CONGRESS CATALOGING-IN-PUBLICATION DATA
Names: Atkins, Jennifer, author.
Title: New Orleans carnival balls : the secret side of Mardi Gras, 1870–1920 / Jennifer Atkins.
Description: Baton Rouge : Louisiana State University Press, [2017] | Includes bibliographical references and index.
Identifiers: LCCN 2017009683| ISBN 978-0-8071-6756-4 (cloth : alk. paper) | ISBN 978-0-8071-6757-1 (pdf) | ISBN 978-0-8071-6758-8 (epub)
Subjects: LCSH: Carnival—Louisiana—New Orleans—History. | Balls (Parties) — Louisiana—New Orleans—History. | Ballroom dancing—Louisiana—New Orleans—History. | Social classes—Louisiana—New Orleans—History.
Classification: LCC GT4211.N4 A75 2017 | DDC 394.269763/35—dc23
LC record available at https://lccn.loc.gov/2017009683

For David

CONTENTS

ACKNOWLEDGMENTS xi

Introduction 1

ONE
"Vive La Danse!"
Balls and Mardi Gras in New Orleans History 10

TWO
"A Most Brilliant Assembly"
Preparing for the Ball and Choreographing Class 30

THREE
"The Age of Chivalry Is Not Passed and Gone"
Tableaux Vivants during Reconstruction 55

FOUR
"A Strange and Silent Group"
Courtly Grand Marches and Quadrilles
in the Gilded Age 91

FIVE
"The Very Maddest Whirlpool of Pleasure"
Ballroom Dancing in the Progressive Era 124

Conclusion 153

APPENDIX 163

Table 1: Popular Carnival Court Families, 1870–1920 163
Table 2: Carnival Court Family Dynasties in Old-Line Krewes
and Tableaux Societies, 1870–1920 171
Table 3: Old-Line Krewe Seasonal Themes, 1870–1916 172

NOTES 179

BIBLIOGRAPHY 215

INDEX 235

ILLUSTRATIONS

The Triumph of Epicurus, engraving of Comus' 1867 parade 20

Rex's throne room, 1897 25

Proteus invitation to "Legends of the Middle Ages," 1888 34

Female guests at the 1899 Proteus ball 47

Women attending an old-line ball in full dress 49

Helen Rainey, 1905 Comus queen 52

Comus' 1873 grand tableau, "The Missing Links" 70

Krewesmen and guests mingling at Comus' 1873 ball 71

Final tableau for Comus' 1870 pageant 79

"Louisiana," 1899 Proteus costume design 84

"Plenty" and "Liberty," Proteus costume designs from 1899 87

Emily Poitevent, 1895 queen of Comus 108

Alice Aldigé, 1907 queen of Proteus 113

Les Mysterieuses tableau 115

"Emblem of the Mysterious" 117

Quadrille, 1822 119

Comus dance card, 1881 129

Proteus dance card, 1906 130

"The Castle Walk" 147

ACKNOWLEDGMENTS

I am indebted to many colleagues for their advice and support in the evolution of this book. Special thanks to Tricia Henry Young, Sally R. Sommer, Suzanne M. Sinke, Rachel Carrico, Shelley Manry Bourgeois, and Gianna Mercandetti, who provided insightful feedback at different stages of the manuscript. The biographical sketches compiled here would not be possible without the incredible sleuthing of Nikki Caruso. I am also grateful for the incredible assistance provided throughout the years by Lucy Escher Kahn, Anna Patsfall, and Bhumi Patel. Additionally, my archival experiences have been unparalleled, in great part because of the archivists, librarians, and curators who have guided me: Amy Baptist, Pamela Arceneaux, John Magill, and Rebecca Smith at the Historic New Orleans Collection's Williams Research Center, as well as Leon Miller and Sean Benjamin at Tulane University's Louisiana Research Collection. Finally, thank you to my brainstorming krewe: Hannah Schwadron, Ilana Goldman, David Atkins, and the littlest one—my Rose. Each one of you has kept this book alive and moving forward. Thank you.

NEW ORLEANS
CARNIVAL
BALLS

Introduction

During New Orleans Mardi Gras festivities in the latter half of the nineteenth century, lavish balls were the culminating celebration of public parades for the oldest Carnival organizations, called old-line krewes.[1] Scholarly attention surrounding New Orleans krewes and Mardi Gras has focused on publicly staged street parades, and historians have argued that the place where krewe tensions, traditions, and frustrations played out was mainly in this arena.[2] However, the Carnival balls (alternately known as *bals masques*) that immediately followed parading were also crucial krewe events. It was in the ballroom theater that krewe traditions and identities were reinforced. As members moved through carefully prescribed behaviors and dances, their tensions and reconciliations were formalized.

Old-line krewes were elite, white, all-male organizations (most established in the 1870s) dedicated to producing spectacular Mardi Gras celebrations consisting of a seasonal public parade, masking, and a private grand ball. The oldest, most prestigious clubs—the Mistick Krewe of Comus, the Krewe of Proteus, the Knights of Momus, the Twelfth Night Revelers (TNR), and the civic-minded Rex—reigned over Mardi Gras.[3] Reigning was quite literal. Each krewe selected a core court: a secret king and dukes along with a debutante queen and maids. The men paraded solo, however. Old-line parades featured huge, brilliantly designed floats on which krewe members costumed as fantastical characters rode above the crowds. Both the floats and the costumes were designed around a theme chosen anew each year by the krewe. A theme such as "Dreams of Homer" or "The World of Audubon," for instance, acted as the consolidating idea and style for that year's festivities, even serving as material for tableau performances at that night's ball.[4] After the parades wound their way through New Orleans' streets amid throngs of spectators, the krewesmen would enter the ballroom to spend the evening socializing, being entertained, and dancing—the zenith of krewe celebrations. Here women joined in the festivities as guests and participated as part of a mock royal court, complete with promenades and special dances. Krewesmen masked as utopian visions of themselves at the ball and carried with them the weight of their group's identity. These performances were for krewe eyes only. This was the secret side of Mardi Gras.

For old-line members, Mardi Gras rituals, especially private balls, conveyed significant information about their place in the world around them. To krewesmen, Carnival "play" was intensely serious.[5] This outlook stemmed from the fact that old-line krewesmen dominated New Orleans cultural affairs and business endeavors before the Civil War even though many of them were northern transplants living in New Orleans for only a few years or a single generation.[6] Despite their northern roots, old-line krewesmen fought in the Confederate army (or served as blockade-runners for the Confederates) and supported nativist, conservative Democrat politics.[7] Not surprisingly, these men lost power in the ensuing Radical Republican government installed in Louisiana during Reconstruction. In attempts to reclaim a feeling of social status and dominance and to minimize the chaotic change they were experiencing, krewesmen retreated to the clandestine workings of their Carnival clubs. There they scripted a romantic image of the Old South, and in doing so, they drew on genteel mores while they masked as gods, kings, and modern-day knights.

The krewe's "ballroom" signifies more than a place: It was also a ritual, a performative ceremony where complex social choreographies inscribed status, power, and identity. The manners and deportment that kept the ballroom running smoothly were distillations of socially constructed actions that translated cultural values into physical movements. Beautifully costumed krewe members executed rehearsed movements that displayed their elegance, body control, and command of appropriate codes of deportment, whether proceeding through a formal tableau presentation or dancing a popular quadrille (a European square dance that emphasized stateliness as dancers moved through interchangeable, geometric patterns). Ballroom protocol was dictated down to the smallest details—an 1889 etiquette manual outlined eight distinct movements and seven shifts of body weight to properly perform a simple curtsy. Curtsies for women and bows for men were often part of salutations at a nineteenth-century ball and in social outings. They were, as William Greene wrote, "the criteria of good breeding."[8] For urbane New Orleanians, these choreographed and dancerly ballroom behaviors embodied and maintained important codes of civil behavior and reflected their perspectives about the world around them. The significance of these ballroom rituals is highlighted by an infamous dispute between two old-line krewes.

Mardi Gras night in 1890 was marked by conflict. The Mistick Krewe of Comus, New Orleans' oldest Carnival organization, prepared for a glorious return to parading after a five-year hiatus.[9] Comus had everything in place: floats were designed and built; costumes were tailored for its secret, all-male membership; the reigning Comus for that year had been clandestinely selected and masked while the queen and royal attendants prepared for the evening ball; the horses were saddled so that the krewe's leader, the captain, and his advisory board of krewe members could lead the parade. As they had for so many years past, the krewe of Comus assumed they would stage the last parade and ball of the season—the highest mark of Carnival status. During the five-year hiatus, however, the Krewe of Proteus had taken Mardi Gras night for its own parade and ball. In 1890, when Comus announced that Proteus would have to return to its old spot on Lundi Gras night (the day before Mardi Gras), Proteus refused. The krewes subsequently proclaimed they would both take to the streets on Mardi Gras evening with their retinues of costumed, masked men on horses and floats. Proteus kept the illustrious French Opera House for its postparade ball, while Comus was resigned to the Grand Opera House. "Unless something is done," the *Times-Democrat* noted, "there will be a jarring rivalry, which will mar the pleasure of the thousands who come to visit us during the gay Mardi Gras season, and of the people of the city as well."[10]

When Mardi Gras night came, the Comus and Proteus parades happened to intersect on Canal Street, blocking both krewes from proceeding. Mardi Gras came to a standstill. Canal Street was an important marker delineating the American from the European sectors of the city, and it was the place where the most spectators gathered. On Canal, the parades went up one side of the street, crossed over the "neutral ground" (the New Orleans term for median), then paraded down the other side. From there, they turned off the busy public thoroughfare and disappeared into the French Quarter, the oldest area of the city where krewes staged their private Carnival balls. It was here, at the crossroads on Canal Street, where Comus and Proteus, in their determination to outstrip each other, turned the parade into an angry public standoff.

Seeing what had happened, each krewe's captain rode into the middle of the gridlock, where a heated discussion ensued. According to accounts of the argument, a masker from the crowd—incidentally, a member of both Comus and Proteus—finally intervened and led the mounted captain of Proteus away from his adversary. Comus and his krewe passed on into the French Quarter, and Proteus followed. Although disaster was averted, the crowds had already begun choosing sides, forcing members of both krewes to restrain jostling bystanders. To the public that night, and to the historians who documented the event, the acquiescence of Proteus to Comus seemed to end the debacle. The conflict was not over, though. In true New Orleans tradition, the battle would be resolved in the ballroom.

The Comus/Proteus conflict put Rex (a third prestigious krewe) into an etiquette bind. Traditionally, Rex's captain, along with the reigning king and queen and courtiers, left his own ball at midnight to visit the Comus ball. There, Comus and Rex leaders promenaded around the ballroom in a double grand march and then retired to a private supper to celebrate the close of another glorious season. This was the tradition. However, Rex began to visit Proteus during Comus' absence. Now that both krewes were active, Rex had to choose between Comus, the oldest, most prestigious krewe, and Proteus, the new friend. Rex decided to honor his allegiance to Comus by visiting his ball first (thereby showing preference), then leaving to bestow a visit to Proteus.[11]

Rex and his queen arrived to applause at the Comus ball. They participated in several rounds of toasts, then bid Comus and his friends good-night. When Rex arrived at the Proteus ball, however, the reigning Proteus (claiming illness) slighted Rex by refusing to greet him. Rex left, infuriated and offended. Never had such rudeness been seen, especially at the Carnival ball, the most prominent social event of the season. Carnival balls were special events where prestigious New Orleanians exhibited their best behavior and manners; the balls were direct reflections of krewe refinement, honor, and general worth. Long tied to ideas of status and respectability, social dance was inextricably twined with manners and conviviality. Social standing was determined by ballroom behavior, where propriety, decency, restraint, and decorum dominated expectations. Dance patterns, partnerships, and physical relationships allowed the krewe to express its best ideals. This time Proteus had stepped over the line.

By 1892, tensions had subsided, and the krewe balls, for a time the site of further bickering, became realms of peaceful solutions. Rex resumed his midnight visits to Comus' ball, and Proteus recommenced its parade on Lundi Gras night, allowing each krewe to attend the other's ball. As guests of honor, Comus, Proteus, and Rex toasted one another, entertained one another, and danced with one another, thus ending their bitter fight with waltzes and wine. Ultimately it was the Carnival ball tradition, with its insistence on composed bodies, attitudes, and the display of refined character that restored order among the krewes. The enforced civility and etiquette of the ballroom was the de facto court where the dispute was resolved. Dancing bound the groups together in harmony as dancers worked together, physically moving through space as partners, drawing on formal elements of dance (upright carriage, geometric floor patterns, courtesy and respect in gentle embraces) to generate a sense of being in sync that likewise reflected their social compatibility. Once the etiquette of the ballroom had been reestablished, krewes again became tranquil and reinvigorated interkrewe sociability by participating in each other's balls as guests. The esteemed Carnival ball was a kind of microcosmic model of krewe activities that revolved around the maintenance of the power and values of elite New Orleanians.

Inspired by my own training as a dance historian and supported by a large body of scholarship from performance studies, dance studies, ethnography, and anthropology that positions dance as a cultural template, I argue that the relevance and identity of old-line krewes are revealed through their dancing bodies. This relationship between identity and the body in motion is based on a fundamental premise: that dance both reveals and asserts social values and cultural attitudes. It can reflect and reinforce what already exists or act as a medium of change. Dance often comments on the values and beliefs that shaped it, "sustaining them or undermining them through criticism of institutions, policies, or person-ages," as anthropologist Judith Lynne Hanna notes: "Thus action and awareness merge."[12] Movement, as dance scholar Cynthia Jean Cohen Bull argues, "emerges from the intricate process of living in society."[13] Iron-ically, dance is often overlooked as a source of information regarding social construction; indeed, it has been long overlooked as a serious subject of scholarly investigation in general. Dance and movement, however, encode sociocultural and political environments into movement and patterns and thus offer rich sites for analysis. As ethnographer Deidre Sklar theorizes, movement is a form of cultural knowledge: "The way people move is more than biology, more than art, and more than entertainment. All movement must be considered as an *embodiment* of cultural knowledge, a kinesthetic equivalent, that is not quite equivalent, to using the local language."[14]

Fundamentally, dance teaches people how to behave within a specific group setting (whether in social, religious, or theatrical contexts) because it contains predetermined protocols or traditions by which people agree to act. The principal customs of dance practices, then, enable men and women to emulate sociocultural expectations, such as gender-specific interactions that become a part of courtship (waltzing, for example). Engaging in a waltz crystallizes social skills on the body, emphasizes interdependent but cohesive teamwork among couples, and demands a constant communication—and adaptation—of bodies and temperaments through space and time. Waltzes, like all other dances, are dialogues that simultaneously contain the com-plexity of ideals and reality. Dance shows us where and how we belong in society and functions as a way for people to experiment with social values. Conversely, dance is also a stabilizing agent and can operate as a means to maintain the status quo: "When change threatens social values and customs, dance can be a conservative force; through traditional forms of dance, indi-viduals may affirm time-honored ways of relating to their neighbors, their institutions, their gods. . . . [B]y dancing in a socially approved way with their peers, individuals proclaim their allegiance to society as a whole—or at least to the values that their subdivision of society holds dear."[15]

This book explores human motion as a site of important sociocultural information and specifically focuses on movement traditions *considered to be dance in their own historical context.* For instance, tableaux vivants (literally "living pictures") relied on meticulously crafted poses to re-create staged renditions of paintings or a story brought to life. They were performed as "theatrical" parlor entertainments, but they also were the choreographic foundation for Delsartean performances (one of the most popular Gilded Age dance practices of affluent Americans).[16] While waltzes, ragtime dances, quadrilles, and one-step partner dancers were widely popular during this time and are easily recognized as belonging to the current dance canon, orchestrated walking and other highly codified movements figured just as prominently into the movement vocabulary of nineteenth-century ballroom protocol. These movement practices, like their "dance" counterparts, were embodied expressions of identity and shared cultural values. As such, they are as germane to this study as a complex quadrille figure. In fact, bows and curtsies (and in the late nineteenth century, grand marches) were movements significant enough to appear in almost every published dancing manual between 1700 and 1930. Likewise, the rituals and preparatory systems surrounding these activities are also crucial elements of interpreting cultural history. In this way, the rules and codes that define Carnival, from planning a Mardi Gras season to getting ready for a ball, act as choreographed strategies and contribute to a dance-centric understanding of the past in relation to the overall zeitgeist of Carnival ball environments.

The following chapters explore these themes and approaches by looking at old-line krewe Carnival balls from 1870 to 1920. The focus is primarily on balls staged by Comus, Proteus, and Momus, since they regularly produced *bals masques.* These events were held in theaters that the krewes converted specifically to retain a stage area while creating an extremely large space dedicated to dancing by laying a parquet floor over the orchestra seats. The Twelfth Night Revelers (TNR) followed the same general format, but organizational troubles led to many closures and revivals; hence that group is cited less frequently in examples provided. Rex also receives less attention due to its semi-civic nature. The identity of Rex, the king of Carnival, was shared publicly each year, and Rex's balls were more akin to a regular society ball of the time—the focus was on ballroom dancing throughout the evening, interspersed with socializing, eating, and drinking. The Rex organization was unique, however, in featuring its krewe court in a separate throne room at the ball. There they "held court" with guests, thus setting them apart from other American society gatherings of the time.

Chapter 1 examines the historical roots of dance in New Orleans' Mardi Gras and the emergence of old-line krewe carnival balls. Chapter 2 discusses the preparations made for old-line balls and the displays of class identity infused into such rituals. The remainder of the book follows the format of the balls themselves. Chapter 3 explores the choreographed tableaux that were performed onstage at the opening of the balls. Tableaux depicted krewe concepts of manhood through costumed performances illustrating the great men of history (both real and mythological). After the tableaux came the formal presentation of seasonal courts through a regal grand march followed by quadrille dancing, the focus of chapter 4. Within these scripted moments, despite being put on display by their fathers for matchmaking purposes, women displayed a measure of performative power through refined body language. Chapter 5 considers the romantic conversations that ensued once the ball opened up for general dancing. The krewe and guests excitedly engaged in waltzes, ragtime dances, and other flirtatious moments that eventually forged the bonds of krewe family dynasties through marriage. The conclusion examines the after-parties attended by many krewesmen—the notorious French balls hosted in Storyville, New Orleans' legalized prostitution district—and highlights the challenges to old-line hegemony that were posed by outside forces.

The krewes' carefully cultivated traditions of dance and codified movement were as much mirrors of the krewesmen's idealized selves as they were escapes into fantasy realms. The choreographed elements of Carnival balls constituted new Mardi Gras rituals and traditions that asserted krewes' claims to elite social status. Moreover, each organization used Carnival pageants to comment on New Orleans (and American) society and in doing so, masked balls revealed krewe tensions about the Civil War, Reconstruction, and modernity, as mock royalty and subjects alike crafted historically and sociopolitically charged identities on the dance floor. Whether considering the complex patterns of the quadrille, the codified walking of the grand march, or the stylized poses of the tableaux vivants, movement traditions examined here reveal that bodies in motion are meaningful, critical tools that offer insight into our past.

ONE

"Vive La Danse!"

BALLS AND MARDI GRAS IN
NEW ORLEANS HISTORY

On Mardi Gras night in 1857, people gathered at the Gaiety Theatre to witness history in the making. Guests, invited by a mysterious, secret "Mistick Krewe of Comus," entered the theater and took their seats. The space was transformed, "decorated with a profusion of hangings, wreaths and festoons of flowers, arranged in a manner more beautiful, if possible, than on the night of the grand ball of the stockholders." According to Comus chronicler Perry Young, the guests were "the elite of Louisiana and the adjacent states," with the "costly costumes of the ladies adding much to the brilliancy of the scene."[1]

While the audience mingled and socialized in anticipation of the night's event, their hosts engaged in a pursuit never before undertaken on Mardi Gras: an organized nighttime parade by torchlight, accompanied by a band of musicians. The Mistick Krewe—whose name was modeled after the character Comus, Lord of Misrule and god of excess from John Milton's famous 1634 masque—selected Milton's *Paradise Lost* as their inaugural theme. Costumed as demons, they wound their way from the corner of Magazine and Julia Streets to the back of the Gaiety Theatre. This was the first "closed" Mardi Gras parade in New Orleans (only members could participate). More than one hundred maskers marched, watched by thousands of spectators whose curiosity drew them to the scene. But this monumental feat did not end with the parade: "Arriving at Theatre alley on Common street they disappeared through the rear doors of the Gaiety Theatre, to reappear on the stage in brilliant tableaux, representing four scenes of Tartarean splendor, followed by a grand ball in the theatre, the parquette being floored over for the occasion. The merry and grotesque maskers made much fun and merriment and enjoyed quizzing their sweethearts and wives to their hearts' content without revealing their identity."[2] In a single night, the Mistick Krewe of Comus delighted the public with a fantastical parade and then amused their friends (and themselves) with a sumptuous Carnival ball.

The ball was a spectacular performance, beginning with the enactment of tableaux vivants. There were four tableau scenes, each of which brought to life a different moment from Milton's play: "Tartarus," "The Expulsion," "Conference of Satan and Beelzebub," and "Pandemonium." Comus used more than one hundred maskers (no two costumes were alike), all of whom the *New Orleans Daily Crescent* noted were "beautiful in their ugliness— charming in their repulsiveness." The newspaper also explained that the night's tableaux were "acted out truly and successfully, in a manner which reflected the highest credit upon the poetic taste and judgment of the gentlemen composing the '*Mistick Krewe of Comus.*'"[3] After the last scene concluded, a final curtain rose to show a cleared stage, decorated only by a gas-jet arch of the words "*Vive la danse!*" suspended in the air. The guests and maskers heeded the illuminated instructions and partnered up for a whirl around the ballroom. As guests flowed onto the dance floor for hours of fun, the krewesmen (still in costume) "dispersed among the gathering and joined in the dance in a manner which showed them to be very gentlemanly and agreeable devils."[4] At its core, Comus stressed merrymaking and entertainment as the foundation of this first ball, yet the outcome was quite serious: "Comus, in the course of a single evening, had recreated Mardi Gras."[5] Dance was at the center of this regeneration.

New Orleans has a long, unique dancing history, tied to Carnival festivities in a variety of ways. The city, founded in 1718 by the Frenchman Jean-Baptiste le Moyne de Bienville, quickly became the capital of French Louisiana. As more Frenchmen, African slaves, and later Spaniards and then Americans arrived in the city, they brought with them their cultural institutions. Although references to Carnival are absent for these early decades, historical documents reveal that dancing was central to colonial life for prosperous European settlers.

As early as 1743, the appointed governor of French Louisiana, the Marquis de Vaudreuil, brought his family, a ship full of furniture, and his Parisian dancing master, Bébé, with him when he relocated to New Orleans. In his new frontier community, Vaudreuil's house was known as a "kind of miniature Versailles, where lavish and elegant balls and banquets proceeded apace."[6] By 1763, Spain had acquired the territory, and balls continued to flourish. The number of places utilized as ballrooms even increased as the French city that loved contra dances now included a Spanish population wild about the newest dance craze across Europe and America: quadrilles, a formal square dance for four couples that emphasized poise through complex floor patterns and partner shifts.[7] Balls were so frequent that New Orleanians became deft at a variety of specific dances: both English and French quadrilles, cotillions, galops, boleros, gavottes, waltzes, mazurkas, reels, and minuets, all of which were ballroom forms that relied on partnerships and formality.[8]

Balls functioned as a cornerstone of European tradition in colonial New Orleans and dominated cultural offerings throughout the year. While the elite held their own private "society" balls, public balls arose in the city as well. In the public ball circuit, diverse social mingling ensued: people from various economic classes, men and women, even whites and free people of color mixed socially. Such encounters were "unthinkable in the streets," but attest to the power of dance as a site of convergence within colonial life.[9] In tandem, as immigration increased and New Orleans continued to establish itself, Carnival gained a foothold. Unsurprisingly, dance was core to Carnival revelry. "At the center of Carnival—indeed, at the center of early New Orleans social life," writes historian Reid Mitchell, "was the dance. Carnival was the season for dancing, but, in fact, so was every other season in New Orleans."[10]

In line with European traditions, the spirit of Carnival dancing embraced fantastical elements of Mardi Gras and included masking. In fact, masking—in the streets and at public balls—was so pervasive in the last part of the eighteenth century that the local Spanish leaders became nervous. At a critical time when Americans were revolting against England and the Spanish hold in Louisiana was still precarious, government officials saw masking as a threat to the state, a tool enemies used to steal political secrets, cause trouble, and commit crimes. The Spanish government frequently banned the festive practice, even as early as January 1781, amid that year's Mardi Gras celebration.[11] Unlike another ban a decade later that outlawed all public masked balls, the 1781 ban had a specific target: "Because of the great multitude of troops and crews from the ships (due to the state of war between Spain and England), and the great number of free Negroes and slaves in the city, the Attorney General recommends that all kinds of masking and public dancing by the Negroes be prohibited during the Carnival Season."[12]

But why were black maskers threatening? During the thirty-nine years of Spanish rule, nearly 29,000 slaves, mostly African, were brought to the port of New Orleans. In 1787 alone, 1,550 enslaved people arrived. Spanish law made provisions for the enslaved: they could hire themselves out for additional wage work; they could purchase their freedom (though only 2 to 4 percent of the slave population was manumitted each year); and abused workers could lodge formal complaints against their masters. This climate led to the establishment of a significant population, a separate class known as the *gens de couleur libres* (free people of color). By 1791, 41.7 percent of New Orleans' black population was free and participating in cultural events, such as nighttime public balls.[13] By 1800, even slaves could join free blacks at the public balls that were held at the Spectacle de la rue St. Pierre ballroom if they furnished a written permit from their owners. According to Carnival historian Samuel Kinser, the balls provided slaves with a chance to utilize "disguise and darkness to have at least a few hours of freedom" despite critics bemoaning that the Spectacle de la rue St. Pierre imitated the white ballrooms.[14] Thus, while black New Orleanians participated to some degree in Eurocentric traditions, they held a potential power to integrate themselves into, perhaps even to undo, the class status and racial values the French and Spanish (and, after 1803, Americans) instilled via society ball traditions. By extension, this overturning of cultural institutions could lead to other institutional revolutions.

The ballroom microcosm inhabited by colonial, European New Orleanians (and, it can be guessed, by black New Orleanians) included a slew of rules and codes of behaviors not to be broken. Within this purview, respectability was a core ballroom value and stabilizing agent. It was at the center of each literal and figurative move. Citizens of Louisiana and the United States engaged in the same general dances with the same general rules, both gleaned from western European traditions of gentility and respectability.[15]

By the mid-eighteenth century, respectable dancing in New Orleans and the United States included formal study and social display. Urbane families enrolled their children in private dancing lessons taught by knowledgeable dancing masters (who were, by the late eighteenth century, mostly French men of noble birth who had immigrated to America to escape the French Revolution). Likewise, private schools began to incorporate dancing into their curriculum alongside Greek, Latin, and trigonometry.[16] The result: cultivated social dance practices flourished.

Ballroom respectability depended on class stratification. Prestigious families hosted private balls at their estates, while wealthy, urban social circles subscribed to a series of private assembly dances held in semi-public spaces (these were sometimes called society dances). Middle-class citizens attended public assemblies.[17] Whether for the wealthy or the middle class, however, all assemblies adhered to a strict set of guidelines: masters or mistresses of the ceremony decided the selection and order of dances, social status determined who danced first, and an endless array of dancing masters and manuals dictated how the opposite sexes should act, including a complex code for inviting a partner to dance. By the mid-eighteenth century, the ballroom played a key role in articulating values of refinement throughout the Northeast, especially in cities like New York, Boston, Philadelphia, and even Pittsburgh, and by the late eighteenth century, southern planter society considered dancing and etiquette lessons paramount in a respectable education. Eighteenth-century New Orleans was just as dedicated as its northern counterparts to cultivating the genteel, even courtly, values and manners inherent in ballroom dancing.

Class distinction was often strictly enforced in American ballrooms by the 1790s. French Creole lawyer and writer Moreau de Saint-Mery (born in Martinique in 1750) resided in Philadelphia from 1794 to 1798, becoming associated during those years with some of the most educated Philadelphians. Of his time in the city, he wrote: "There is a great deal of snobbery in Philadelphia, where classes are sharply divided. This is particularly noticeable at balls. There are some balls where no one is admitted unless his professional standing is up to a certain mark." Moreau continued: "At one of the balls held February 23, 1795, to celebrate the birthday of Washington, I begged Mr. Vaughan, my near neighbor, and my colleague in the Philosophical Society, to buy me one of the tickets of admission. But he replied that since I was a *storekeeper* I could not aspire to this honor."[18] Here, we see the emergence of a particularly American idea: status based on business rather than birth. Without royal bloodlines, American citizens made distinctions among themselves grounded in the democratic ideals of the self-made man, especially after the American Revolution. The Protestant work ethic merged with genteel manners in a distinct relationship that was performed on the ballroom dance floor. Amid the rules of behavior and knowledge of most fashionable dances, a man or woman's prestige was marked on the body: dancing skill and deportment evidenced who was polished and who was not, further implying the economic status that would make such polishing possible. Therefore, decorum and success in the ballroom (especially through dancing) testified to one's economic stature and created a respectability that often led to political influence. George Washington, after all, was a deft dancer who used dances like the minuet to exhibit his thoughtfulness and commanding presence. In the ballroom, and by extension in daily life, good dancing cultivated social cachet, which could realistically lead to currency in political or other cultural realms. Without birthright to automatically determine status, dancing became a means through which Americans set themselves apart and prospered.

This meant that dancing was equally important to men and women. While women jettisoned themselves into good marriages through flirtatious but proper interactions on the dance floor (courtship is one of the most obvious reasons for social dancing), men could display for other men good breeding, sensibility, and acumen by dancing well. Balls and assemblies were formatted so that dancers occupied a central dancing space, but nondancers surveyed the terrain from vantage points around the room. Essentially, wallflowers were actively engaged in sizing up dancers and in mingling with other, equally polished guests. For George Washington and the men who aspired to be like him, proficient dancing garnered attention that meant surrounding people watched and respected each graceful move. This instilled in spectators a confidence in particularly masterful dancers and elevated men like Washington to a revered, trusted status. In this sense, dancing and ballrooms were important in developing social, cultural, political, and even masculine identity. For New Orleanians at the turn of the nineteenth century

—Creoles and newly transplanted Americans alike—ballrooms were critical to understanding the world around them, especially as European traditions like Mardi Gras clashed with American cultural attitudes. The ballroom was a shared space of understanding where multinational dancers navigated these tensions.[19]

The first ballroom built in New Orleans specifically to house public dances, La Salle Condé (the Conde Street Ballroom), opened in the French Quarter in 1792 and offered Carnival balls as early as 1802. By 1805, there were more than fifteen public ballrooms, and by 1815, there were another fifteen.[20] By the 1840s, there were more than eighty ballrooms operating in the city, and soon admission prices to the balls "varied from $1.50 a couple to the $6.00 charge for box seats at the Orleans Theatre."[21] Many venues hosted two to three balls a week during winter, and some had as many as five dances a week during Carnival. Dancing commenced around 7:00 p.m. and lasted until daybreak.[22] These balls were extremely vivacious (though not always decent for proper company) and often acted as sites of performing race and nationality within the multicultural city—places where Spanish, French, English, and American dancers incited national pride (and often, brawls) by championing dances from their homelands.[23] The nationalism evident in the ballroom was amplified during the many times ownership of Louisiana changed hands. Reigning government officials hosted formal balls for the incoming rulers, who returned the favor with balls of their own for the retiring leaders. For New Orleans, manners and dancing were at the center of political exchanges and daily life.

Despite rumors to the contrary, Americans did not suppress the New Orleans penchant for dancing after taking possession of the territory through the Louisiana Purchase. As W. C. C. Claiborne noted to James Madison in a 1804 letter: "Upon my arrival at New Orleans, I found the people very Solicitous to maintain their Public Ball establishment, and to convince them that the American Government felt no disposition to break in upon their amusements (as had been reported by some mischievous persons) General Wilkinson and myself occasionally attend these assemblies."[24] Americans, at least initially, seemed content with the cultural traditions already present in the city and even began to add to the scene with their own dance customs, such as replacing prestigious governor's balls (exclusive dances that honored the king's birthday) with balls that honored George Washington. These became the new dancing traditions in New Orleans. Quickly, however, subscription/society balls emerged as alternatives to the public assemblies and began to lay the foundation of exclusivity in New Orleans dancing practices by following the northern—that is, "American"—way of socializing. As Benjamin Latrobe noted about his experience at an 1819 subscription ball during Carnival time: "I have never been in a public assembly altogether better conducted. No confusion, no embarrassment as to the sets having, in their turn, a right to occupy the floor, no bustle of managers, no obtrusive solicitors of public attention."[25] Social exclusivity in New Orleans was beginning the shift from Eurocentric, Creole practices to American ones.

Early New Orleans Carnival rituals included two other dance practices, both European in nature: the *bals de bouquet* and the *bals de roi*. Both were Creole family institutions and, accordingly, select affairs. The *bals de bouquet* were a series of dances that elected bachelors to act as party king. The bachelor king at each dance selected a queen to reign by his side for the evening, and subsequent parties—which always included a hefty amount of quadrille dancing—selected new royalty for the evening. The ritual continued each week until the close of Carnival season.[26] The *bals de roi* (king's balls) were similar; they originated in the European Twelfth Night celebrations, which featured *gâteau des rois*. These "king cakes" determined who would reign for the night, depending on which guest's piece of cake contained a hidden golden bean. As with the *bals de bouquet,* mock royalty hosted the following dances where new kings and queens were "crowned."[27]

Whereas Mardi Gras during French and Spanish rule consisted mainly of masked balls and private dancing parties, a shift to public celebrations and parading occurred during American rule in the early decades of the nineteenth century. The earliest Carnival parades were defined by loose, rambling processions on foot through the French Quarter and a courting tradition where women donned their finest gowns and rode through the streets in open carriages. Other, more organized events appeared in 1838 as men masked as knights, harlequins, Turks, and Indians and then rode horses or marched through the streets.[28] Throughout the 1830s and 1840s, organized, secret groups of men paraded on Mardi Gras day and retreated to private balls, but none of the groups persisted for very long.

Perhaps the first affluent, concrete Carnival tradition in New Orleans was the performance of Daniel Auber's opera *Gustave III*, or *Le bal masqué* (The masked ball).[29] Auber's opera debuted in Paris in 1833 and featured a spectacular ball scene choreographed by Filippo Taglioni as the crowning moment within the last of its five acts. The dancing section was so popular, in fact, that the fifth act—and sometimes only the ball scene itself—was often updated to suit the latest tastes in dance style and then presented as a stand-alone performance.[30] When *Le bal masqué* debuted in New Orleans in 1840, it was the dancing that drew audiences, so much so that the performance developed into a Carnival ritual wherein Creole maskers paraded around the French Quarter and then arrived at the opera house just in time for a unique finale: a grand march of maskers followed by a galopade dance that included cast *and* willing audience members.[31] Then, everyone slipped away to various balls for the rest of the evening.[32]

The galopade was an international sensation at the time and was still prevalent decades later. In his 1859 treatise, dancing master Edward Ferrero wrote that the admired dance was:

> the easiest of all dances to learn, being, as the name implies, simply a gallop, though rapid in its movements. It is said to have sprung from the Hungarians, and was introduced into France by the Duchess of Berry during the carnival of 1829. It became famous as the termination of the mask [*sic*] ball at the French opera. The Germans use it instead of the chassez all at the close of the quadrille, and bound off into the galop with the greatest exuberance of spirit. It can be made very pleasing and entertaining by the dancers, in couples, forming a column. The whole party then follow the leaders, or head couple, through a variety of serpentine courses, now winding themselves in circles, and anon unwinding to create new ones.[33]

It was wildly popular, even associated with royalty and aristocracy, as evidenced by the following news clipping: "Lord Ranelagh and Lord Lowther are traveling together on the continent. The Emperor of Russia paid these young noblemen marked attention during their residence in his capital. They were invited to a grand ball, given by his Imperial Majesty; and Lord Ranelagh is reported to have distinguished himself by his elegance and grace in the famous Parisian galopade."[34] The galopade's lively character, coupled with its embrace by royalty, was certainly a draw for any opera audience who loved to dance, especially for a New Orleans audience with strong French roots. As part of Carnival, the lively *Le bal masqué* finale enabled Creole audiences to extend (and participate in) their own Mardi Gras traditions, enhancing their own sense of cultural and urbane exceptionalism.

By the 1850s, however, many prominent New Orleanians, Creole and Anglo-American alike, viewed Carnival as disreputable. They retreated to their own mansions for parties and private balls and viewed with disdain the general public who were consumed with violence, pranks, lewdness, and drunken behavior. To counter such practices, the socially privileged participated in their own partying. In addition to dinners and dancing, masked gentlemen called on ladies and friends on Mardi Gras evening. Thus, dancing, masking, courting, socializing, and fantasy continued, though definitions of acceptable or proper activities varied from group to group.

Then, on Mardi Gras night in 1857, an uproar: a group of men calling themselves the Mistick Krewe of Comus staged New Orleans' first organized, public, citywide parade, followed by a private ball. More than one hundred maskers marched. This procession was closed, with only members allowed to participate, but the event was meant to entertain the people of the city. Interestingly, Comus' route wound mainly through popular American streets, bypassing the older Creole city spaces. Added to that, no Spanish or even French names appeared on Comus' membership list. This infuriated Creoles, who were also resentful that Comus spoke no French and invited only a smattering of established Creoles to the postparade Carnival ball at a non-Creole theater.[35] To affluent Creole families, Comus' decisions disrespected European habits of good breeding in New Orleans. Animosity spread, strengthened by Comus' implicit statement that they now ruled festivities. By making the Comus parade and postparade ball the zenith of Mardi Gras events, Comus "asserted symbolic authority over the whole celebration."[36] Comus, after all, was no earthly king—he was a god.[37] The intent was clear. A new hierarchy had emerged in New Orleans, and at the top were Comus members: white, Protestant Americans.[38]

The arrival of Americans to New Orleans, as we see here, resulted in cultural rivalry. Eventually this conflict lessened through business exchanges and social intermingling in ballrooms, even intermarrying. But despite the

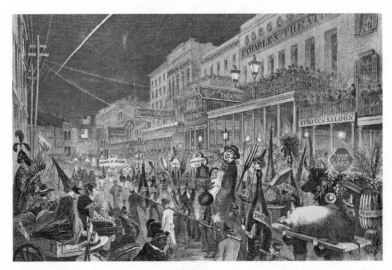

The Triumph of Epicurus. An engraving from *Frank Leslie's Illustrated Weekly* of Comus' 1867
parade. Courtesy The Historic New Orleans Collection, acc. no. 1974.74.5.

mitigation, Anglo-Americans prevailed in acquiring political and economic
power in the city, and old Creole families retreated to the background. Mardi
Gras and dancing, unsurprisingly, were central to this narrative.

Although Comus successfully took center stage in Mardi Gras of 1857,
the Americans' power, wrestled from long-standing traditions not their
own in a city only recently called home, was not absolute. Through their
shaping of the Carnival krewe model in particular, Anglo New Orleanians
volleyed between cultural domination and appropriation in their attempts
to control the city, the Creoles, and the new immigrants, especially when
even larger threats—sectionalism and the Civil War—emerged in the 1860s.
As historian Lawrence N. Powell noted, close examination of krewesmen
reveals them as a "governing group there that's never really felt entirely in
control. They've tried to rule, but this has been a city too unruly to rule."
Powell argued that the "organized parade is something to kind of assert
their primacy and to say, 'Well, we can be arbiters of culture.'"[39] As a public
statement of cultural authority, riding atop horses and, later, floats acted as
visual support of American krewesmen's ascent within New Orleans life,
but this public display might have also carried with it the precariousness of

that power. Previous generations saw Creole families dictate New Orleans culture, society, and politics from private spaces, but the Americans needed to proclaim their power publicly, and Mardi Gras parades served as the perfect cultural device for this process. From the Civil War to World War I, there were four major Mardi Gras parading groups: Comus, Rex, Momus, and Proteus. All began as Anglo-American krewes.[40]

With the new public parades followed by private balls, modern Mardi Gras emerged, defined by these earliest organizations known as old-line krewes, who fused Creole with southern traditions, all rooted in their own northern sensibilities. Take, for instance, a group of businessmen from Mobile, Alabama, who relocated to New Orleans in the early 1850s.[41] Back in Mobile, they had been part of a group called the Cowbellian de Rakin Society, which intermittently paraded around town on some New Year's Eves while clanging cowbells. After their ramblings, the group ended the night with a private ball. In 1852, the Mobile group visited New Orleans and participated in a parade. In 1853, they returned to participate in a masked ball. Thus, when some of these men permanently relocated to New Orleans, they had already engaged in the New Orleans way of celebrating Mardi Gras, but they also brought their Mobile past with them. The first New Orleans krewe, the Mistick Krewe of Comus, was founded in 1857 by former Cowbellians, with the aid of their new New Orleans friends who had relocated from the North.

During the early decades of the nineteenth century, as New Orleans settled into its new American identity, businessmen from around the country filtered into the bustling multicultural port in the hope of sustaining successful business opportunities. Many of these men were northerners intent on turning their accounting and legal backgrounds into flourishing cotton, sugar, tobacco, and manufactured-goods trades.[42] For entrepreneurs, New Orleans was a good and exciting bet. Situated near the mouth of the Mississippi River, the port connected New York, California, and the Caribbean, and it "stood fourth in point of commerce among all the ports of the world, with only London, Liverpool, and New York ahead."[43] Additionally, New Orleans had an ever-expanding population: in 1806, there were 12,000 people; 41,000 people in 1820; 46,310 residents in 1830, with waves of German and Irish immigrants arriving in the 1840s (providing cheap labor and therefore laying the foundation for the business boom of the next decade). By 1850, New Orleans—the fifth-largest city in the United States and "excluding Baltimore . . . vastly larger than any southern city"—had 116,375 people.[44] Among the city's newcomers were the Comus founders: brothers Joseph and William Ellison, J. H. Pope, S. M. Todd, Franklin Shaw Jr., Lloyd Dulaney Addison, Charles H. Churchill, and A. W. Merriam. Mardi Gras historian Errol Laborde dubbed this group the "Men Who Made Mardi Gras," and Augusto Miceli described them as "aggressive, strong-minded individuals who had achieved success in their new home."[45]

Pope, who suggested the name "Comus" for the group, was born in 1827 in Brooklyn. By the 1850s, he owned Pope's Pharmacy on the corner of Jackson Avenue and Prytania Street in New Orleans. This is the spot where the krewe's founding members gathered to formulate their new Carnival idea.[46] Churchill—born in North Carolina and described as a "modest, vigilant, intelligent and faithful man, and respected in all the relations of life"—and Addison (born in Kentucky) were in the hardware and sugar/molasses trades, respectively.[47] Todd, born in Utica, New York, in 1815, moved to New Orleans in the 1830s before going on to Mobile, where, as an accountant, he became the city's treasurer and then comptroller before moving back to New Orleans in 1854. As the owner of a paint business, Todd likely provided supplies for floats, scenery, and costumes, but also important, he was Louisiana's oldest Mason grand master and possibly ignited the mystic rituals that Comus cultivated through its secret membership and masked balls.[48]

Merriam and Shaw were also influential in Comus' early years. Albert Walter Merriam was born in Ware, Massachusetts, in the late 1820s and later became a lieutenant colonel in the Continental Regiment of the Louisiana Confederate Military.[49] In New Orleans, he renovated a building at the intersection of St. Charles Avenue and Canal Street, creating a gallery of shops along with an extensive billiards area. This place, named Crescent Hall, became Comus' "reviewing stands," a specially demarcated spot where Comus' female courts and distinguished guests positioned themselves. From the balcony, they watched the parades pass below, a tradition that lasted for decades and came to include krewe court toasts. According to Laborde, Merriam may have begun the "reviewing" tradition when, in 1874, as the parade approached Crescent Hall, he left the merriment and, from the gallery of his property, saluted each float as it passed. Unfortunately, after that same parade (followed by a tableaux ball and postball supper), when Merriam retired to his home he suffered a stroke and died.[50] Merriam's fellow krewesman Franklin Shaw Jr. was Comus' youngest founding member. Shaw was born in New York City in the 1850s, became a produce and commission merchant, and operated Frank Shaw, Jr. & Co. in New Orleans. He was the krewe's first treasurer and accordingly represented the "young male merchant class that typified Comus membership." Unsurprisingly, when the Civil War loomed, Shaw enlisted in Louisiana's renowned Washington Artillery unit and, like many other krewesmen, staked his claim with the South and the future of his business.[51]

The Ellison brothers, however, were perhaps the most remembered of Comus' founders. Joseph Ellison, born in Louisville, Kentucky, lived in Mobile before being listed as a "commission merchant" in New Orleans with the firm of Pope, Ellison, and Co.[52] He was a captain in the Civil War and defended New Orleans against Butler's and Farragut's invasions. Along with his older brother William (a New Orleans cotton broker born in Pittsburgh), Joseph raised Company C of the New Orleans Confederate Guard to defend the city. In fact, Joseph Ellison became the commander of Company C.[53] During a trip to the North to raise support for the Confederate troops, he was captured by Union soldiers and arrested on espionage charges. He was imprisoned in the Dry Tortugas for the remainder of the war. Obviously dedicated to New Orleans and the Confederate cause, Joseph Ellison was also committed to making Mardi Gras respectable, hence his founding of Comus—and its public "associate," the Pickwick Club—with prestigious leaders from the uptown, American sector of New Orleans.[54]

While the Mistick Krewe of Comus (MKC) was born in the late 1850s, the other old-line organizations did not begin to emerge until after the Civil War. During Reconstruction and in the early 1880s, four other important krewes formed: the Twelfth Night Revelers (TNR), the Knights of Momus, the Krewe of Proteus, and Rex (a semi-secret, civic-minded Mardi Gras club). The TNR entered the scene in 1870 and took up the *bals de roi* as the main component of their Mardi Gras revelry. Thus, they opened the Carnival season on Twelfth Night (January 6, the Christian feast of the Epiphany and the official first day of the Carnival season) with a ball and selection of a Carnival court.[55] Momus, named after the Greek god of satire and mockery, organized in 1872 and debuted with the theme "The Talisman," taken from Sir Walter Scott's romantic 1825 novel by the same name. The third group, Proteus, organized in 1881 but premiered in 1882 and named themselves after the oracular Greek god of the sea.[56] Their inaugural theme was "Ancient Egyptian Theology." Both Momus and Proteus were offshoots of Comus. Momus came about because the Comus waiting list was too long; Proteus (supposedly following a suggestion made by the Comus captain) eventually formed because it took too long to get into Momus.[57] Momus was comprised of younger men from Comus families.[58] Proteus' members were mostly Cotton Exchange men and, like Momus, were younger than Comus krewesmen.[59]

These were highly secret organizations, but in 1872 a handful of businessmen (some from Proteus, Momus, and Comus) created a new krewe, Rex. As "King of Carnival," the partially masked Rex served as the old-line krewes' public persona.[60] Rex issued annual proclamations that businesses and schools should close to join the celebration, thereby turning Mardi Gras into an official New Orleans holiday.[61] Another critical role early in Rex's history was to act as host to important northern visitors, thereby assuaging lingering postwar tensions. As historian Henri Schindler pointed out, the Carnival traditions Rex instituted were steps in modernizing Mardi Gras but also attempts to "formalize the healing of the post-Reconstruction era."[62] Rex acted on behalf of all the old-line krewes and was a visible, more accessible presence during the Carnival season. Importantly, because Rex's identity was exposed, the other old-line organizations could maintain their secrecy.

More reconciliatory attempts surfaced at the Rex ball, which favored a traditional format focused mainly on dancing and socializing. In keeping with the organization's civic duties, Rex invited prominent nonkrewe New Orleanians and influential out-of-town guests to the ball, enabling Comus, Momus, and Proteus to remain out of many spotlights while still networking and interacting with various aspects of the city through Rex channels. At the Rex ball, men wore white tie and tails instead of masks and costumes, a throne room housed the season's royal court and encouraged guests to pay their respects to the year's reigning king and queen of Carnival, and a separate ballroom supplied copious opportunities for dancing in the eve-

The throne room at Rex's 1897 ball, where Rex and his queen held court.
Daily Picayune, March 3, 1897.

ning. This decision to veer away from the established old-line ball format meant that the themes performed in other old-line tableaux vivants (often responses to contemporary social and political issues) remained protected, hidden from nonkrewe eyes. By the end of Reconstruction, old-line krewes had developed lasting customs that operated as smoothly as their actual dancing.

But why did so many new krewes materialize during this era? Simply put: the affluent, white, mostly Protestant men who had taken control of New Orleans in the 1840s lost much of their political power during the years of Reconstruction through their attachment to and participation in the Confederate cause as well as their adherence to staunch Democrat politics during a time of Radical Republican rule. Krewe involvement became a way to wrest back control of their sphere. As self-proclaimed kings—gods, even—elite krewesmen, now firmly identified as southerners and New Orleanians, constructed a world for themselves where they still reigned and could champion their ideals through a code of chivalry. Their move was made during a critical moment when Reconstruction threatened class structures. To escape this vulnerability, which also threatened krewesmen's familial prestige, old-line krewes relied more heavily on the traditions they were establishing in the realm of Mardi Gras, underscoring Rosary Hartel O'Brien's argument that "this period began with the aristocracy's forced decline into an insecure, repressed group which became more exclusive as it fought for authority."[63]

Confederate defeat and the resulting changes in the social order spurred further developments in modern Mardi Gras rituals and firmly established the hold that old-line krewes had over New Orleans Carnival. Eventually, parades and balls during Reconstruction even began to heal the wounds of the Civil War. Not only did krewes use Mardi Gras to reiterate traditional southern ideals and come to terms with their loss, but parades and balls also ironically functioned as symbolic sectional reconciliation. The splendor of krewes' public parades and the exclusive mystery of their private balls began to attract national attention. Northern tourists visited New Orleans for Mardi Gras and, if prestigious enough, were even hosted by various krewes. These new northern friends became an indispensable part of Mardi Gras tourism and keeping Carnival alive.[64] As Karen Trahan Leathem noted, alienation of southern elites by Reconstruction led krewes to exert indirect powers through Carnival activities. Eventually, this outlet resulted in krewes regaining social dominance, especially through their tactic of using southern honor as grounds for inviting prestigious northerners and military officers to krewe balls, thereby exercising "noble effort to remain gentlemanly."[65]

Thus, the modern format of New Orleans Mardi Gras solidified into a triad of masking, parades, and balls; the latter two were krewe organized and in appreciation of social prestige. Masking, of course, could be hypothetically enjoyed by all. Anyone with resources could costume in the streets. And any group of people could organize a parade; however, by the late 1870s, emerging krewes had such a hold on the general public that two main roles crystallized for Mardi Gras parades: bystanders—tourists and the people of New Orleans—were relegated to spectators while krewesmen elevated themselves to magnificent paraders on floats; they literally towered over others while often drawing on classical literature, myths, and contemporary politics to entertain, even educate (or propagandize to) their audiences.

The parades, though they stood as a public acknowledgment of krewesmen's education, splendor, and wealth, were but one component of social prestige in New Orleans. The Carnival ball, prestige's second factor, was a private affair between one krewe and another. Balls became the arena where prominent New Orleanians reaffirmed their status. Regardless of their economic or political standing with other New Orleanians, the socially esteemed krewes proclaimed themselves kings and queens of Carnival, New Orleans' most important cultural institution. In this sense, Carnival balls were arguably the most important aspect of old-line Mardi Gras.

On Mardi Gras night, every ballroom in the city was open as crowds gathered to celebrate their last masked dance before Lent began.[66] Perhaps this is why so many rituals surfaced in the execution of krewe Carnival balls—traditions marked the end of one period and the beginning of another. Krewesmen's daughters, for instance, "grew up" at Carnival balls. If on a krewe court, they were presented to society as eligible women, thus emerging from the Carnival season like a butterfly from a cocoon. For men, their names might comprise a short list of krewe members to be chosen as that season's kings, dukes, and committeemen (all honors). Women married to krewe members, meanwhile, were flattered by being asked to the dance floor by their masked men, and all other guests, though consigned to the balconies as spectators, were honored by receiving an invitation to the event. Throughout all of these bequests of status on the elite, by the elite, dancing united ideals and practice as men and women displayed their manners, propriety, and smoothness on the dance floor. Krewes waltzed into Lent with a sense of dashing gentility, honor-bound respectability, and the security that all was well.

But as much as the krewe Carnival ball created a space to experiment with and solidify group values, it also revealed tensions. Krewesmen had lost some of their money, property, and political power during the Civil War. Reconstruction was no kinder to them. Prestigious New Orleanians were troubled to see black men enfranchised, even holding government positions, and women taking new, publicly active roles in greater numbers. Although disappointment prevailed outside of Mardi Gras, in the privacy of their own balls the krewes orchestrated every moment so that men and women were in positions that supported ideas of white, patriarchal, American superiority as the cornerstone of good society. Carnival balls became a space wherein culture according to krewe ideals reigned, but it was a magical realm of ephemeral fantasy, not a daily reality. The very act of regulating the balls as circumspectly as krewes did spoke of a lingering apprehension over impending chaos. Comus, for example, stressed merrymaking and entertainment as core underpinnings of their first ball in 1857, which presented four tableaux vivants and then opened the floor to general dancing. Over the years, however, as Comus krewesmen encountered adversity in war, politics, the economy, and even on city streets, Carnival balls assumed more rigid confines than their early festive persona. Balls became serious events that scripted even more serious social and cultural negotiations, like social debuts, courtship, and generational legacies in the making. As such, the balls themselves developed into an evening of multiple rituals and performative elements, always beginning, as Comus did for its very first ball, with tableaux vivants that illuminated the seasonal theme. As the krewes felt increasing external pressures from Reconstruction policies and lost more power in the non-Carnival world, their balls reflected a tightening of traditional values.

Gilded Age balls instituted a formal krewe court, which served as a presentation for socialite daughters in the guise of maid. Each year, new women were chosen from among the krewe members' children, introduced into formal society, proclaimed eligible for marriage, and trained to act like proper ladies. In fact, in 1871 TNR went one step further and selected a queen to reign at the king's side (a clumsy attempt the previous year had yielded no queen).[67] After that, queens and court maids became standard at Carnival balls. Krewe court women, while symbolizing readiness for marriage, revealed the potential for krewesmen's daughters to live like real-life princesses, even if only for a Carnival season. They also revealed krewesmen's abilities to provide such a lifestyle and to produce daughters worthy of queenly status. Thus, the women selected became symbols of krewesmen's virility, prestige, and honor. The Carnival ball, then, morphed into another arena for krewesmen to display their achievements and, through their daughters, offer alliances to other equally prestigious men.

By the 1890s, call-out dancing became an additional ball component. In call-outs, select women were invited by special honor to join a krewe member on the dance floor. These women, often krewesmen's family members, were partitioned off from the rest of the guests in a call-out section—a few decorated seating boxes at the back of the dance floor but still in full view of the other guests. By their positioning in a special space, the privileged call-outs were put even further on display. Committeemen would escort each woman to her masked man, who played the part of mysterious lover for a dance or two. The exhibitionist nature of these ceremonies was further amplified by pushing all other guests up into the balconies. This change made clear that each krewe was the performer for its visitors from other illustrious krewes—bodies on the dance floor became a measure of who belonged and who didn't, while bodies in the balconies further defined the membership standards of social exclusivity.

What resulted was a ritualized format that bespoke old-line krewes' multiple desires: Carnival balls that adhered to tradition but allowed for (sometimes improvisational) creativity and contemporary commentary. First, costumed krewe members entered the theater and performed tableau scenes ("living pictures"). Then, the krewe presented the court, and both court and masked members engaged in a grand march (a promenade around the stage and parquet area, sometimes several times). After that, the royal court members and then call-out women participated in a few quadrilles and waltzes. Later, the court retreated to a private supper while lingering krewesmen and guests migrated to the dance floor for fun until dawn. This crystallization of Carnival ball rituals evolved over time as an amalgam of cultural, historical, and physical influences, but the ball's lasting presence as a core old-line tradition reveals its importance to krewe identity. In fact, the ball was so important that it often occupied krewesmen's lives throughout the year. Preparations for the ball were extensive and constituted a performance of krewe identity, as we shall see in chapter 2.

"A Most Brilliant Assembly"

PREPARING FOR THE BALL AND
CHOREOGRAPHING CLASS

I n 1877, while America focused on the end of Reconstruction or the
Compromise of 1877 and Rutherford B. Hayes' presidential victory,
krewesmen in New Orleans had more pressing concerns that Mardi Gras
season: two invitations to the Comus ball were unaccounted for, either
stolen or misplaced. The faux pas was grave. Missing ball invitations meant
that a nonmember might be able to penetrate the carefully crafted krewe
world. According to Robert Tallant, the "blood of New Orleans aristocracy was curdled with wrath and indignation and chilled with horror that
some outsider might get in."[1] Exclusivity grounded krewe activities, and the
regulation of tradition was a key component of successful balls. At the
center of this solidarity, and especially of concern to the krewes, was the
guest list.[2] Uninvited guests had the potential to upset the old-line krewes'
status quo, to potentially disrupt the hierarchy that krewes strove to keep
intact.

Comus committeemen checked and rechecked the guest list. They poured
over delivery confirmation receipts and perused the short list of returned
invitations that would go unused (guests unable to attend were forbidden
from transferring their invitations to someone else). Invitation protocol was
so strict that the missing invitations were sure to leave a breadcrumb trail,
but despite the krewesmen's best efforts, the invitations remained at large.
Anxious, the krewe promised a reward through newspaper advertisements:

REWARD—$2,000!

Whereas, two invitations to my festival, each numbered 22, have been stolen by some disloyal subject, now, therefore, be it known that a reward of $1,000 each will be paid by the keeper of my privy purse for the return of the same to the custodian of our royal archives.

This done in the twentieth year of our reign, Anno Domini, 1877.

COMUS[3]

Luckily for Comus, the invitations never turned up in the hands of a stranger. The admit cards that accompanied each invitation (and were required to gain entrance to the ball) were never used. Still, krewe circles were ruffled.

Recovering the lost invitations was important to Comus because the krewe relied on selectivity and secrecy. To krewesmen, this cultivation was key. Old-line krewes articulated their sophistication and affluence—the most crucial aspects of their identity—through sumptuous Carnival balls and refined but conspicuous displays of material consumption. The finest clothes, costumes, sets, float designs, even invitations, proclaimed that they were cultured, prosperous men. In turn, these attributes constituted a group ideal of modern gentility that played out through spectacular Carnival pageants, reassuring krewesmen that they stood at the apex of New Orleans culture.

In their dominance over Mardi Gras, and by extension over all of New Orleans, old-line krewes carefully choreographed their class identity through decisions about the most prominent social event of their year: the krewe Carnival ball. Ball preparations were meticulously scripted. A full year was sometimes necessary to make sure that every element fell into place exactly as it was meant to—one of the reasons why a missing pair of invitations could cause such a ruckus. Critically, krewe exclusiveness often emerged through physical articulations of class consciousness, such as in embellished Parisian-designed invitations, opulent theatrical settings, selective guest lists, and ball arrival "performances."

The first step in preparing for the ball was the selection of that season's theme, along with designs for invitations and costumes. These decisions were, of course, made by men, especially by the krewe's leader, the captain.

Captains operated with the assistance of hand-selected krewesmen who
served on secret committees and as advisors when not engaged with their
normal professional duties as cotton merchant, bank president, coal manu-
facturer, or lawyer. Selecting the next year's theme came fast upon the heels of
each season. After captains solicited krewe members for ideas and consulted
designers, artists created float and costume plates around interpretations
of the main theme and then brought to life these visions in papier-mâché
tableau paintings (which served as float sides for parades and as performance
scenery at balls), lithograph invitations, jewelry, costumes, and more.

Some krewes even dispatched select members to France in order to secure
Parisian artists to join the production team. Until World War I, Comus'
costumer was Chalin of Paris, who was killed in action.[4] Despite this loss,
Comus continued to have court jewels and mantles crafted in Paris into the
1930s. Additionally, costumes were extravagantly expensive, costing up to
$8,000 for a cast of 125 men. For this reason, krewes were especially careful
in choosing their designers. The tableau car builders, for example, passed
their Comus affiliations down the family line.[5] Sons inherited the trade
and lucrative Comus contracts from their fathers.[6] Rex was also known to
engage Parisian craftsmen. For the 1883 season, the organization imported
the following from France: 128 costumes (costing $6,000, including shoes,
jewels, head coverings, and prop weapons), $150 worth of queen's jewels,
more than $400 worth of decorations, $1,000 in horse saddles and harnesses,
and more. The grand total was around $7,600.[7] Rex member George H.
Braughn traveled from New Orleans to Paris and personally inspected the
materials.[8] As time progressed, each season boasted increasingly elaborate
designs for floats, costumes, and ball scenery. Flourish and dazzle became
standard characteristics of krewe products, which came together for full
effect at the ball. In fact, newspapers reported year after year that each krewe
created and presented "the most brilliant ball ever."[9]

Early invitations were hand-delivered and, in the case of Rex, printed in
French. They were simple and straightforward; they designated the ball's
time and place. Often, the top of each invitation was illustrated with classical
motifs and symbols: masks, lyres, flutes, flowers, and ribbons.[10] Invitations
were "strictly personal" (meaning they could not be given away) and had a

number that corresponded to the krewe's master list. An admittance ticket for each guest also accompanied each invitation. Krewes called these proofs of social status "admit cards." Occasionally men's admits were blue while women's were pink. Moreover, women's invitations contained an additional treasure—a dance card, complete with a small pencil on a string for filling in gentleman dance partners' names. Dance cards were treasures unto themselves and were often reconfigured in some creative way to unveil the night's list of dances.

From the 1880s to the early 1900s, invitations experienced an arc of extravagance. They had become as lavish as the balls themselves and were effective in hinting to guests the sumptuousness that lay in store. As intricate pieces of art and krewe keepsakes in their own right, Gilded Age invitations were die-cut, lithographic wonders. Some were designed and crafted by Parisian artists, but many krewes used local artists, as well.[11] The invitations opened up to reveal new illustrations reflecting the krewe's seasonal theme, often scenes of enchantment or romance. Paintings of chivalrous knights, bacchanalian feasts, military conquests, or sylph seductions graced the invitations' inner leaves. In the 1890s, Rex began distributing favors—inkwells, fans, brooches, bonbon dishes, vases, and the like—with each invitation. Leonard Huber noted that twelve thousand of these prized possessions were distributed in 1903, but like many other Mardi Gras traditions, this custom ended with the advent of World War I.[12] Around 1902, Rex abandoned the elaborate lithographic, three-dimensional invitations in favor of a sleeker, more modern style. New invitations, made in New Orleans, were printed in bold black letters on thick, white card stock. At the top of the invitations was Rex's now legendary royal coat of arms in purple, green, and gold. It took other krewes a few years, but eventually they all followed suit. By the 1910s, the lithograph treasures were passé, but invitations to prestigious old-line Carnival balls remained prized items.

While invitations were being designed and printed, krewes established a yearly invitation committee in order to formulate their guest lists. Committee members (appointed to their posts by the captain) arbitrated "who was in and who was out" and spent the months before Carnival determining which New Orleanians were worthy of attending the ball. In secret, the committee-

The Proteus invitation to "Legends of the Middle Ages," 1888, displays the lavish style of old-line invitations. *Top:* The invitation arrived folded, resembling a medieval chalice. *Bottom left:* The outside of the invitation once fully opened. *Bottom right:* The inside of the invitation, complete with splendid scenes of knightly adventures. Courtesy The Historic New Orleans Collection, acc. no. 1960.14.52.

men (often unknown to even their own krewe) deliberated over names, occupations, and social reputations. Acting as an "encyclopedia of social biography," the invitation committee sorted through each krewe member's list of personal invitations (usually, about twenty per member), organized the nominations for call-outs (members were allowed only a handful of these), and scrupulously considered the character of all potential guests. If a person was found unworthy of attending the event, the committee asked the nominating krewesman to submit an alternate name for consideration.[13] Like those of the membership committee, the invitation committee's duties were serious, and, even though its members were anonymous, participating on the invitation committee was an esteemed role within the krewe. The captain took great pains in selecting the group, carefully choosing "members who are familiar with the social history of Old New Orleans and also members who are abreast of the times."[14]

Naturally it was notoriously difficult to secure invitations to old-line balls. Rex was the only krewe to distribute out-of-town invitations, but even for multigenerational New Orleanians, getting your name on the invitation list was, like everything else, an arduous process. Even as early as 1859, the *Daily Picayune* noted about Comus that: "Men go about, taking as much pains to secure an invitation to the great ball, as if they were electioneering for some fat office; supplications, introductions, recommendations, all are put in motion, and even bribery would be attempted if it could affect the thing. But it is all of no avail."[15] That same year, one Comus member exclaimed:

> I am in my carnival costume, it's a hey day for us all to enjoy, everybody is making the most of it, all the balls last night were a jam, and the crown of all is the coming "Mystic Krewe of Comus" tonight. The mysterious preparations have excited every one's curiosity, owing to a few who penetrated into the last ball. It is difficult to get invitations to the dance, every one has to be certified to, by a member, and many of the fair ladies are asking their lords to "join the Krewe" so as to command invitations, and many have been rejected today, it being a day of culling, so I hear a member say (James Robb). The Varieties Theatre is to be well guarded tonight, as a lot of invitations have been stolen.[16]

As we see from this incognito krewesman's report, invitations could not be bought in any manner. Guest lists were the first step in enforcement. Even after the ball, a selected group of krewesmen gathered to sort out which invitations were used and which were not. They checked each presented admit card against the invitation list to make sure that guests did not waste or transfer their privileged possession. Recalling the fears of the missing Comus invitations leading to a possible intruder, guests who were found to have given away their admit cards were sometimes placed on a blacklist, never to be invited to that krewe's ball again.[17]

This planning of guest lists, themes, invitations, and balls in general was relatively similar from one krewe to the next, but settling on a king, queen, and court members varied widely. A reigning court for each old-line ball became standard after 1887, eventually including dukes, maids, pages, and cup bearers in addition to kings and queens. Each year a krewe committee or ballot (both secret) determined anew who would reign as king. The kings were masked, as were the dukes, furthering the mystery of krewe membership for ball guests. The exception to this was Rex, leader of the civic-minded Mardi Gras organization by the same name, who wore a faux beard and wig instead of a full facial mask. Because of his partial "exposure" and his public role as King of Carnival, each year's Rex had to be a prominent citizen who could afford the exorbitant costs associated with reigning: a slew of social parties, gifts for court members and his queen, and having a tailored costume made especially for him.

Whereas kings took center stage during the all-male parades, it was the queen and her court who commanded the spotlight during the Carnival balls. Unlike men, women did not veil their faces, though they did wear traditional "masks" of a sort: they costumed as men's feminine ideal in couture gowns and expensive jewelry. Perry Young cautions that "rare and delicate judgment must ever be exercised in the selection of the courts, as the ladies are never masked, and must be the most beautiful and in all other ways the most pleasing element of the scene."[18]

Some queens and maids were selected solely by the captain; others were chosen by committees. Some krewes allowed the king to choose the queen and then permitted both monarchs to select their own attendants. As queen of Carnival in 1891, Bessie Behan personally selected four maids and four dukes for her Rex reign, though now the organization chooses the entire court.[19] Once selected, court women learned of their royal role through

Christmas or New Year's Day morning visits from krewe members.[20] Select krewesmen called on the maids first, and then the queen, presenting each with a scroll and asking the women for the honor of their acceptance with the utmost formality. Recalling her New Year's Day visit, Bessie Behan explained that she was totally surprised when the Rex men arrived at her Garden District home. "My father may have known ahead of time, but he never told me," she explained.[21] As these visits make clear, most krewes decided on royalty in advance. Two groups, however, the Twelfth Night Revelers and the Knights of Momus, waited until the actual ball to reveal their court choices.[22] By the turn of the twentieth century, many of these royal identities were confirmed at birth, at least for the baby girls who were born to outstanding old-line krewe members.

Dorothy Spencer Collins, former Comus queen, explained that being selected for a krewe court depended on a father's participation in the krewe: "That is why at the Annual Luncheon for the Merrie Queens of Comus I drink a toast (using my father's jeweled cup—he was No. 1 in 1914) to 'Our Fathers Who Art in Comus.' I had the great honor of being Queen in 1915."[23] Collins later revealed that the real authority behind her reign was Mr. "Buzz" Walmsley, "the power behind the Throne of Comus—'the King and Queen maker.'" Collins remarked: "Every year his eldest daughter Myra Loker (now over 90 years old) is at the Queens of Comus luncheon, looking so pretty and her family always sends her a white orchid for the occasion, and she looks every inch a Queen."[24]

In 1915, Mr. Walmsley honored the Spencer family by choosing Dorothy as Comus' queen, despite the fact that a prominent tableaux society, the Elves of Oberon, had also asked her to be their queen.[25] In addition to the Elves' request, friend Sadie Downman, Rex queen and thus queen of Carnival that same year, asked Dorothy to be her Rex maid. Dorothy had happily accepted her friend's offer without knowing that their friendly arrangement would never come to fruition. Despite Dorothy Spencer's decision to be Rex maid, her fate was decided by men:

> One night Mr. Willie Dufour came to see my father and they were sitting in the Library. There was quite a long, low conversation and finally my father's voice was raised emphatically. "She cannot be Queen of Comus. I have accepted from you the honour of her being Queen of Oberon and she cannot

be Queen twice in the same Season." Then Mr. Dufour, equally empathetic, "Walker, if you don't permit her to be Queen of Comus I will withdraw my offer for Queen of Oberon. I won't have Dorothy hating me the rest of her life." This went on and on with me hanging breathlessly over the upstairs banister. Well, finally Mr. Dufour won his point and I was Queen of both balls my debut year.[26]

Dorothy's tale makes clear that choosing a queen and royal court was a juggling maneuver, especially for men who were members of multiple krewes. Perhaps because of situations similar to Dorothy Spencer Collins'— and likely because the pool of krewe daughters remained limited—Comus eventually developed a strict policy. George Janvier, who became Comus captain in the 1930s, inherited the Comus protocols and traditions of the early twentieth century. Concerning the selection of queen and court, Janvier revealed that Comus began to choose the season's female court members according to a board decision. Janvier wrote: "We maintain a family record card system by which there is a pink card kept on each member. He fills this out himself, giving the names and ages of all members of his family. We keep these up to date so that we know the exact family status of each member. Some members list their grandchildren and this is sometimes of help."[27] Janvier also noted that Comus queens could no longer reign at another ball the same year, though the Twelfth Night Revelers and Momus were exempt from this protocol since they choose their queen at the ball itself. Further stipulations included a maximum of eight maids on a court and no more than two previous court appearances by a woman becoming queen of Comus.[28] Janvier's document reveals the growing complexity of krewe codes. Rules were central to krewe activities, and built into this system was the understanding that, whether a member of the krewe or a queen elect, the core principle for all Carnival events was secrecy.

By the late 1890s, female court participants were selected from among that season's debutantes, furthering the ideal inherent in krewes' scripting of elite class identity. Because of this, some Carnival and debutante social engagements became intertwined. Social rules stipulated that debutantes entertain peers (in this case, other krewe members' daughters) with brunches, dances, and social calls. These social engagements were added elements of the choreographed exclusivity that formed krewe identity. Queen of Carnival

1904, Josie Halliday, admitted that she and her friends had a Cinderella existence, including being privy to the best education and frequent travels in Europe.[29] Halliday's father, Rex in 1906, owned all of the ferryboats in the city, and the economic and social standing garnered by her father enabled Josie to engage with the cream of New Orleans' society. As a debutante, Josie regularly attended the opera, private suppers (presumably at the homes of other debutante families), and respectable plays, and enjoyed chaperoned carriage rides.

But luxury came with duties. According to Halliday, once a debutante was introduced to society, she was expected to visit the homes of New Orleans' most illustrious citizens. "Every family in good social standing had an 'at home' once or twice a week," noted the ex-queen. She explained that callers left their cards in big bowls, presumably located in the foyer for young women to peruse when alone and for guests to easily access when they entered the house.[30] One can easily imagine how the number of calling cards blatantly proclaimed each family's social prominence for all visitors to see. Bowls overflowing with cards were certainly marks of popularity. This conspicuous display could also be a method by which each debutante could measure her social worth.

Accordingly, old-line krewe family daughters spent much of their life preparing for their hopeful debut at the Carnival ball. Because certain families expected their daughters to reign in the family krewe (or at least to serve as maid), krewesmen's daughters were given training befitting their future roles and were taught to cultivate ladyhood. Certainly, rearing a royal daughter began at home through lessons passed on from mother to daughter. Etiquette was also part of school instruction. Krewe daughters attended the very best girls' schools in the city, where teachers instilled proper codes of femininity alongside lessons in literature and mathematics. Dorothy Spencer Collins recalled that her Newcomb High School French teacher, Clarisse Cenas, "sent me into the hall to drink six glasses of water in punishment for having crossed my knees in class. As I left the room she hissed, 'Mademoiselle, will you cross your knees when you are Queen of Comus?'"[31]

Dancing lessons were likely available to wealthy families, too, though records do not allude to this information. Only one dance teacher, Ms. Tharp, was mentioned in literature left behind by krewesmen and court women, and only one other dance "professor" materialized in the archives. He was J. Vegas. Little is known about either of these teachers, but for Tharp, at least, it may be safe to assume that she, like the krewe court training specialists who emerged in the mid-twentieth century, might have been a ballet mistress or even a previous krewe monarch.[32]

Beyond dance teachers and private educational institutions, there was a more accessible method for krewe daughters to learn deportment: dance manuals. Dance manuals were among the most popular of published texts in the mid- and late nineteenth century and offered advice on current dances, fashion, etiquette, and romance.[33] Dance teachers across America at this time either authored the instructional guides or relied on dance manuals to keep up with the latest fashions in dance.[34] Thus, in one way or another, potential krewe queens and maids could master their movements and learn to project a regal manner befitting their status by studying dance manuals. Even though there is no direct mention of how krewesmen's daughters prepared for their Carnival reign, it is a reasonable assumption that because of their proliferate nature, nineteenth-century dance manuals were likely a part of krewe court women's experience and at least reveal *what* occurred at Carnival balls. In line with the etiquette and "how to" manual craze of the nineteenth century, dance manuals outlined the organization, techniques, step sequences, styles, and manners present in balls across the United States, including those staged by the old-line krewes.

Dance manuals upheld the standards prescribed by a larger, genteel society, which krewes articulated in their own social relationships. Learning the multitude of rules associated with behavior, carriage, and dancing at balls was important because, as dance historian Elizabeth Aldrich observed, the "ballroom was a microcosm of the society at large; in these areas of Terpsichore, general, everyday social behavior was distilled and focused more intensely than normally occurred elsewhere."[35] For krewe court women, especially queens, this microcosm entailed the young women's entrance into society, their eligibility for romantic courting, and their new role as public representation of their father's status and reputation.

Dance manuals, of course, discreetly addressed this serious business linked to courtship and family respectability in the ballroom. The gravity of ballroom behavior and body language was underscored in the 1866 publication *The Ball-Room Guide:* "It is in the ball-room that society is on its very best behaviour. Everything there is regulated according to the strict code of good-breeding, and as any departure from this code becomes a grave offence, it is indispensable that the etiquette of the ball-room should be thoroughly mastered."[36] For this reason, a debutante's promenade, wave, curtsy, pose, and walk, in addition to her performance of the standard ballroom dances, became symbolic statements of gentility for krewe court women and of their suitability for continuing genteel values beyond their debutante years and into a new role as wife.

Just as krewes conferred status on select New Orleanians by selecting them to be mock royalty at the annual Carnival balls, the theaters in which the balls took place added glitz and glamour to the scene, heightening even more the relationship between krewe functions and affluent status. The most popular Carnival ball venues were the French Opera House in the French Quarter (previously known as the New Opera House), the Washington Artillery Hall, and the Athenaeum. Exposition Hall, the Grand Opera House, and the Varieties Theater were additional spaces used throughout the decades, but the most popular theater by far was the French Opera House.

The French Opera House, which burned to the ground in 1919, was the center of Creole opera outings and of New Orleans cultural affairs. The Greek Revival structure, designed by James Gallier Jr., was built on the corner of Toulouse and Bourbon Streets in 1859. Henry Pitot, direct descendant of James Pitot (a noble Frenchman and early New Orleans mayor), recalls his childhood memories of the theater. Besides attending French operas, Pitot noted that he attended a Carnival ball at the French Opera House when his sister, Emily, was a maid. Like other New Orleanians, Pitot lamented the theater's loss. Of the fire, he said: "I remember the morning that it burned. . . . [I]t was one of the most disastrous things that ever happened to the French Quarter."[37] In its heyday, the French Opera House was magnificent, inside and out. It was a shining beacon in a city that had long considered itself comprised of a distinctly cultured people. For krewes, the theater added another stratum of prestige to their already multilayered reputations for lavishness.

Fundamentally, the opera houses and theaters that old-line krewes used to stage their spectacular Carnival balls were transformational sites of opulent fantasy. Once a krewe had engaged a theater for its upcoming ball, members set about converting the space into a magnificent, otherworldly ballroom. Through decorations, thrones, mirrors, and a parquet that covered the orchestra seats (creating a floor flush with the stage), they changed their surroundings into a mythical realm.[38] Krewesmen draped stair bannisters in velvet, adorned rows of seats with silk ribbons, and enhanced the theater space with elaborate décor (linked to the season's theme) that guests could admire up close. The theater became a place of wonder and awe, with the stage and accompanying "ballroom" as primary focus. Thus, the krewes fashioned more space for their tableaux, grand march, and dances than they did for their guests. Rules relegated visitors to the balconies while krewesmen and their female royalty occupied the entire ground floor, except for the stage and dancing space. Since the parquet floor covered the orchestra pit, musicians arranged themselves in a back corner (or high in a balcony when the theater was especially crowded); the special box seats for queens and maids were positioned on the side. This area was far enough away from the stage to allow for the grand march and other performances but was not entirely tucked under the balcony. Guests, after all, needed visual accessibility to women in order to admire them. And, once call-outs were fully institutionalized in the 1890s, krewes established a roped-off section on the side of the dance floor where call-out women could watch the tableaux and court presentations, then be available for their own special dances. With all of these demarcated spaces in place, the krewes took control of the theater, created hierarchy among themselves, and, perhaps most importantly, manufactured an arena where floormen regulated everyone's comings and goings. In this way, the theater was not only transformed into a fantasy-scape, but was also shaped into a labyrinth that the krewesmen patrolled and knew how to maneuver. It was their turf.

As with the theater's physical alteration to reflect the season's theme, old-line krewes calculated and planned every detail of the Carnival ball, including the tableaux vivants that opened each ball. The tableaux were intricate and required rehearsals, which krewe captains often opened to all krewe members. Rehearsals were important because (in addition to training the cast) the captain finally divulged the season's theme and float designs to the general krewe.[39] The main business of the rehearsal, however, was to practice the tableaux, which were specific and complicated and required systematic training. For the first Comus ball, krewesmen met nightly in their den (the individual krewe warehouse where the floats were assembled). At these clandestine rehearsals, each man received a number and stood in an area designated by chalk circles on the ground. When the captain blew his whistle, the men moved into their respective positions and poses. Cast and court members methodically practiced and memorized their choreographed entrances, gestures, and exits. Understudies likewise learned various roles so that, on the night of the ball, they could quickly jump into a part if a krewesman was missing, injured, sick, or worse: drunk. Krewesmen also learned how to form complex drills and highly structured, geometrical marches during these rehearsals. Eventually, they admitted female court members to the process so that the women could learn their own entrances and floor patterns alongside the krewesmen in preparation for the court's grand march that immediately followed the last tableau.[40]

Once captains settled on a theme, designers created the costumes, lithographers crafted (and krewesmen delivered) invitations, set designers decorated the theater, and the tableaux were cast and rehearsed, the real drama began. First came the parade, after which the ball commenced. Some ball guests, excited to claim a special seat for themselves, left the street parades early—if they went at all—and flocked to the theater in their ball attire.[41] These early arrival performances could cause quite a commotion. Krewe friends sometimes arrived a half hour to an hour before the theater doors opened. While waiting, guests often contended with uninvited people (women, for the most part) who showed up in anticipation of jostling their way into the ball. In 1860, there was even a group who attempted to gain entrance by forming a (now infamous) "flying wedge" of female bodies. Desperate women used every trick to their advantage, including feigning fainting and, in 1868, shouting "Fire!" in order to get through the front doors. Luckily, Gen. P. G. T. Beauregard and Col. James McCloskey arrived on the scene, "restored order," and kept the event from getting completely out of control.[42] During these scuffles, many women tore their dresses and were obliged to return home. An 1869 article in *DeBow's Review* described a typical scene, which occurred at 8:00 p.m., quite some time before the "magic portals" of the French Opera House were opened: "Ladies were there—refined and delicate ladies—who were pushed, smashed, shoved and had their dresses torn—more, 'mussed,' but who heroically through it all held on to the places they had won, refusing to yield to the pressure of the surging crowd, who every moment grew larger, holding all their waiting and their trouble cheap if they could only obtain that for which their soul longed—a good seat."[43] Committeemen tried to control the situation by politely turning away uninvited guests.

Despite the possibility of unruly crowds, guests' grand entrances were so spectacular that in addition to guests and uninvited hopefuls, other New Orleanians lined the street to watch the carriages full of krewe friends come and go. Spectators gawked at the latest fashions and ball guests. To put it another way, this parade of "status performance" was instrumental in displaying opulence. It was clear: servants conducted ladies and gentlemen of the upper echelon about town to the most exclusive soirees while social standing relegated others to the dirty streets. Carriages equaled status.

Ball guests, however, could not come and go as they pleased; their entrances and exits were specifically choreographed. Krewes went to great lengths to have the evening run smoothly, including dictating exactly how carriages should approach the individual theaters that housed the krewe balls. Outlines of guest arrival protocol became more complicated each year, so much that krewes posted notices in the local newspapers.[44] For their 1897 ball at Exposition Hall (later called the Washington Artillery) in the 700 block of St. Charles Avenue, for example, Rex stipulated:

> Guests will enter by way of St. Charles street entrance only. They may retire by way of either the St. Charles or Carondelet street portals. Under no circumstances will guests be allowed to enter by the Carondelet street entrance.
>
> At the St. Charles street entrance carriages will approach the Palace from the direction of Canal street, and after their occupants have alighted retire beyond Julia street.
>
> Household troops will see that these orders are rigidly carried out, and no carriage permitted to unload its passengers until facing properly.
>
> Guests will please instruct their drivers how to drive in and how to drive off, and thus save much confusion.
>
> If persons who propose to attend the Royal Reception will carefully read these rules and regard them they will save themselves and the committee much trouble and annoyance.[45]

These directions, of course, were not the only rules laid down by krewes. Once in the theater, guests could not leave until the tableaux had concluded. Likewise, if guests *arrived* during a tableau performance, they had to wait until after the grand march to gain admittance, along with those who had only received admit cards for the ballroom dancing portion of the evening.

Although watching guests arrive at the ball was certainly a sight for spectators, the arrival of the queen was especially magnificent since she was accompanied by fanfare befitting royalty. The *Times-Picayune* described the arrival of the queen of Comus in 1915: "Before the ball began gorgeously clad outriders clattered down the asphalt pavement of Bourbon street. In their wake rolled a line of fancy equipages, drawn by four horses, and the crowds gathered in front of the French Opera House made way in obedience to the herald's call announcing the coming of the Queen."[46] Krewes staged court arrivals that harkened to the elaborate, affluent pageantry of royal entrances in the Middle Ages.

Once the carriages deposited their stately cargo, the ball guests began their ritualized entry into a krewe-created world. The first step was to make a grand entrance into the lavish theater. In remembering the brilliance of the French Opera House during Carnival, one journalist described the foyer, a "red tapestried room": "Gracefully curved tiers of boxes, elegantly adorned with crimson damask, rise one above the other. Magnificent mirrors in gold frame are hung in each side of the proscenium. Handsomely carved rails, with newels of turned and oiled mahogany, sweep upward to a natural cypress wainscoted landing, deep enough for at least 12 persons to 'stop and gossip' (a Creole sport). Even the radiators are 'richly bronzed.'"[47] In this sumptuous space, guests were met by men in white tie and tailcoats, the reception committee—often older family members, respected friends from other krewes, or young krewesmen being trained in gentlemanly etiquette—who collected admit cards at the door and served as surrogate hosts for the costumed krewe members. The reception committee was charged with discreetly determining that each guest was indeed the person whose name was hand-printed on the card.

Committeemen frequently worked their way up through the ranks. John M. Parker recalled that he was young when he began working on reception committees, which often included additional duties for krewesmen-in-training. He remarked: "I remember Mrs. George Denegre used to have the court supper at her house. She had three or four of us wait on the tables for her. She could have hired waiters, but she wanted us to be there."[48] Another committeeman, William G. Nott, whose father was a member of the Boston Club, also started young, but his formal entrance to krewe activities began with program writing for several krewes and extended from there.[49] Krewes maintained exclusivity throughout their events, allocating roles to krewesmen and their eventual successors.

This was no different for krewesmen's Carnival ball guests, who were also expected to adhere to prescribed notions about behavior and social positioning. Once guests entered the theater, committeemen escorted them to "their place": call-out women to the parquet, ladies to the first balcony, gentlemen to the second balcony.[50] Positioning women on the first balcony was a smart move by the krewes. This vantage point gave women unobstructed opportunities to scope out the scene and watch the evening unfold, which in turn made it possible for them to praise the krewe's infinite taste the following days while dining out with equally superior friends or when sitting next to other women at an ensuing ball. As the *Daily Picayune* noted in 1900: "The Proteus ball attracted to the French Opera House last night a most brilliant assembly. It is estimated that fully 3000 people were present, if not more. The theatre was filled completely, long in advance of the hour set for the rising of the curtain."[51]

What was there for a "brilliant assembly" of three thousand guests to do? Gossip. Gossiping, as well as surveying (and being surveyed by) other guests, was integral to preball identity performances. Seeing and being seen confirmed status, and whether a woman was on the parquet, the first balcony, or even higher, her social standing was measured by everyone around her.[52] Noting who was present from one ball to the next was a sport in itself, not just in New Orleans but across all of high society at the time. The New York Opera season provides one example, where being seen with the right people and in the right fashion was sacrosanct. Within the space of New York's Academy of Music, moreover, attendance not only "bestowed distinction" but also marked socialites as being members of an elite class who possessed financial and material wealth, as well as cultural knowledge.[53]

Female guests at the 1899 Proteus ball gossip, survey other guests,
watch the krewe, and read their tableau program during the performance.
New Orleans Times-Democrat, February 18, 1899.

These distinctions were furthered in the seating arrangements of the theater:
only the most affluent New Yorkers could obtain access to the prized box
seats, whereas everyone else occupied seats according to their own social
rank and financial standing. From each vantage, men and women could
view (and gossip about) those more well off than themselves. Being seen
and talked about was as important to these class performances as the actual
opera itself.

Gossiping, scrutinizing characters, and performing social status revolved
in large part around fashion. Nineteenth-century fashion was integral in
expressing individual character and moral identity.[54] By dressing properly,
men and women acknowledged their conformation to social standards as
they simultaneously sought to define those standards for themselves. Balls,
of course, were prime sites for testing and reaffirming class status through
fashion displays. As a mark of class distinction, krewe women eagerly learned
all they could about the latest fashions from New York and Paris, and in doing so, they consumed aesthetic ideas that, when executed on their female
form, would catapult them into the strata of the modern, luxurious woman.

Through the latest and most elegant clothing, women made themselves distinct. Dressing well set ballgoers apart from people who could not afford such finery and, by extension, occupy the same social circles. In this way, high fashion cemented ball participation as members of a bound group via conspicuous consumption.[55] The white tails and ball gowns worn by Carnival ball guests became a performance of class-consciousness and solidarity.

Women's dress in particular was extreme in its display of class. High heels, multilayered long skirts, long hair, and restrictive corsets were fundamental accoutrements, but it was the corset that most denoted class style. Ethnologist Marianne Thesander argues that the nineteenth-century corseted body reflected self-restraint and restrictive sexual morality. It "literally locked women into a role in which it was almost a duty to be attractive."[56] Since a woman's schedule and employment determined fashion, the tight-laced corset became the ultimate symbol of prestige.

For social events like Carnival balls, the right dress, corset, shoes, and gloves became a pressing matter for women. Since most ball guests used their time before the tableaux to chat and survey their companions, individual women could effectively use fashion to set themselves apart, thereby creating further hierarchy within the ranks. Prosper Jacotot, a Frenchman who visited New Orleans in 1877, remarked that, for Carnival, "these holidays are the occasions for exhibition of feminine clothes with desperate competition among the elegants." Prosper noted that "all of this is done in an orderly manner" and concluded that "it is too bad that it is not Mardi Gras everyday."[57] Besides friendly, feminine competition, women also used fashion to their advantage in snaring eligible bachelors. Men's presence at krewe events solidified their manly status as respectable and rich, so women were free to flaunt their feminine attributes in the hope of securing a husband.

All of these elements, however—from clothing, to flirting, to establishing personal character—had rules. The first guidelines, of course, were outlined by the krewes. As with invitations and arriving for the balls, krewes published strict standards in the newspapers. The following 1897 reminder from Rex was typical: "FULL EVENING DRESS IS ABSOLUTELY REQUIRED from all guests. Gentlemen with colored suits or overcoats and ladies with hats or bonnets WILL UNDER NO CIRCUMSTANCES BE ADMITTED TO THE BALLROOM."[58]

The "most brilliant assembly" of women attend an old-line Carnival ball in full dress. *New Orleans Times-Democrat,* February 27, 1900.

Since krewes stipulated that their guests wear *costume de rigueur,* committeemen only admitted gentlemen in white tie and tails, no tuxedos. Women had to don floor-length dresses and most often chose décolleté gowns. Any deviation from this prescription meant that guests were turned away at the door or, in cases of small infractions, relegated to the third (highest) balcony, their faux pas publicly acknowledged. "Ladies with bonnets, and not in evening dress," declared Comus, "will be conducted to the upper tiers and not allowed on the dancing platform."[59]

While fabulously attired guests graced the balcony, krewesmen were expected to conform to dress codes, as well. Committeemen, or "black coats," wore boutonnières to set themselves apart. Krewesmen from the parade and tableaux were required to remain in costume. And the reigning monarchs . . . they had their own rules. Rex disguised himself with fake beard, mustache, and sideburns. Other kings of old-line organizations wore masks. Most kings generally costumed in the style of western European Renaissance rulers.

In addition to a scepter and crown, kings bore a mantle, "based on cloth of silver with an ermine border and designs made of sequins and rhinestones."[60] Royal attire also included trains, specific to each krewe and up to fifteen feet long.[61]

The regal, brilliant costumes of the kings were rivaled only by those of the queens reigning at their side. Josie Halliday, 1904 queen of Carnival, reminisced that "the Queen of Sheba had nothing on me, my dear." She remembered: "I was dripping with jewels. Crown, miles of necklace, brooches, bracelets, jeweled scepter!" Her gown, which was made in Brussels, was handmade lace (she later used it to make bridal veils for herself and some friends). Halliday remarked that her French hairdresser, whom the whole court used, put her hair "up in a pompadour over a rat. They all wore rats then. Ghastly!"[62] Despite the change in hairstyles through the decades, the queen mused: "Was I beautiful, you want to know? Well, what young girl isn't? Especially when she's having a good time. But, my dear, if you have a figure and personality that's all that counts."[63] Adding to the illustriousness of these haute couture garments, old-line krewes often employed Parisian designers to make the queen's dress, even into the first decade of the twentieth century.[64] Bessie Behan, 1891 queen of Carnival, described her gown: "Oh, mine was a handsome gown. Tight, tight. It showed the curves. Heavy white satin, embroidered with gold butterflies, and with little gold cords in the puffs of the sleeves. The Medici collar was of gold lace."[65]

Just as there were hierarchies and status delineations within the world of the krewes, kings and queens dressed to adequately reflect these differences. One such difference was that only two krewes, Comus and Rex (at least before the early 1890s), bedecked their queens with all the royal accoutrements befitting a Renaissance monarch: crowns, necklaces, bracelets, and jeweled belts (stomachers), in addition to a mantle, train, and jeweled scepter. The other krewes focused more on fine gowns and crowns. As one journalist noted: "In the early days, according to Miss Lucia Miltenberger, second queen of Atlanteans at the turn of the century [1892], only queens of Comus and Rex came equipped with jewels, crowns, and mantles. Their gowns were laced up the back in Scarlett O'Hara style and they wore trains."[66]

From the 1890s on, columns upon columns in local newspapers described old-line queens' dresses in detail for all of New Orleans to read, exemplified here by the *Daily Picayune*'s description of Momus' 1897 queen: "The queen of the evening was Miss Lydia Finley, a tall and stately brunette. Miss Finley's dress was beautiful and rich, well befitting one of such exalted rank. It was of white satin, trimmed with handsome lace and pearl ornaments. A long court train of yellow velvet, lined with pale blue satin and bordered with ermine was suspended from her shoulders, and hung in rich and sweeping folds."[67]

Appropriately, the quantity and detail of news coverage reflected the status of krewes in relation to one another. That same season, May Schmidt, befitting her rank as queen of Comus, was described in richer detail than her counterpart queens:

> Miss Schmidt wore an exquisite gown of royal magnificence, after the unique style of the court of Marguerite de Valois. The robe was of royal satin duchesse, cut en traine and richly trimmed. The skirt was a marvel of beauty, the front being richly embroidered in threads of woven gold and silver in delicate designs representing the shells of the sea. Each round was gemmed with diamonds and mounted pearls. The corsage was cut en point and garnitured in rich embroidery of gold and silver in the same beautiful fairy shell designs as the skirt. The sleeves were the real Marquerite de Valois, being made of rarest Point d'Alencon lace, through which glimmered threads of woven gold and golden beads, each tiny puff being emphasized in this graceful arrangement.

But this was not all that was noteworthy about Miss Schmidt. The paper continued:

> The collar was rich and rare, standing high after the type set by the lovely Valois, and yet showing the graceful swan-like throat and neck of the beautiful queen. This collar was a gem of art, and was formed entirely of diamonds and pearls wrought together in a way that would have been deemed magic art in even the famous Aladdin's court. The crowning glory of this magnificent gown was the court train of rose geranium velvet, exquisitely embroidered by hand in gold and precious stones, and bordered by broad bands of princely ermine. It was lined with rich white satin brocade wrought in golden threads, and every turn of the graceful wearer was like a flash of sunlight from those far-off realms where fairies dwell.

And this description only includes her dress! Further illustrations went on to discuss Schmidt's ostrich fan, whose tips were "mounted in mother of

Elegant and ornamental, 1905 Comus queen Helen Rainey poses in full
regal garb, befitting her status at the top of the old-line hierarchy. Courtesy
The Historic New Orleans Collection, acc. no. 1978.226.

pearl and gold," a handkerchief made of Point d'Alençon lace, her diamond crown, her gem girdle, and her scepter. According to the report, her "tout ensemble made up one of the richest and most beautiful toilets ever worn at a carnival ball in New Orleans."[68]

Observing the proper protocol, krewe maids dressed fashionably, richly, but without the royal jewels of their reigning counterpart, befitting their role as attendants to the queen. While maids' dresses were certainly beautiful, newspapers filled their columns with descriptions of the queen and simply listed maids' names. The most common description of their dresses, if printed at all, was that maids wore white. Still, it is reasonable to assume that maids were more elegantly dressed than the guests, separated by the honor of krewe court identity, their debutante emergence, and their entrance into the courting scene. But just as court women's gowns echoed their status, so, too, did the guests' ball gowns, which were superior to the nonkrewe Carnival balls staged in public ballrooms. To be sure, women at the old-line balls dressed well beyond the means of a woman outside of the krewe stratum.

While guests waited for the ball to begin, they occupied themselves with talk of fashion, gossip, and other social pleasures, but krewesmen prepared for the evening in a much different fashion. At the appointed time, well in advance of the parade's start, krewe members (often, after eating at Antoine's or another fine New Orleans restaurant) gathered at their den. There members donned their costumes and then reported to their designated float (if they were riding) or to the appropriate meeting place for maskers who walked the route. When the parade was ready to "roll" (commence), an appointed person checked each costume and krewesman, enforcing sobriety at each stop. Finally, the floats and maskers took to the street, fulfilling their public commitment while anticipating their private party to come.

When parades neared the end of their route, krewes found themselves in the French Quarter. It was difficult for throngs of people to follow the parade down those narrow streets. Because of this, floats easily dropped members off at the stage entrance of the opera house, where the krewe mysteriously disappeared into the bowels of the theater. There they changed into their cast costumes and readied themselves for the tableaux.

With the preparations meticulously organized and carried out with a level of specificity befitting the prestige and intricate opulence of old-line krewes, the guests having arrived and found their assigned vantage points in the theater, and the krewe members having donned their costumes, everything was set for the commencement of the ball, beginning with the tableaux vivants. "A most brilliant assembly"—not just urbane guests but also distinctive krewesmen—converged to celebrate and create old-line traditions. Conversations quieted and lights dimmed. Every preparatory detail contributed to this moment as the first strains of music flowed through the space. Finally, the curtain began to rise, revealing a stage full of krewesmen who would use their bodies to continue the choreography of class that old-line Carnival balls relied upon. Commence with the tableaux!

THREE

"The Age of Chivalry Is Not Passed and Gone"

TABLEAUX VIVANTS DURING RECONSTRUCTION

In 1900, after more than a decade of retirement from public parading due to financial strain (though they still hosted balls), the Knights of Momus returned full throttle to the Carnival scene with an Arthurian theme for their comeback. The *Times-Democrat* hailed the fifteen-float pageant as a success that was thoroughly "imbued with the true Carnival spirit—that gay, glad, mad, merry, indescribable something which has made the great midwinter festival of New Orleans unique and unapproachable."[1]

After the parade, guests arrived at the French Opera House to find an atypically sparsely festooned theater. Despite the meager ornamentation, Momus' spectators were abuzz with anticipation of the coming tableaux, selection of the queen, and masked dancing. As they waited for the performance to begin, guests mingled or perused the evening's program, designed in the form of a gray shield with an illustration that depicted Arthur receiving Excalibur.[2] After the guests had arrived, the Momus krewesmen quietly entered the theater through a back door and quickly changed into cast costumes. They made their way to the stage wings as the orchestra began its overture. Little did anyone know that they were about to experience the last great gasp of a changing tradition—the opulent Carnival krewe tableau performance.

When the curtain finally rose, the first tableau that came into view was a vision of King Arthur and his great knights. Momus clad its cast in rich silk and velvet costumes; it spared no expense in approximating the grandeur of Arthur's realm. Once the last knight (Galahad) joined the circle, a light appeared onstage, and the Holy Grail slowly came into view, "floating in through the air, shedding its red effulgence throughout the banquet hall."[3] The tableau shifted: "Suddenly the hall grew dark and a soft red glow of light moved through the darkness and the thing that shone was in the form of a goblet, but no one could see clearly. They knew, all of them, that this, that they almost saw, but could not see, was the Holy Grail. It passed on again across the hall, and the red glow was gone."[4] Seemingly from nowhere, Momus and four attendants emerged from the shadows. They appraised the scene for several minutes, and then the curtain fell.

When the curtain rose again, the remnants of King Arthur's glorious court had vanished, and in its place, an even better one appeared—that of Momus on his throne, surrounded by his krewe on either side. Stately Momus descended to center stage and dispatched his Lord High Chamberlain to choose the queen from among the court women. Once the queen (Miss May Waters) was paired with her king, Momus crowned his beauty and attached her train; the royal couple then returned to the throne, where they were joined by their dukes and maids and the previous year's royalty. All together, they composed the final tableau and saluted their admirers. It was, as the *Times-Democrat* wrote, "A Dream of Chivalry."[5]

This "Dream of Chivalry" and other scenes like it unfolded in secret, performed by krewesmen for their family and friends. After lavish parades through the streets, old-line krewes retreated to ballrooms where, with the exception of Rex, they staged elaborate tableaux vivants—choreographed performances that illustrated concepts from their annual theme.[6] The tableaux opened krewe balls and often included scenes from mythological battles, chivalrous adventures, famous paintings, or great works of fiction. Through this format, krewesmen relied on their public parades to elevate their social status among the city's residents while the private balls functioned as performances of prestige among themselves and their guests. Tableaux were the first glimpse into the annual articulation of krewe identity, and each scene onstage—the most prevalent themes revolved around romantic legends, ancient literature, or exotic adventures—cultivated a sense of utopian fantasy that remained throughout the entire ball. Through their tableaux, whose main purpose was to entertain guests, krewesmen were also able to utilize a facet of Carnival long embraced by Europeans: the ability for pageants to delight spectators while reflecting contemporary concerns, issues, and perspectives on everyday life. This was especially important during the heyday of tableaux in Carnival balls, the 1870s—during Reconstruction, when krewesmen grappled with the changing, often chaotic world around them but could craft their own immortal, fantastical worlds through tableaux vivants. Because tableaux vivants theatricalized "living pictures," krewesmen posing onstage dramatized their identity and mores in personal ways: through their bodies.

Static "living pictures" have been dramatic concepts since the late medieval period with possible links back to ancient Greek theater.[7] By the fourteenth century, tableaux vivants were popular enough to be regularly incorporated into medieval mystery plays and, later, Renaissance pageantry and *ballet de cour* (especially to celebrate royalty). These spectacles were ceremonial in nature. In late eighteenth-century Europe, tableaux shifted into a modern form and began to take their inspiration from art and history. The "living pictures" were accomplished through physically choreographed poses onstage, complete with costumes, scenery, and the latest theatrical technology: colored, calcium lights. Even then the purpose was threefold: entertainment, moral instruction, and the formation of identity.[8]

In 1830, tableaux vivants were introduced to the New York stage, and by the 1880s, they had been married to dance in a distinctive way that quickly permeated American culture: through Delsartism. François Delsarte, French master of musical theater, oration, and aesthetics, developed a scientific system of elocution and dramatic expression in the 1840s that linked spiritual with physical states. Delsartism spread from France to America, where Genevieve Stebbins (a student of Delsarte's only American pupil, Steele Mackaye) popularized American Delsartism —a blend of Delsartean principles and physical culture—on the New York stage in the 1880s and through her own teachings.[9] American Delsartism stressed gentility and refinement through neoclassical posing but also included vigorous drills, pantomimes, and processions that posed amateur actors (many of them women) as Amazons, Athenians, Greek statues, and other characters inspired by antiquity. Stebbins especially accented this aspect of ancient Greek poses and pantomime within the American style, and her teachings proliferated. American Delsartism spread into mainstream entertainment and education, even into political performances, such as suffrage parades, and notably influenced modern dance. Both Isadora Duncan and Ruth St. Denis, movement innovators at the turn of the twentieth century, studied Delsartism and married it with aesthetic dance and pageantry, fundamentally infusing American concert dance with Delsartean principles.[10]

The presence of tableaux in American popular culture was also widespread—as exercise, education, and dramatic training in settlement houses for working-class children and adults but also as upper- and middle-class parlor amusements, theatrical acts, and charity fund-raising events, mainly performed by women.[11] Writers Louisa May Alcott, Edith Wharton, and Harriet Beecher Stowe inserted tableaux as poignant plot moments in their fiction.[12] By the 1850s, tableaux were popular fixtures of New Orleans entertainment, where they often featured dancing and large production numbers that included female warrior characters who performed drills and geometrically patterned marches.[13] Soon thereafter, tableaux, dance, and elocution became deeply intertwined facets of New Orleans society, so much that instruction in all were features of upper-class children's upbringing, even into the twentieth century.[14]

In addition to being presented onstage, in private parlors, and as part of children's education, tableaux vivants also surfaced in late nineteenth-century society balls.[15] This is not surprising, considering that hosting balls was an important social duty of prestigious women in the nineteenth century and that, in general, women dominated tableau performances. Cultured New Orleans women were no exception. They staged charity balls and tableaux to raise money for disabled soldiers, orphans, and upkeep of Confederate graves.[16] On January 10, 1915, a front-page spread in the *Times Picayune* ran the headline, "Society Women Who Participated in the Roses of Shiraz Dance at the Charity Ball," accompanied by a photograph of women in costume grouped into a multitiered tableau scene. One of the performers was Sadie Downman, queen of Carnival that same year.

Inserting a tableau or two into a ball program enabled women to literally take center stage at their own events. These performances permitted women to reimagine themselves and to enact public, idealized female roles. Through tableaux, they could experiment with traditional perceptions of the female body and femininity.[17] For these same reasons—reimagining themselves in idealized ways and experimenting with identity—tableaux vivants were also a perfect performative medium for krewesmen. Because of tableaux's use of high art and connection with entertainment and cultural values, staging scenes connected to seasonal themes enabled krewesmen to act out their fantasies while strengthening their solidarity and commitment to fraternal group ideals.

Accordingly, tableaux vivants were powerful opening statements for old-line Carnival balls. Once krewe members arrived at the theater and changed into their stage costumes, they were ready to perform. The evening's orchestra played an overture to quiet the crowd and then switched to a commanding piece of music to accompany the first tableau. Once the curtain rose, the audience saw the krewe's interpretation of a familiar literary passage, moment in history, or replication of a specific artwork that characterized the season's theme. Curtains dropped between each scene so the krewe could ready the stage for the next tableau while the orchestra continued to entertain guests with live music.

For Comus' first ball in 1857, krewesmen enlivened their "Demon Actors in Milton's *Paradise Lost*" theme with four tableaux: "Tartarus," "The Expulsion," "Conference of Satan and Beelzebub," and "Pandemonium." The tableaux began at 10:00 p.m., when "the Mistick Krewe appeared on the stage, in full glare of the lights."[18] "Tartarus" showcased a bounty of characters: three fates, three furies, three harpies, three gorgons, and seven miscellaneous characters (including Minotaur and Chimera), all presided over by Pluto and Proserpine. The performers were "arranged in classic attitudes" and "flooded with colored lights in a manner most beautiful to behold." The second tableau illuminated eight main characters, including Isis and Osiris and a "host of other infernals." The third tableau represented the conference of Satan and Beelzebub. The final tableau, "Pandemonium," was "a most magnificent spectacle." This time Satan, flanked by Sin and Death, presided over the passions (Gluttony, Vanity, etc.). The *New Orleans Daily Crescent* reported: "The different tableaux were arranged in accordance with descriptions in Milton's immortal poem, and they were acted out truly and successfully, in a manner which reflected the highest credit upon the poetic taste and judgment of the gentlemen composing the 'Mistick Krewe of Comus.'"[19]

Most early tableaux were intricate and presented several living pictures onstage for the audience to admire. The krewe captain signaled curtain movements with whistle blows, and posing actors held each scene for anywhere from thirty seconds to several minutes. If the audience raved enough, the krewe might even provide multiple encores.[20] Sometimes, performers would even break their pose and dance onstage or into the audience, as was the case with Comus' third ball in 1859. The theme that year was "The English Holidays," and in the third tableau, "Christmas," the stage was set with a feast, Christmas tree and decorations, and even Santa Claus himself. Within the scene a Harlequin beckoned for everyone to join the festivities, "and every now and then he would dance out among the people and cut up his antics in the midst of them."[21] The living picture was alive indeed.

Comus occasionally added grand finales. For the 1860 theme "Statues of the Great Men of Our Country," krewesmen presented nine groupings of characters representing famous men such as Christopher Columbus, William Penn, and John Calhoun. After the nine tableaux concluded, the krewe characters enacted a tenth scene that incorporated a grand march from the stage to the dress circle (the border with the audience where special guests were seated). The lines of krewesmen then split in two and marched back to the stage along opposite sides of the theater. Once back at the tableau site, the men mounted faux-marble pedestals, with each character arranged in chronological succession. The *New Orleans Daily Crescent* described the sight: "For a few minutes all thus stood, in statuesque attitudes, and motionless as if really statues," adding that, at the termination of this scene, the "whole performance was enthusiastically applauded, in all the masculine parts of the house."[22]

Momus and Proteus sporadically replicated the elaborate grand finale practice, as well, indicating that the final tableau could include more action than the standard repertoire of sculptural shapes. For Momus' 1891 theme, "Palmer Cox's Brownies," for instance, two tableaux were followed by a third in which "the Kingly Knight" Momus emerged from a tree and sent messengers out to the four corners of the stage in order to summon brownies to a ball. Without a curtain drop, there was a blackout, and then the lights came up to illuminate a brilliant ball setting, complete with walls, columns, tinsel, and flowers.[23] This elaborate ending was not only a formal transition into the dancing portion of the evening; it was also self-reflexive. Krewes referenced their balls through tableau finales and, in doing so, effectively tied their present frolics to the grand mythos they presented onstage.

Unlike some of the popular parlor or theatrical tableaux vivants, there was no spoken narration to accompany the staged scenes at Carnival balls. Instead, krewes distributed keepsake programs to guests. These programs explained the context surrounding each tableau and aided in further immortalizing tableau personae. Sometimes, as in the case of the 1878 Comus program, the keepsakes could be quite thick, taking on a booklet format rather than a program of a page or two.[24] Programs could even contain drawings of the individual masked characters, which was especially useful for guests in the high balconies who might not be able to distinguish among the various figures in the performance. Ball programs were additionally engaging because they outlined the program order and entertained guests with poetry and illustrations that related to the night's theme.

Generally, seasonal themes comprised four categories (with some overlap): "Great Men," "Fairytales and Folklore," "The Exotic 'Other,'" and "Arts and Nature." Often, "Great Men" themes revolved around men of epic proportions, including figures from history, especially antiquity and Louisiana's past, and classical mythology or literature, such as "The Classical Pantheon" (Comus 1858) and "The Aeneid" (Proteus 1884). These were neoclassical in look. "Fairy Tales and Folklore," which were more romantic in aesthetic, centered on enchantment and European legends. Some of these pageants were based on specific fairy tales, fables, or nursery rhymes, like "Pinocchio" (Momus 1916), "Mother Goose's Tea Party" (TNR 1871), and "Aesop's Fables" (Momus 1908). Others were more general, like "The Fairy Kingdom" (Comus 1902) or "Tales of Childhood" (Proteus 1900).[25] Occasionally, pageant themes rendered "the Other" through exoticism by "going around the world." These pageants depicted sultans, czars, and emperors, or they centered on a particular far-off country, such as "The Moors in Spain" (Momus 1883) or Comus' 1892 "Nippon, The Land of the

Rising Sun," which focused on Japan and whose ball displayed "all the soft hazes, the curious customs and legends of that distant and wonderful clime."[26] "Arts and Nature" designs were perhaps the most whimsical, depicting flowers, musical instruments, the seasons, and even the senses (these last two themes were, in usual old-line style, represented by floats, costumes, and tableaux that depicted antiquity, heroes, gods and goddesses).[27] Through tableau performances, old-line themes lured spectators into a surreal world of sumptuous scenes and, by the nature of the timeless themes themselves, immortalized the performances (and performers).

Costumes were important in conveying the grandeur inherent in these remarkable tableaux. Whether or not a part of the tableau cast, all krewe members made costumed stage appearances for the final scene. This last tableau was the mechanism for the unveiling of the king and court before the commencement of the grand march. The attire krewesmen wore for these moments held significant symbolism. Designs were fantastical and opulent, just as other production elements of the ball. Though no known photographs of actual tableaux exist, old-line krewes left behind copious original costume sketches to peruse. These plates, designed by esteemed artists in close consultation with krewe captains and other members of the ball organizational committees, provide a descriptive glimpse into the development and anticipated action of tableau roles.[28] For pageants that focused on animals or food, the costumes were wildly imaginative. For human characters, costumes often reflected the real-life characters old-line men sought to cultivate: krewesmen as heroes and women as either beautifully sensual or as virtuous symbols, with people of the world (nonkrewesmen, in other words) as "Other." Sketches of heroes show men richly clad, draped in elegant fashions that often included capes and elaborate headdresses. Moreover, male characters were poised for action with noble faces, wielding swords and other weapons. Female characters were often draped in revealing dresses, depicted as passive or offering services like wine or food. Other sketches presented the female body as impenetrable. These drawings costumed female characters in togas and metal breastplates and armed them with spears, shields, and arrows, in line with the symbolic virtues extolled by the character in a pageant that likewise honored the bravery of great men. Characters from far-off lands were predominantly (and generically) Asian. Their costumes were just as fantastical as those of other characters, but their costume sketches often depicted menacing faces with slanted eyes and exaggerated styles of facial hair. Sometimes the characters were part animal.

By costuming as passive women or (without much regard for authenticity) as indigenous people from other races, ethnicities, and cultures, old-line krewes symbolically proclaimed their own superiority, even within the costumed characters that were not center stage during the performance. Members of the supporting cast, of course, were important to krewe identity in that they buttressed the main characters: knights, gods, and kings who asserted power over their respective fictitious dominions just as the old-line kings did over other krewesmen and as old-line krewes did over Mardi Gras. As noted by Carnival historian Karen Leathem, krewe pageants sculpted male images around themes of conquest and power while men assumed their places as make-believe warriors, kings, and rightful rulers of society.[29] This domination was reinforced by the nature of the performance itself. Fairy tales and stories of enchantment, argues Steven Swann Jones, not only offered psychological instruction to audiences but also inculcated audiences with social values and bolstered prevailing cultural traditions: "They promote marriage and the patriarchal family structure as dominant cultural institutions. They depict roles and behavior patterns considered socially appropriate for each gender and for each age group. They encourage industry and moral virtue (such as following the golden rule) as routes to securing material and financial success."[30] Tableau performances, through theme, costume, and gesture, enlivened a space where krewesmen could retreat from the concerns of their time and instead choreograph themselves into ideal roles.

To achieve their ideal, krewesmen most often relied on a specific type of enchantment to stage their identity: the hero of chivalric romances. Tales of courtly love and medieval romance were popular topics for krewe tableaux, including themes that stressed kingly munificence, knightly honor, bravery, and brawn.[31] Tableaux thus championed manly characters who saved damsels in distress—the ultimate chivalric and romantic action. As a 1924 Comus ball booklet stated about the krewe's 1917 theme, "Romantic Legends": "Romance must ever appeal to man, and Comus[,] attentive to the wishes of his faithful subjects, has chosen for this parade the great love epics of all times."[32]

Whether characterized by king or knight, chivalric themes revolved around a concept of manhood that required an ostentatious expression of specific qualities. Chivalrous masculinity rested upon the idealized knightly code in which men were brave warriors (defenders of home and country), champions of virtue and courtly love, faithful to God and king, generous, merciful, and ready to sacrifice themselves for honor, truth, and good. The code also required that heroes test their strength and prevail against supernatural creatures (dragons, evil knights, sorceresses, and the like) and thus attain spiritual enlightenment. As Steven Swann Jones noted, adolescent-category fairy tales (stories in which heroes leave home to find themselves and their manhood) result in the creation of a new domicile—a new life for the knight and his female prize. Likewise, in the category of adult fairy tales (stories where mature male protagonists explore moral and philosophical dilemmas), narratives usually concluded with a renewed balance of domestic tranquility.[33] A knight, then, was expected to rule over his own territory—the home—with the same expertise he demonstrated in battle.

This same expectation of ruling home and battlefield permeated mid-nineteenth-century masculine standards, as well. Honor was a core virtue in this recipe, especially in the South, even after the Civil War. During Reconstruction and in the years afterward, the "Lost Cause" movement intertwined nostalgia for the past, remembrances of the war, and hopes for the present to cultivate a romanticized ideal of a southern manhood entrenched in honor. This ideal (understood to be white) was supported by local communities but also in some of the most popular southern fiction of the time, such as Mark Twain's *A Connecticut Yankee in King Arthur's Court* (1889). As with Twain's work, romantic, artistic renditions of chivalric subjects in the last half of the nineteenth century often surfaced in connection to Arthurian legends. Edgar Fawcett's drama *The New King Arthur* (1885) and Edward Burne-Jones' painting *The Beguiling of Merlin* (1872–77) are examples. Poetry was especially fertile ground. Tennyson's "Idylls of the King" (1859), William Buchanan's "Merlin and the White Death" (1864), and Matthew Arnold's "Tristram and Iseult" (1852) were notable publications.[34] Although romantic legends were popular in the arts across America by the end of Reconstruction, gender codes did not necessarily match. Northerners were preoccupied with the idea of the self-made Christian man. They saw southerners as effeminate and falling short of emulating the northern standard.[35] The return to chivalry in the South, then, energized the idea of southern men at a time when they had lost so much. For old-line krewe members, tableaux served as a vessel for this reinvigoration, promulgating the chivalric code as a core of southern manhood.

As much as old-line romances stressed the chivalric code, they especially emphasized the bonds of brotherhood. The brotherly relationships between tableau characters of knights, heroes, and kings reflected the real-life bonds of brotherhood that krewesmen formed in war. Through utopian visions of the past and the presentation of female tableau characters as championing Confederate values, krewesmen romanticized Confederate participation. This was especially important considering that some krewe members fought for the Confederacy. Essentially, tableaux such as these relieved any lingering guilt over the war atrocities that might have been committed and then punished during Reconstruction. In keeping with the general "Lost Cause" image of Confederate veterans in the New South, a status as defenders of the Old South allowed old-line peers to revere and memorialize Confederate veterans as noble knights who fought to protect their families and the New Orleans way of life.

In commemoration, the Historical Committee of the Mistick Krewe of Comus reported that some of their members, "as patriotic as convivial, donned the gray, the billiard cue exchanged for the musket and the cozy card room for the bivouac. The bloody episode of the Civil War, well remembered by most of us, brought death to many members of our Club." The 1897 krewe booklet noted that the "chivalrous" Chas. De Choiseul died in Richmond while the "gallant" Gen. A. H. Gladden (a Comus president) fell at Shiloh.[36] Through tableaux and in knightly roles, krewesmen recast their past and praised themselves for their involvement in what the historian Bertram Wyatt-Brown termed the "morally purifying nature of military action."[37] In turn, this chivalrous past culminated in krewesmen's genteel manners at balls. In fact, these gentlemanly ways were so impressive at the 1859 Comus ball that one journalist even exclaimed that "the Age of Chivalry is not passed and gone."[38]

Tableau performances equated to choreographic maneuverings that provided space for krewesmen to more clearly appreciate the sacrifices they made while coming to understand more about the emerging causes and values they wanted to embrace in shaping their identities anew. Romantic portrayals of knights and chivalry provided a shared narrative from which krewesmen could script their new selves while sustaining a sense of group power and prestige. In part, the script not only reconstructed krewesmen as their ideal but also countered the political realities of Reconstruction that surrounded them every day, alluding to the serious play aspect of their performance. Even as early as 1860, for instance, Comus staged a plea for sectional compromise with its pageant "Statues of the Great Men of Our Country," presumably protecting its economic interests as leaders in the cotton business. The krewe presented figures from American history who hailed from all regions of the country: George Washington, Andrew Jackson, Daniel Webster, John C. Calhoun, and more. In displaying a shared history for parade-goers (native New Orleanians and northern tourists alike), Comus spoke across the lines of a national debate in order to comment on how to best protect their local concerns. The *New Orleans Daily Crescent* was on hand for the parade and wrote: "The Mistick Krewe of Comus, who have for several years past, on each recurrence of Shrove Tuesday, or Mardi-gras, totally eclipsed all other festive bodies in the richness and originality of their masquerading and in the splendor of their entertainments, on this occasion eclipsed not only everything else, but even their former selves."[39]

Reconstruction was, of course, a tense time. New Orleans was a site of Radical Republicanism, and Democrats in the city (many of them old-line krewesmen) attempted to overturn Republican dominance by swaying people to vote for their own candidates. More extreme measures of resistance to Republican rule surfaced in the formation of the White League, a paramilitary group whose membership overlapped with that of some krewes. Animosities exploded on September 14, 1874, when 3,500 armed men from the White League attempted to oust the local carpetbag government by attacking the metropolitan police and deposing the governor. This "Battle of Liberty Place" not only precluded Carnival the ensuing year but also marked the near end of krewesmen's declining control over local politics.[40] President Ulysses Grant's federal troops arrived in New Orleans and forced the White League to surrender, and although the following Carnival season "opened earlier and more brilliantly than ever before,"[41] it seemed that Mardi Gras was now the main realm where krewesmen held direct power.

The last gasp for krewesmen's overt political power came with the 1896 mayoral election. In 1896 Charles Janvier, that year's Rex, emerged from Carnival season and led a reform group to take back control of the local government, which had been tampering with salaries and the balance of power. Janvier's prestige and good reputation swayed many New Orleanians as he backed Comus member Walter C. Flower for mayor. Flower, "a man of wealth and education, a merchant," had been president of the Cotton Exchange and, like Janvier, was involved in the famous Hennessy investigation.[42] Flower (and Janvier) reflected the politics of the most prestigious krewes. Under the victorious Flower, a new charter that followed the ideology of the Municipal Reform League was put into place and assured the men of Comus, Rex, Momus, and Proteus of their political influence. After this and content with the demise of the old politicos (known as the "Ring"), krewes retired from direct political engagement altogether, and subsequent political machines refrained from disturbing krewe interests.[43] Krewe members' attention then shifted solely to social involvement in the finest schools, clubs, churches, and neighborhoods.[44]

After the tumult of the war and Reconstruction, krewesmen retreated to their clandestine Carnival organizations and began to engage in a "closed system" of social exchange. Segregation from the rest of the world equaled exclusivity, which equaled safety and even a sense of power.[45] From this equation emerged a need to articulate class-consciousness: wealth alone no longer corresponded to krewe status. Now, prestige was a crucial ingredient in how old-line krewesmen measured their worth. And with prestige came another element of their developing social and cultural capital: discernment. Through an elevated appreciation of art and by being cultural connoisseurs (as displayed through their tableau performances), krewesmen created a special identity for themselves, separate not only from the racial and ethnic minorities on the outskirts of their system but also from other upper-class New Orleanians not worthy of (or interested in) krewe membership. To institute themselves as New Orleans' highest cultural emissaries, old-line krewes began to use the idea of exceptionalism to cultivate tradition, legacy, and staying power.[46]

Old-line krewes' focus on sociocultural status reflected their "gentlemanly agreement" code, reinforcing club membership as an "organized effort to retain social power within a castelike social stratum."[47] Krewe activities were important in preserving the esteemed reputations and alliances that the white, (mostly) upper-class, (mostly) Protestant krewe families previously cultivated.[48] But krewe events also served as an outlet for another need: sociopolitical commentary. Battered by the war and then Reconstruction, krewesmen needed to bond over pleasurable activities that also galvanized similar worldviews through tradition and ritual. The Carnival ball was a prime site for engaging in both requirements, especially in tableau performances.

From 1860 until the end of Reconstruction in 1877, old-line krewe themes, unveiled in the parades and then further presented through tableaux at the ball, often served this double purpose: they provided both whimsy and entertainment for Mardi Gras festivities while also using Carnival as a performative space of political commentary. In performing sociopolitical perspectives through their cultural institutions of tableaux, old-line krewesmen during Reconstruction reconstructed *themselves,* like phoenixes emerging from the ashes of Confederate, Democrat defeat and floating (literally, in parades) into a new era of order, peace, and even power. As historian Reid Mitchell points out, New Orleanians used Mardi Gras in part to assuage the wounds of the battlefield: "For them, recovery from the war required the revitalization of Carnival," including Rex's rule, among other krewe activities, which "met a desire for a kind of symbolic victory amid actual defeat."[49] Defeat didn't end with the war, however, and political satires during Reconstruction pageants provided additional moments for performing krewes' political frustrations.[50]

Out of all the Reconstruction years, 1873's Carnival season stands out most as political performance. Three clear examples of krewe political satire exist: TNR's "The World of Audubon," Momus' "The Coming Races (Entwicklungsgeschichte)," and Comus' "The Missing Links to Darwin's Origin of Species." While no descriptions of the tableaux remain for the TNR and Momus pageants, their theme, costumes, and float designs at least reveal *the ideas* that played out onstage that night.[51] TNR's theme, "The World of Audubon," was an outward celebration of the renowned ornithologist and artist John James Audubon, who lived and worked in New Orleans in the early 1820s. Krewesmen were costumed as owls, parrots, pelicans, doves, and more. Beneath the many bird costumes, however, was another message: a failing state government, including satires of the legislature as "The Crows in Council," complete with a "Carrion Crow with carpet-bag in hand."[52] The pageant "burlesqued the Republican Party," while commenting on the fraudulent oath taking of two politicians to the office of Louisiana governor just months prior.[53] Likewise, Momus' "The Coming Races (Entwicklungs-geschichte)," though less overtly satirical than TNR, mocked Darwin and even Audubon through the krewe's "master history," thus staking a claim with the other old-line krewes in political resistance. Momus' topsy-turvy world commented that scientific theory had a devastating effect on civilization: floats carried women clad in breeches, male crustaceans were assaulted by their female counterparts, sharks were descendants of lawyers, and scholars had sheep faces.[54]

Comus' 1873 pageant, "The Missing Links to Darwin's Origin of Species," provides even more detail. In this pageant, krewesmen dressed as various animals of Darwin's evolutionary chain, from sponge and mosquito hawk to elephant and baboon. Main characters—escorted by personal squires dressed as asses—walked the parade route in exaggerated papier-mâché an-imal costumes representing the carpetbag government. Many of the animal masks went so far as to caricature specific government officials. A tobacco grub signified President Grant while Benjamin Butler was mocked as a hyena. A snail and a leech stood for members of the Louisiana legislature, and a bloodhound's head bore the likeness of the local superintendent of the metropolitan police.[55] Satire, a prominent feature of even today's Mardi Gras celebrations, allowed old-line krewesmen to safely jest about Reconstruction politics while embedding their concerns in harmless entertainment. But satire, as we know, is rarely innocent or benign. By its very nature, satire uses humor and exaggeration to criticize and even ridicule. "The Missing Links" literally embodied Comus' attempts to work out this formulation and, by extension, the mechanisms that old-line men could safely employ to explore (and grapple with) problems in the world around them.

As a satire, the costumed "Missing Links" pageant made visible krewes-men's central concern over racial politics. Comus presented its version of the "Missing Link" as a hybrid animal, a half–black man, half-gorilla crea-ture who played the banjo. According to historian Reid Mitchell, Comus'

Harper's Weekly engraving of Comus' 1873 grand tableau, "The Missing Links."
Courtesy The Historic New Orleans Collection, Gift of Harold Schilke
and Boyd Cruise, acc. no. 1953.69.

satire clearly pitted the krewesmen against the era's "two most progressive
strands of thought"—the Radical Republican government and Darwin's
evolutionary philosophy. Mitchell argued, in fact, that the "krewe held up
the contemporary political and social order as unnatural" through their
pageants, both publicly in the street and privately in their tableaux.[56]

Later that night, at their Carnival ball, the Mistick Krewe continued
their parody through tableaux presented at the Varieties Theater. The first
dramatization, which introduced lighting techniques that made images
appear and then dissolve, began with a scene from the bottom of the sea. A
sponge, coral, alligator, crab, and dolphin glittered next to a mermaid, seal,
and walrus.[57] This scene was replaced by the second tableau, which flaunted
a crowned gorilla as the completion of Darwin's chain. Various animals—a
grasshopper, an orangutan, a beetle, a locust, and more—bowed to the gorilla and danced with delight. Yet, one figure conquered the stage: Comus,
radiantly costumed, standing tall in the center of the stairs, unyielding to
the animals around him.

Costumed krewesmen and female guests mingle at the ball following
"The Missing Links" tableau. *Scribner's Monthly* engraving, "Carnival Balls" folder, Louisiana
Image Collection, Louisiana Research Collection, Tulane University.

Comus made his point. He clearly stood apart from the rest of the world, even from the rest of man's evolution and the platform of Reconstruction. He was superior, and he ruled by divine right. As the audience drank this in, the tableau shifted. The *Daily Picayune* stated: "The arm of the Grasshopper moves! A strain comes from the fiddle, the music strikes a march—beasts, fish, bugs, birds, and creeping things start out upon the dancing-floor, the living mass of the audience surges down to meet them, and word is given for the ball."[58] Once on the dance floor, alligators, gorillas, mock gods, and ladies alike intermingled for waltzing and conversations, furthering group bonds and solidarity through socializing and ballroom embraces.

Tableau images such as the ones performed by Comus in 1873 were not uncommon but by no means solely dominated Reconstruction media. Supporters of Emancipation depicted African Americans with dignity and respect, even fortitude, and championed equal rights through drawings and writings. These were, of course, mostly northern artists. Take, for instance, Thomas Nast's engraving *Franchise*, in which a black Union soldier, dressed in his army uniform, stands atop a set of stairs, holding himself up on crutches (he has only one leg). The artwork, published as a centerfold in the August 5, 1865, issue of *Harper's Weekly*, shows the soldier accompanied by Columbia, a classically robed figure representative of American government. *Franchise* was paired with *Pardon,* which illustrated famous southern soldiers and politicians kneeling at Columbia's feet, begging forgiveness. The caption posed a question from Columbia herself: "Shall I trust these men, and not this man?"[59]

While positive images in popular culture sought to rally support for black rights, many Americans still tense about Emancipation and its aftereffects opposed enfranchisement and sought to bolster their view through media portrayals of African Americans that built upon stereotypes and fed on fears of the "black menace" and "black peril." Racial caricatures peppered printed newspapers, even in the North, which often stereotyped blacks as much as southern culture did. Out of all racialized performances during Reconstruction, minstrelsy was by far the most popular. Minstrelsy—(mostly Irish) white performers in blackface performing dances and skits that stereotyped African Americans and slave culture—began appearing in theaters in the late 1820s. Within twenty years, minstrelsy became the most popular form of American entertainment, appearing often in New Orleans and dominating stages until the advent of vaudeville.[60] After the Civil War, mixed minstrel troupes included black and white performers, though everyone was still required to wear blackface. As variety performances, minstrel shows disseminated singing, dancing stereotypes of the "happy slave" through burlesques and comic sketches that included shuffles, bucking, and the popular "Jump Jim Crow" made famous by Thomas "Daddy" Rice.[61] Importantly, minstrelsy stood at the center of a contentious debate about race, class, and institutionalization. It was adored by general audiences and loathed by abolitionists, and, like Comus' 1873 "Missing Links" tableaux, it revealed core tensions about race and politics in nineteenth-century America.

Following the tumultuous "Missing Links," "The World of Audubon," and "The Coming Races (Entwicklungsgeschichte)" pageants in 1873, the ensuing season was seemingly docile. Beneath its calm exterior, though, citywide political and racial tensions had actually percolated to a boiling point. While old-line krewesmen masked for Mardi Gras, they publicly revealed their racial attitudes through parallel participation as members of the White League in the explosive 1874 riot. Because of the battle, the city canceled Mardi Gras for the following year, and most krewes tempered their criticisms. The exception was Momus, who staged "Hades: A Dream of Momus" in 1877. This was the last overt political krewe satire, a last stab at the Republican Party that was then making an exit from New Orleans politics. "Hades" literally demonized major government departments with Satan (wearing Grant's face) ruling his empire from a grand throne, surrounded by snakes and monsters. To conclude the pageant, Momus depicted a sinking "Ship of State." The vessel was engulfed by flames with caricatures of famous northerners: abolitionist lawyer Wendell Phillips, Union major general Ben "Beast" Butler, and former vice president Schuyler "Smiler" Colfax, among others.[62]

Reconstruction, a nationally strained period of transition, raised questions about difference and belonging on a multitude of levels—socially, economically, politically, and so forth—and just as tableaux vivants revealed krewe tensions about politics and race, the Carnival ball stage was also a space where krewesmen confronted their sociopolitical views about women. With the formation of the National Woman Suffrage Association (NWSA) and the American Woman Suffrage Association (AWSA) in 1869, the issue of women's rights reemerged with vigor, creating an additional political front against which conservative white men contended. In other words, American women's activism caused further chaos for krewesmen already swimming in political change. In tableaux, of course, these tensions manifested through the body; male krewesmen costumed as grotesque women, which likely intensified both the entertainment value and heinousness of the "women" presented onstage. Grotesque female characters in ball tableaux served as both humor and a warning for what women should avoid.

Literary theorist Mary Russo argued that men's anxieties about women and women's bodies, especially in relation to the power of reproduction, created a mystique about women's physicality. Russo contended that this apprehension of the womb—the grotto-esque element of femininity— evolved into the idea of grotesque, where the images usually associated with women's bodies (and by extension, women's nature) included hag, witch, medusa, bearded woman, fat lady, hottentot venus, and evil seductress, not to mention the "Shrieking sisterhood" of the suffragists.[63] Old-line krewes used this same imagery to caution women against "bad" behavior while also lauding krewesmen's own manhood. As historian Judy Hilkey has argued, the "idea of manhood was given force, poignancy, and positive meaning in part by counterpointing it with a pejorative notion of the feminine."[64] Manly strength, bravery, and protection were not only clarified but also justified and required when juxtaposed against the threat of grotesque women.

Take, for instance, Comus' 1877 season theme, "The Aryan Race." For this, Comus traced men's heroic history from Greece through the Crusades and into the grandeur of urban America. Floats began with Comus, followed by "The Feast of Isis," "The Empire of Rome," and "Charlemagne," even a hunting party and a tournament, moving through time and leading up to the last float, number twenty-four. That float, "Our Future Destiny, 1976," exhibited the Aryan race a hundred years from the pageant and was focused on a monumental political change: women voting. This was, in fact, a satire. Comus' hidden message, which became clear in that night's tableau performance, was that it had no desire to see women participate in the American political landscape.

After the parade, in the private tableaux of the Carnival ball, Comus staged five scenes. The first four tableaux illustrated the evolution of man and civilization. Tableau one, "Roman Wedding—Second Century," unveiled twenty "gayly dressed figures, handsomely grouped in wedding fashion"; the second tableau, "Baptism of Clovis—Fifth Century," featured fifty characters who "made a fine display of this imperial ceremony." The third tableau, "Court of Justice—Twelfth Century," used thirty actors, and "Science, Literature and Art Dominates War," the fourth tableau, comprised of fifty men, staged the character of War, who, "lay at the feet of the peaceful conquerors."[65] Finally, the curtain rose on the fifth scene, titled "Woman's Election in 1976." According to the program for that evening, this was Comus' vision of man's future:

An Election Day in 1976 when woman is fully enfranchised and in control and possession of all branches of the government and man has no vote or voice whatever in government; Woman has risen to a standard of perfection in government and business that leaves Man's highest capacity in the nursery and kitchen. On the left, Woman conducting an election; on the right the nursery and kitchen with Man in his proper sphere. In the central background Comus and his Court deriding Man in the nursery. In the side background the Past Ages mournfully regarding the end of Man's influence in the world.[66]

Comus' futuristic picture was a flip-flopped reality of empowered women and emasculated men. According to the *Daily Picayune:* "All the figures of the Krewe, superior women occupying the left and abject men the right. Comus and court were above looking down upon, laughing and ridiculing the scene."[67] The tableaux presented a nonsensical, but even more importantly, an improbable outcome. Strikingly, even within this world Comus is set apart. The krewe not-so-subtly used humor to remind their audience where the sexes belonged—men at work and women in the home. This sentiment was timely. In 1878 Congress responded to suffragist demands by forming House and Senate committees to debate the issue. Surely some krewesmen envisioned their playful Election Day scene from the previous Carnival season.

Krewesmen, of course, were not alone in this viewpoint. American society in general was torn over the idea of women voting, and popular culture referenced antisuffragist views through cartoons and other humorous modes, gaining even more traction around the turn of the century. In fact, twelve years after Comus' "Aryan Race" production, a similar sketch appeared in the manual *Tableaux, Charades, and Pantomimes.* The book described the scene, aptly titled "Woman's Rights": "A domestic scene, in which the duties of the sexes are reversed. One man should be at the wash-tub; another paring potatoes and rocking the cradle with his foot. A woman should be reading the newspaper leisurely; another with pen over her ear, should be poring over some accounts."[68] Interestingly, in the manual this scene is followed by one that pictures a gypsy woman reading palms and foreseeing futures, followed by "Signing the Pledge," a tableau wherein a drunkard commits to temperance while his female family members, including his wife, helplessly plead to the world around him. Contextualized in this way, the guide presents images of women, if not completely ridiculous, then only in control of tomfoolery.

While general tableaux in popular culture allowed for the possibility of women playing their own roles, old-line ball versions relied on krewe members to portray female characters. Journalist W. G. Bowdoin observed that in the 1901 Carnival, "no women take part in these street parades. The female characters are taken by chosen youth and the selection is very critical. The costuming is cunning and appropriate."[69] Likewise, Mardi Gras historian Henri Schindler has remarked that "every female character in the float designs was brought to life by an all-male cast; no matter how delicate or feminine the costumes might appear, they were worn with delight by generations of the most prominent businessmen in New Orleans."[70] Although Bowdoin was possibly impressed and Schindler certainly looked back in time with admiration, local *Daily Picayune* journalist "Catherine Cole" (writer Martha R. Field) penned her own thoughts. In her assessment of Momus' 1880 spectacle, "A Dream of Fair Women," which depicted Mary Queen of Scots, Cleopatra, and other famous historical women, Cole wrote that "they attempted to portray a 'Dream of Fair Women,' but I confess my imagination was not vivid enough to fancy 'fair women' in the lot of gorgeously appareled brawny men who hid their beards and moustaches behind false faces. Adieu! It was a perfect nightmare. The disillusion was most complete."[71]

The absurdity of the "Dream of Fair Women" performance was no doubt hilarious, but it hid a deeper meaning that the *Daily Democrat* noted—the "sad fact that most of these heroines of Momus have played a sad part."[72] As observer George Augustus Sala noted in his travelogue, the krewe struck a "Tennysonian chord." But what Sala also noted, like the *Daily Democrat,* was that the female characters portrayed the worst moments that defined these women. The only exception was the final subject, Josephine, who, as Sala pointed out, was a "Creole" empress whose "sweet memory is yet revered" in New Orleans.[73] As for the other characters: Delilah was seen cutting a drunk Samson's hair, Dido was poised on the funeral pyre, Judith was beheading Holofernes, Cleopatra was poisoning Marc Anthony, and Mary Queen of Scots was descending to her execution. These "Fair Women"—all captured at a distinct moment in time—referenced woman's inconsistency or treachery, her seductive, grotesque nature.

This selective editing of women's lives was common. The nature of a tableau freezes an entire narrative into a single, poised moment, but those chosen moments also delivered key messages. Where women were concerned, the central lesson was that women constantly undermined men's achievements through feminine trickery. As Mary Chapman has shown, the "woman as seductress" theme was common in tableaux vivants. In Louisa May Alcott's novel *Little Women,* for example, we see female tableau characters as gender commentary, symbolizing the evils of American womanhood through powerful portrayals of their womanly wiles: as a governess looking to undo the "supervisory gaze" of her male employer or as Judith, whose sex appeal lured enemy Holofernes to his death.[74] Krewes went a step further and staged a variety of seductress levels, all of which implied that, if man was taken in by women's schemes, he would eventually be able to rectify the situation by punishing her for her waywardness. Tableaux vivants (like many images in the visual arts) cautioned audiences that any woman who lashed out against male power would face consequences. In the selective artistic editing of their lives onstage, women immortalized in tableaux would be forever trapped in the moment when they suffered at the hands of men. These moments underscored a perspective where female bodies were "objectified as signs of virtue gone awry."[75] "A Dream of Fair Women," then, was as much a warning to women as it was a spoof on history.

As much as these tableaux both parodied and resisted political woes, old-line tableau performances also presented utopian counterparts beyond chivalrous knights to offset the hags and gorillas, murderesses and monsters. While krewesmen's forays into chivalric territory established a sense of gentility that pervaded group identity in everyday life, they also employed neoclassical allegories to represent the values that gentility championed. Two-thirds of Comus' themes referenced heroes and gods from ancient Greece and Rome, as well as great men from American and Louisiana history. Almost a quarter of Proteus pageants did the same, as did a handful of Momus pageants.[76] In contrast to romantic images of sensuality, individuality, compassion, bravery, and honor, the masculine ideal in neoclassical tableaux championed virtue, beauty, reason, truth, humanism, and education in the liberal arts—all characteristics of a privileged class. Moreover, whereas krewe members masqueraded as knights and warriors in their romantic tableaux, they assumed the roles of gods and conquerors for their neoclassical performances.

Like most visual arts of the day, tableau performances did not portray specific myths from antiquity. Rather, gods and heroes symbolized the noble character from general mythology. Krewes even extended those noble characteristics into portrayals of famous and brave men from Louisiana's own past. Focusing on character enabled krewesmen to stage one particular moment of a hero's life or to present a series of moral lessons without being bound to the particulars of the stories or to chronological accuracy. Generalized mythological references also enabled krewesmen (like artists of their time) to avoid "overly sensual or pagan" meanings, as well as allusions to the possibility of violence and male desire that often accompanied specific myths, thus protecting the image of female chastity that tableaux conveyed.[77]

An excellent example of this general usage of ancient mythology is Comus' 1872 theme, "Dreams of Homer." For this year, Comus staged four tableaux. The first, "The Judgment," featured Venus, Juno, Minerva, and Paris. "The Combat," with Diomede, Menelaus, Ajax, Thersites, Mars, and Hector, composed the second tableau, and the third, "Trials of Ulysses—The Odyssey," showed Ulysses returning to Ithaca after a twenty-year absence. The final tableau showed the "Battle of Frogs and Mice," wherein a Louisiana local, King Pontchartrain, mitigated the comical clash.[78] On February 14, the New Orleans Daily Picayune relayed that "the curtain drops to rise again in a few minutes. Gods, goddesses, warriors living and dead, giants, mice, frogs, and crabs join in a grand march, led by Comus and mingled with the audience."

While the scene was humorous, krewesmen staging themselves as victorious warriors was serious business. Krewesmen not so subtly claimed power by concluding their tableaux with the triumph of a figure close to home (Pontchartrain). These tableaux were successful because they showed gods and great heroes at poignant moments. By associating themselves with classical mythology, krewesmen literally embodied their self-constructed identity as great men. This symbolism was not understated. The fact that krewesmen physically emulated great masterpieces of art and literature through tableaux that guests could easily recognize was in itself "an implied sense of status."[79] This also intimated a sense of southern-ness. A continued reliance on classical literature reassured krewesmen that nothing need change and created a common bond of reference among educated, cultured southerners, even when the North had moved away from the practice toward educational investments that formed the bedrock of future progressive reforms.[80]

Krewes were especially successful in linking neoclassicism to class status and southern-ness when they equated themselves to great figures from local

The sixth and final tableau, "Louisiana—Her Founders and Defenders,"
for Comus' 1870 pageant, "The History of Louisiana from 1539 to 1815."
Courtesy The Historic New Orleans Collection, acc. no. 1959.32.

history. The Mistick Krewe of Comus' 1860 and 1870 seasons were notable
performances in this regard. For their 1860 pageant,"Statues of the Great
Men of Our Country," Comus choreographed a captivating sight:

> Carlos Patti led the orchestra with 100 musicians and when the curtain rose
> on the first historical group, Patti gave us a new Potpourri for the occasion,
> Misses Cellia and Jesse Crisp (aunts of the Present G. A. Senator) sang the
> Star Spangled Banner. The equestrian statue of Gen'l Jackson was staged to
> perfection.... The statues soon broke ranks, and Patti's music brought them
> all to tripping the "light fantastic toe" and in a few moments COMUS and
> his Mystic Krewe disappeared into the air, and Terpsichore had taken his
> and the Krewes place.[81]

A decade later, Comus again associated its krewe with greatness for the
1870 season, "The History of Louisiana from 1539 to 1815." In the last tableau, "Louisiana—Her Founders and Defenders," all of the characters were

arranged on various pedestals and faux-marble staircases; this was a grand testament to the krewe's admiration for Louisiana men, and also for themselves. For this performance, the Mistick Krewe literally put their visions of great men up on pedestals for the guests to appreciate. Accordingly, this was no small, static picture. One newspaper described the scene as "grand in the extreme, and of gigantic proportions," as the base of the tableau platform alone was 35 feet wide and 21 feet tall and was covered completely with men posing as Napoleon, Bienville, De Soto, and others, with Andrew Jackson at the top.[82]

As the illustration shows, multiple platforms display the white "statues" who stand erect with open chests and feet apart. Men are firmly planted where they stand. The bodies possess verticality, an association that often ties performers to Enlightenment ideals, a performance of Western culture at its finest and a bedrock of ballet through the ages. The stance also evokes parallels between the ideal spectator—assumed to be heterosexual, white, and male (the quintessential old-line krewesman)—and the male performer (in this case, the same demographic as the ideal spectator). In Michael Fried's argument about male representation in paintings (apt for tableau comparison and extended to male dance performances by Ramsay Burt), the "theatrical" model is one that "makes a claim on spectators." A "theatrical" painting or performance elicits interest in what the principal figure is doing; audiences want to see what the performer "sees." In short, spectators identify with the intensity, intent, and identity of the male performer. Juxtaposed against this, the "absorption" mode has an inward focus. By being completely absorbed in what he is doing, the performer allows the audience to take in the formal, aesthetic qualities of the art form and, in doing so, may invite an erotic gaze despite his conformity to male norms of self-sufficiency and detachment.[83] Absorption leads to feminization while theatricality equals dominance. Comus' tableaux champion the theatrical; krewesmen clearly dominate the scene with their bodies. Characters claim their space, even extending the space around them (and thus their own presence) with doffed hats and an assortment of manly implements: guns, swords, and staffs. Characters look out past their viewers, commanding the audience's attention with confidence. They are strong; they are grounded; they are timeless.

According to the *New Orleans Times* of March 2, the scene was "the most perfect, beautifully conceived, and handsomely grouped tableau ever witnessed in the country." And, despite its lasting longer than the other tableaux, the krewe brought it back for an encore in response to the thunderous applause from onlookers. By creating their image as such, old-line krewes literally and figuratively linked themselves to a mythologized past, a romantic vision that conceived of krewesmen as the embodiment of refinement and education—gentility's apotheosis. They were perfect southern gentlemen.

Onstage, towering marble statues connected krewesmen's image of southern gentility to heroic deeds, dominance, and whiteness, all through grand scenes that relied on carefully controlled bodies. This correlation is clarified even more when considering a man closely affiliated with old-line society and lauded throughout the South: Robert E. Lee, incidentally nicknamed the "Marble Man" for his impeccable outward restraint and exemplary behavior.[84] Lee was a parental, community, and regional authority, a model of propriety, control, and genius (with a cultlike following throughout the generations). He believed in Christian sacrifice, decorum, order, avoiding self-absorption, and in a "superiority that was tied to the cultural prescriptions of white society." As Nina Sibler points out, these elements "marked him as what nineteenth-century white Americans considered a 'gentleman.'"[85]

For old-line tableaux, the link between old-line culture and whiteness was very literal. Krewesmen achieved the look of a white, classical marble statue by powdering their skin with precipitated chalk, donning layers of white fabric fashioned into a toga, and striking an elegant, noble pose. Not only did they reference marble statues, long thought of as the most refined and sophisticated artistic creations, but performances also demonstrated krewe connections to ideals promulgated through classical marble statues; whiteness—as artistic material and skin color—attached male bodies to power, prestige, and cultural enlightenment. As such, tableaux were static expressions of class solidarity, communicated through moral instruction embedded in theatrical entertainment. As social scientist John MacAloon has pointed out, cultural performance is not merely entertainment or simply a cathartic indulgence; it is about self-definition and preservation of history and myths, and it functions as a portal to change.[86] Through the 1870 Comus tableau, "Louisiana—Her Founders and Defenders," krewesmen artistically *and physically* achieved the goals MacAloon lays out.

Effectively, these tableaux achieved the same objective as visual artists of the day. That is, "marbleizing" their masculine ideal enabled krewes to create an arresting moment when, through robust, muscular strength, krewesmen physically embodied their choreographed version of their ideal selves. The act of posing impressed this feat upon their audience while the performers used their bodies to build dramatic and emotional tension. Simultaneously, the marble men garnered audience appreciation for their theatrical achievements. Tableaux were at once both art and life. By the end of the performance, krewesmen instilled virile images in their audience's minds, and in turn, guests equated krewesmen with the figures they represented, further entrenching masculine ideals as a shared group value.

Old-line values, though focused predominantly on men in tableaux, also addressed representations of women. Naturally, in this chivalry-based fantasy world with heroes of mythical proportions, all women, even goddesses and queens, relied on men's love, men's protection, and men's brawn to shield them from the phenomena of their mystical worlds. In tableau performances, female characters referenced male heroes. This was especially true for the idealized female characters: sublime goddesses and picturesque maidens. The idealized feminine iconography, of course, was a blueprint of what krewesmen wanted their women to replicate. "A symbolized female presence both gives and takes value and meaning in relation to actual women," argues historian and mythographer Marina Warner, "and contains the potential for affirmation not only of women themselves but of the general good they might represent and in which as half of humanity they are deeply implicated."[87]

While grotesque female characters symbolized what krewesmen saw as the worst of womanhood, the converse iconography of woman as sublime encouraged female audience members to dismiss any personal sacrifices as they persisted in supporting their men. Naturally, this femininity represented krewesmen's ideal woman—attractive, delicate, leisurely, and, in accordance with the normal gender codes of the day, selflessly devoted to their homes, their husbands, and their husbands' values.[88] Wyatt-Brown has argued that this "familiar stereotyping of Southern ladyhood" was a socially indispensable means of ensuring "at least outward submission to male will."[89]

Not surprisingly, these idealized images occurred precisely at the time of the women's movement, when women were rejecting the docile, domestic image in favor of professional independence and voting.[90] Sublime women subverted the headstrong suffragist and restored order to a world in flux. That krewesmen's goddesses also symbolized nationalism emphasized this point even more.

The most extreme example of the idealized Carnival feminine was, as historian Karen Leathem pointed out, when men masked as angels: innocent and pure, angels were the pinnacle of ideal womanhood and served as a sharp contrast to women's involvement in political activism.[91] Though angels were an often-embraced feminine ideal, krewesmen mostly preferred to portray the sublime through female characters in chitons and togas, classical statuesque women often accompanied by partial armor, shields, and staffs, or even the United States Constitution, comprising what Warner has termed "Armed Maidens," hailed as "invulnerable epitomes of the nation."[92] Comus, for instance, staged tableaux that included Minerva (1858), Venus (1869), the fair maiden Louisiana (1870), Goddess America (1874), and Juno (1878). In fact, Comus' 1878 pageant, "Scenes from the *Metamorphoses* of Ovid," presented several mythical figures with women rivaling the male characters in stature and plot prominence. The first tableau of that evening's ball presented the entire dramatis personae from the literary work: "On a throne in the background sat Jupiter and Juno; on the right, Athena and Arachne, Circe and Ulysses, etc.; on the left, Cadmus and Hermione, Latona and the Lycians, Apollo and Daphne, etc.; in the centre, Bacchus, the Daughters of Minyas, etc." Through tableaux, the physicality of these idealized women starkly contrasted the grotesque body. Whereas the grotesque was comical, bawdy, and exemplified the ravages of worldly toil, the Armed Maiden was an ethereal embodiment of classical form. The classically inspired figures were "monumental, static, closed, and sleek, corresponding to the aspirations of bourgeois individualism."[93] In this way, krewes produced a female counterpart to their marble men.

Female characters' transcendent representation in tableaux further intimated class status and enlightenment, galvanizing krewesmen's wives, daughters, and female friends as integral to the development of krewe identity. The classically feminine characterizations onstage conceived of

"Louisiana," an 1899 Proteus costume design and a prime example
of Marina Warner's "Armed Maiden" concept. Carnival Collection, Louisiana
Research Collection, Tulane University.

women as ethereal and morally uplifting, especially considering their placement, often center stage poised on platforms, sometimes even overlooking
the male roles.[94] The goddess Flora, for example, surveyed her garden kingdom in Comus' third tableau in 1869. "She occupied the same elevated position that had been assigned to her mythological predecessors, and from her
cap, which was full of earth's most beautiful productions, she showered down
upon the heads of her subjects handfuls of God's earthly jewels. Around her
were grouped representations of the flower kingdom," and in the front center
was a giant nose that served as a pedestal for god Comus.[95] By staging Flora
thus, a figure as core to the scene as the krewe god himself, krewesmen made
an artistic spectacle of female presence. They overtly linked the delicateness
and decorativeness of flowers to women, specifically to their women, who
would be watching from the audience and drawing forth meaning from the
stage before them.[96]

Krewesmen's lauding of the female, though, went far beyond tying her
to beauty. Women embodied the greatest virtues of civilization, even civilization itself. Because these female characters often symbolized ideas of
Creation, the State, and the Country, krewesmen essentially correlated
female sexuality to a nationalistic fervor, with krewes as the preservers and
defenders of this ideal.[97]

The illustration of the feminine ideal as a transcendent symbol mirrored
the cultural trends of the time. The most commonly employed ideal of
woman in 1870s American art was the use of the feminine form as allegory,
symbol, or metaphor, employed as "a poetic strain in American painting."
Many classically inspired paintings depicted "visions of an Arcadian past,"
highlighting the "arrangement of beautiful, classically-clad maidens" as "allegorical and quasi-mythological subjects. Their features were idealized, their
costumes vaguely antique," and painting techniques essentially "defined the
women as occupying an otherworldly, symbolic, or 'ideal' realm."[98] Krewesmen, in keeping with this imagery, imbued their feminine icons with an
American essence of democratic values and history. Comus' sixth tableau
of 1870, for example, surrounded Louisiana and her daughter, beautiful New
Orleans, with characters Cotton, Sugar, and Rice, linking the products that
made krewesmen wealthy to woman's fertility.[99] The scene was a sensation
and brought down the house with rapturous applause, which, as the *New*

Orleans Times noted on March 2, necessitated an encore showing. Louisiana, as the central character of that season's theme, reappeared with her daughter on the stage platform for the finale. Lording over the rest of the characters, she held a shield and a wheat "staff"; she defended the krewesmen's economic interests.[100] Even thirty years later, the symbolism still held weight. Proteus, for their 1899 pageant, "E Pluribus Unum," borrowed Comus' characters Sugar, Rice, Cotton (complete with crown and dollar-sign scepter), and Louisiana with her wheat staff to join a throng of armed maidens and allegorical figures.

In 1874, the Mistick Krewe took their symbolism even further. The theme was "The Visit of Envoys from the Old World and New to the Court of Comus." The cast included Europa, Britannia, Louis XIV, and a host of other characters, leading up to American roles. Float eighteen featured Liberty mounted on an eagle.[101] That night at the ball, the first tableau unveiled the Goddess America, who straddled two buffalo and surveyed the state of her country. Krewes not only referenced their world through female characters of the city and state, but they now tied themselves to the positive, progressive image of modern America. Like American painting, sculpture, and murals of the time, krewes constructed a female ideal that looked back to antiquity for morals while operating in the modern age; these womanly images bridged the past with the present in order to make sense of a rapidly changing American society that was continually adapting to new economic and technological situations.[102] Similarly, the core values that this tableau stressed were mainstream American ideals: liberty, independence, progress, justice, and modernity. Krewesmen used the visage of powerful women and infused them with male-centric ideas of America.

The sublime female, as bastion of male thought, was a powerful image of victory precisely because she rallied behind man's causes.[103] For krewesmen, the causes were many: protecting the South through Confederate participation, coming to terms with Confederate defeat by romanticizing their participation as having been noble, sustaining a sense of nobility through genteel values presented in Carnival balls, and contending with a radically changing political landscape on local and national levels. In this way tableaux enabled krewesmen to recover and sustain their sociocultural refinement and class status despite Confederate and even Reconstruction defeat. The

Proteus costume designs from 1899: "Plenty," holding arrows and a cornucopia, and "Liberty," wielding the Constitution. Both are dressed in chitons and represent krewesmen's sublime goddess/American ideals. Carnival Collection, Louisiana Research Collection, Tulane University.

choreographies themselves were informed by classical aesthetics, which added a sense of tradition to the scene, as well as underscored the serious nature of the tableaux.

By the late 1880s, neoclassical and romantic art waned in American popularity, replaced by a decorative style and technique that looked to America's ties with European artistic models. Perhaps because of their now-entrenched position as southerners, krewesmen continued to foster a genteel tradition and so remained attached to the ideals associated with these aesthetic styles.

But the 1880s did see changes in the ball tableaux, mainly through modifications to the format. Presumably, staging several tableaux (which cost many thousands of dollars) had become too expensive to mount alongside parades, and so krewes reduced the number of tableau scenes they presented.[104] In streamlining tableaux, however, krewes maintained their cultivated projection of kingly munificence and luxuriousness. Beyond money, another prompt to change was that guests were more enthralled by the romantic connotations of mock court "marriages" and the flirtatious dancing that followed than in absorbing moral lessons from tableau productions.[105] Consequently, where mythic heroes once stood in the spotlight of the calcium glow, krewe courts soon took center stage at the balls. Taking their lead from the TNR, the other krewes shifted to producing a two-scene arrangement that first presented the krewe and then unveiled the court. A prime example was Comus' 1893 pageant based on Flaubert's *Salammbo*. According to the February 15 coverage in the *New Orleans Times-Democrat*, the krewe arranged the masked characters in various groupings under the proscenium; spotlights illuminated one group at a time for the audience. The second tableau that night was a court scene. The curtain rose to show an arrangement of maskers who were poised, ready for the royal dances to begin. Comus, front and center, walked to the proscenium box, claimed his queen, and escorted her to the stage to pose for all guests to admire. Then the ballroom dancing began.

Proteus presented a similar ball that same season. Again, the *Times-Democrat* was on hand and described "a preliminary toning down of lights, and a swift rush of shadows over the parquette and boxes[;] then as the curtain rose a flash of incandescent light fell upon the stage like the sun breaking through a cloud at midday."[106] Despite being the single tableau of the evening, the scene, which revealed masked krewesmen and Proteus on his throne, "was a superb picture—a vision which dissolved only too soon."[107] The stage was made even more spectacular by colored lights that were thrown about, momentarily resting on various maskers. After a few minutes, Proteus emerged from this flashy landscape and escorted his queen to center stage. The entire group then commenced with their grand march. The following year, the *Times-Democrat* exclaimed that Proteus had "killed the virulent tableau. But he has done it astutely. He has recognized it as an essential part of a Carnival ball, but he has had the good sense to see that, like spiced fish roe, it retains its individuality as a good thing only when taken in small portions."[108]

During the first few years of the twentieth century, old-line krewes further distilled their performances. By 1905, their balls presented a single court scene that featured krewesmen and the year's honored queen. Although simplified, magnificence remained a defining characteristic, and most court tableaux were still enchanting and otherworldly. Amid lush scenery, the element of fantasy was ever-present. Within this new structure, krewesmen created their very own gardens of Eden, and in the case of Comus in 1902, the scene was complete with peacocks, silk thrones, and brilliant lighting.[109] This simplification of theatrical productions denoted that the days of grandiose Carnival ball tableaux vivants had already passed.[110]

Momus in 1900, with its depiction of King Arthur and the Knights of the Round Table, was a last gasp in a long line of lively, lavish tableaux, but it did not signal an end to krewe identity based on chivalry and classical inspirations. Indeed, though old-line krewes in the Gilded Age relinquished their primary focus on serial tableaux in favor of another spectacle—that of queens and maids of the magical krewe kingdom—the ideal they championed through tableau masculinity remained a cornerstone of self-identification. Even sixteen years after Momus' great Arthurian performance, Proteus presented their pageant "Sherwood," which boasted a twenty-float arrangement, including "Robin Rescues Marian" and "Richard the Lion-Hearted." Their parade ended at the French Opera House, where the ball commenced with the presentation of a single tableau. Though the sole scene of the evening, it was no less exquisite than past tableaux and no less significant in representing krewe mores: "It was an hour or more after the parade when Proteus announced that he was ready to mount his throne and receive his guests. The curtain ascended and revealed a picture of rare elegance and grandeur. The entire stage had been converted into a great throne room, the architecture and arrangement of the romantic feudal time, the period of crafty John's reign, of infamous memory in a line of mighty kings."[111] From Comus' first tableau in 1857 to twentieth-century court-scene performances, krewesmen invested in tableaux as an artistic, aesthetic (and entertaining) representation of their gentlemanly position within their elite class status. Within this realm, chivalry was "not passed and gone" but rather a mainstay buttressed by classical attitudes of legendary size.

The heyday of old-line tableaux vivants is central to understanding how krewesmen created and performed group values. For old-line organizations, tableaux were useful ways of mitigating anxiety, adapting to modernity by fomenting and expressing cultural values, reinforcing such ideals within a performance among peers. In effect, krewe tableaux became embodied political theater.[112] Krewesmen defined for themselves a cohesive, postwar world vision through tableaux vivants—a vision that pushed back against new government policies while it praised the old-line stratum of New Orleans men as ultimate sovereigns.[113] Tableaux vivants, then, physicalized and embodied old-line krewe ideas in ways that clarified their stances about Reconstruction through bodily participation. At a time when New Orleans underwent tremendous changes in politics, old-line krewesmen reconstructed their own identity by choreographing themselves into valiant knights and heroic statues onstage. As "marble men," krewe members allayed their fears about Confederate defeat, racial equality, and women's rights through tableau performances. At once timeless and timely, krewesmen nobly embodied their roles as kings and gods of their private Carnival realm.

FOUR

"A Strange and Silent Group"

COURTLY GRAND MARCHES AND QUADRILLES
IN THE GILDED AGE

The krewe of Comus' ball on Mardi Gras night in 1884 was a very special
occasion. Despite their theme of "Illustrated Ireland," their focus that
evening largely rested on another place—the American South. The French
Opera House was lavishly decorated, lit by colored gas jets. To the right of
the stage were box seats festooned with ribbons, flowers, and relics of the
South's glorious past: bugles, floral swords, and Confederate silk belts. Most
importantly, the seats were occupied by the daughters of Confederate leaders
Stonewall Jackson, Robert E. Lee, Jefferson Davis, and D. H. Hill.[1] After a
few serenades to these special female guests and a tableau presentation, it
was time for Comus and his men to formally laud the "five Confederate
virgins," the maidens of the South.[2]

When the second curtain rose, Comus and krewe began their grand
march from the stage around the ballroom floor. The "most beautiful effects
were produced by the winding procession," which stopped when the captain
blew his whistle, with the marchers then grouping themselves in geometrical patterns.[3] From the balcony guests' vantage, the grand march was an
impressive weave of costumed bodies, an intricate web of masked figures.
Once the march ended, Comus led Mildred Lee to the dancing platform,
and his court members each selected a partner from among the remaining
Confederate women: Mary Lee, Julia Jackson, Varina "Winnie" Davis, and
Nannie Hill. The couples commenced with a quadrille, and after dancing,

the courtly krewesmen presented their partners with individual keepsakes to remember the occasion.[4]

In a souvenir booklet for the 1924 season, Comus noted that the 1884 ball was extraordinary: "Indeed, never was the South better represented, the maids being, with one exception, daughters of Confederate Generals." The report continued, "Jefferson Davis as well as Lieutenant General D. H. Hill were counted among the distinguished guests, and amid scenes of unrivaled splendor Comus reigned until the 'wee sma' hours of the morning."[5] As historian Reid Mitchell observed, the appearance of Confederate legends—"nobility" to their admirers—was important to the Comus ball in that their presence accentuated the dignified, romantic appeal of the Lost Cause.[6]

While not acknowledged at the time, the Confederate maidens became known as Comus' first female court, with Lee as the reigning queen.[7] Before 1884, Comus personally chose a partner while his dukes selected women from among the crowd, all for the first quadrille. Reigning kings made these choices at the ball, but in the case of Lee and her companions, the Comus krewe decided beforehand that they would invite the Confederate daughters to join the royal quadrille. Accordingly, the daughters of the South were the first predetermined group of women chosen as krewe court companions; they began the Comus dynasty.[8]

In 1892, Comus again championed southern femininity by elevating Confederate court maid Winnie Davis to queen. Winnie was well known to New Orleans socialites. She even provided letters of introduction for her friend, 1883 queen of Carnival Susan Richardson, who was traveling to Paris.[9] Winnie was especially popular among old-line krewes for her feminine expressions: she graced southern, private upper-class tea parties as the guest of honor and appeared at Lost Cause events throughout the South. She frequently visited New Orleans, where she mingled with illustrious Carnival families and became a symbol of the "true womanhood" of the South. According to Cita Cook, Winnie Davis "learned to keep silent and smile regally" as members of the southern gentility "projected onto her their most cherished dreams and values."[10]

The year that Winnie Davis was Comus queen was the season of "Nippon: The Land of the Rising Sun." In keeping with their Japanese focus, Comus provided silken kimonos and colorful jewels for the female court to wear to the ball.[11] Though her jewels were dazzling, Winnie Davis herself was the sparkling center of the ball. According to the *Times-Democrat,* Davis was "the personification of queenly grace and dignity and when she moved along the stage and bowed right and left to Comus and the dignitaries of his court her manner was so exquisitely gracious that the audience, moved by a common impulse, broke out into enthusiastic applause."[12]

It is obvious that Davis was a popular choice. In fact, the *Times-Picayune* noted that "the selection of the beloved 'Daughter of the Confederacy' as queen of the God of Mirth was the happy signal for thousands of war veterans to sound off their famous rebel yell after 27 years of unreconstructed silence."[13] As Comus queen, Davis represented the feminine component of lingering romanticism associated with the Old South. According to the *Times-Democrat:*

> It was a gallant and touching tribute to the ulterior recollections of that head cause, from the ashes of which have sprung, phoenix-like, such blessings of amity and peace, that the daughter of the Confederacy, Miss Winnie Davis, should have been chosen from among all of the beautiful women of the Southland to be the Queen of the godly Comus. Had she been born upon Mount Olympus and reared among its preternatural grandeurs, it would seem that this beautiful Queen could not have been more stately, dignified and graceful.[14]

Through their choice of Winnie Davis as queen, old-line krewesmen symbolically reincarnated an image of Confederate glory in an age of growing nationalism. This image, a nod to "gallant" New Orleans men—the self-proclaimed local nobility—lauded a past steeped in honor, prestige, and masculine virtues, the virtues often performed in Carnival ball tableaux. This image could not stand alone, however. No matter how deeply it referenced a male-dominated realm, the reputation of New Orleans men as modern and chivalric rested in great part on the unchanging support of genteel southern women.

As we have seen, krewe tableaux vivants were spectacular performances of identity. But once they concluded, it was time for another old-line ball highlight: the unveiling of the seasonal krewe court, which featured debutante daughters who reigned as queens and maids. The presentation contained an impressive grand march that included the court and entire masked krewe, followed by special royal maskers' dances (mostly quadrilles) reserved for court members only. The pomp and circumstance of the grand marches and quadrilles emphasized the formality and regality of the evening since the court members, especially the women, were the central focus of the spectacle. Through the concept of the "polished pedestrian"—smooth and elegant displays of everyday movement sculpted into regal body language that set the performer apart from onlookers—krewe courts generated a modern monarchy in the kingdom of New Orleans.[15] By selecting their daughters to represent the feminine aspect of krewe royalty, old-line men buttressed a femininity that championed traditional family values. At the same time, this representation worked to dampen a prevalent and potentially threatening feminine role of that era: the suffragist.[16] The presence of a polished pedestrian quality acted as a physical metaphor for the execution of such social codes.

Often, Carnival balls doubled as a marriage market; krewesmen put their daughters on display so that young, eligible, and equally prestigious krewesmen could take notice.[17] In this ritual, the physical presentation of ladyhood—through acceptance of that role or in defiance of it—was an important tool for daughters. Engaging in courtly personas was a way for women to test out their taste for adulthood and the expectations that accompanied it.

Most often, krewe court daughters chose to bolster the ideologies set in place by their fathers. As one newspaper clipping stated: "The Carnival queens of New Orleans have been a strange and silent group, using the bow and the smile instead of the vocal cords."[18] Through their polished pedestrian movements, krewe queens actively engaged in supporting a past that lauded their men's bravery in battle and savvy in business, while the presence of queens also justified krewesmen's masquerades as kings. The virginal bodies that graced the courts provided symbolic evidence that krewesmen needed to continue their old ways—to defend and champion the women and children of the New South. By accepting (and relishing) a court role, krewesmen's daughters proclaimed to their social peers that women still needed, and wanted, chivalrous protectors. And through krewe courts, Comus and his kin provided opportunities for women to "costume" as men's idealized woman. Carnival queens were corporeal proof that New Orleans' refined culture had survived the war intact, perhaps even stronger than ever. By embracing this symbol and Carnival role, krewesmen's female family members furthered the image of krewe families as guardians of the Old South.

Whether consciously aligning themselves with krewe values or using the Carnival ball as a springboard to explore their own womanly voice, court queens and maids were not simply pawns; they were not powerless. Although the queens were bound to traditional ideals through scrupulously drafted bodily behaviors, their mastery of such language also held potential for feminine independence. They found ways, even within a male-dominated process, to manipulate the royal image and carve out some sense of personal power. This was particularly evident in the pomp and circumstance of the grand march—a regal display of dance for all guests to admire. Potentially, this was a moment for queens and maids to make decisions about how the world would see them.

Tableau performances cemented class solidarity through thematic presentations of heroic men, and as such, they were arguably the most important aspect of Carnival balls early on. However, krewe courts transitioned into the spotlight during the latter part of the nineteenth century as krewesmen sought to ensure a continuation of their social power through krewe family intermarriages. For this reason, Carnival court rituals became instrumental to krewe identity. Perhaps it is no coincidence that as New Orleans entered the Gilded Age, old-line krewes amped up the lavishness of their balls by focusing on court presentations. More than simply being a Carnegie or Rockefeller, they were kings who ruled alongside gorgeous queens.

Perhaps obviously, there have been special roles for men since the earliest Carnival pageants. Each krewe celebrated one member by allowing him to don the costume of Comus, Lord of Misrule (TNR), Proteus, Momus, or Rex. For one evening, they were more than krewe kings; they were gods. Additionally, krewes selected seasonal dukes and knights as part of the krewe court, and by the turn of the century, they instituted pages, thus initiating young boys into the fold—boys who themselves might reign as kings one day.[19] But women were not entirely absent, even during the Carnival balls that surfaced shortly after the Civil War.

The first female Mardi Gras krewe court emerged from the original Twelfth Night Revelers' ball in 1870 and established TNR's tradition: using a bean hidden inside a cake to determine who would reign that evening.[20] In 1873, Rex staged a ball at Exposition Hall, where Rex arrived with four heralds, twenty courtiers, and bearers of the royal crown and orb. Rex and his attendants marched twice around the ballroom before Rex walked up to Mrs. Walker Fearn and designated her as queen.[21] Later in life, Fearn recalled that she had worn her second-best dress that night—a black silk gown. She reminisced: "Of course no thought of being queen ever entered my head. I expected to visit all the balls that night, and had only dropped in for a while to see what girl would be chosen queen, feeling as excited as the girls themselves over the issue."[22] While Mrs. Fearn and her infamous "second-best black dress" are well remembered, the selection of a matron to rule alongside Rex was restricted to that single year. Every season afterward, Rex (like other old-line krewes) chose a young, unmarried woman as his consort.[23]

By the 1880s, all old-line krewes had female courts. In 1881, Momus chose his first queen at the ball when he asked Elise McStea to dance the royal quadrille with him. In 1883, Proteus marched out and designated Susie Richardson as the first official KOP queen and cemented the krewe's queen selection process by presenting her with a gala badge. Comus joined the trend the following year with the first predetermined court, his Confederate Court that honored Mildred Lee, Mary Lee, Julia Jackson, Winnie Davis, and Nannie Hill. Soon, krewes began to extend their royal focus and added maids to the ritual. By 1903, the standard across all old-line krewes was to honor one queen and four maids for the season at hand.

The significance of krewe courts (and thus the grand march and royal maskers' dances) grew with each season. Masked as gods, kings, and knights, male courtiers symbolized extreme manly power, and because of this, the image of court women needed to reflect an extra-elevated status, as well.[24] Subsequently, krewes began intertwining Carnival rituals with previously separate debutante events in the 1890s and in doing so further solidified the social importance, and perhaps even virginal quality, of their female queens and maids.[25] But New Orleans socialites were distinct in some ways from other American debutantes of the time.

High society was much the same throughout most Gilded Age metropolitan centers, and many affluent Americans flocked to New York City during the social seasons to participate in elite gatherings and entertainment.[26] Newspapers spoke of dances, receptions, teas, charity events, and dinners that prestigious parents hosted for their soon-to-be equally prestigious children, mostly daughters. These parties occurred during two separate social seasons: winter (which, like Mardi Gras, ended with Lent) and summer (usually held in leisure communities like Newport or Saratoga, or, later in the century, Europe). In New York City, the winter social season began with the opening of the opera; like krewe membership, opera season tickets were handed down from one generation to the next. Certain families were established facets of the social scene. Every place had its ultra-elite, as in New York, where families such as the Vanderbilts, Morgans, and Stuyvesants reigned as social leaders, with Mrs. Astor as the empress.[27]

Debutantes seemed to be thoroughly enveloped in these established practices, with events for debutantes and nondebutantes being listed together in society sections of the newspaper. For all social gatherings, newspapers printed the hosts' names, along with their home addresses, which imparted a sense of status for readers thoroughly acquainted with the city's geography. Names of urbane guests—in the case of debutantes: friends who "assisted in receiving" guests, usually five to eight women—also appeared alongside the time, place, and nature of the event. By 1880, December was marked as debutante time, when the young women debuted in coming-out receptions—a supper in the 1870s that changed to a tea in the 1880s—and then made a secondary entrance via a ball, the Patriarch's Ball in New York City and junior cotillions in other cities. As with Mardi Gras krewe courts, American debutantes wore white gowns for their receptions and dances.[28]

The balls served as evidence that the debutante had mastered important social skills that would enable her to contribute to the group as a thriving member while they also displayed her as distinctive. Usually, a debutante was presented to the audience by her father or escorted around the ballroom by an esteemed young man, after which she and her young escort commenced with a dance. This might have been a german (a round dance whose mutable formations supported frequent partner changes), cotillion (early form of quadrille), or lancer (quadrille variation, also popular at old-line balls).[29] As with other genteel nineteenth-century dances, these choices underscored that "individual pleasure arose from participation in hierarchy, social interdependence, and group unity."[30] A debutante's promenade and ballroom dancing reflected refinement, elegance, control, excellent manners, physical poise, polished dancing, and confidence. And while men presented their daughters at the balls, women were the ultimate social gatekeepers; they organized most balls (with few notable exceptions) and facilitated every ritual leading up to the dance: afternoon calls with the debutante to the homes of ball guests they would invite, teas and receptions, and chaperoning the debutante whenever she was in the company of men.[31]

While New Orleans debs did participate in general dances and tea parties leading up to their debut, their formal entrance into society did not occur at these events. Instead, their coming out unfolded through the mysterious and notoriously secret ritual of the Carnival ball, with coronations and masked men.[32] Thus, a young woman's entrance into society was sometimes made through the guise of Comus queen or Momus maid, a revered and royal status elevated well beyond socialite.[33] While a debutante's status often emanated from her father's success and reputation (as it did for debutantes elsewhere in the country), New Orleans debutante rituals veered away from standard practice. A New Orleans debutante's most prominent event was not arranged by her mother but instead by a group of mysterious men. Moreover, she was not introduced to society by her father or even a respectable young attendant. Masked gods and kings, not mere mortals, escorted the women into their adult lives, all within an opulent world of the imagination. The link of Carnival ball traditions to Old World European culture, in conjunction with debutante rites, amplified the prestige of a New Orleans debutante's social standing and further underscored the seriousness of the play at hand—presentation in a fantasy krewe world reaped real benefits in everyday life.

The growing exclusiveness of krewe court traditions produced another outcome, as well—the emergence of the ultra-elite, a handful of New Orleans families. These krewe court dynasties associated with the names Fenner, Claiborne, Hardie, Buckner, White, Legendre, Richardson, Maginnis, Levert, and Rainey passed the status of krewe king and queen down from one generation to the next.[34] Of primary importance to these court families was a dual lineage: one that could be traced back to prestigious historical roots, and another that centered on future generations' krewe involvement. Mary Orme Markle reminisced in her memoirs that, when she was a baby, her parents "drank to my charm, good nature, beauty. I was born to be a 'Southern Bell' [*sic*]. [T]hey vowed I would become queen of Comus ball someday which I was in 1914."[35]

One member of the ultra-elite was Josephine Maginnis, Comus queen in 1893. Josephine (born Mary Josephine) came from a prominent New Orleans family headed by her grandfather, Arthur Ambrose Maginnis. The son of Irish immigrants, Maginnis hailed from a family whose lineage included lords, foreign court ministers for Great Britain and Ireland, and famous soldiers. Born in Baltimore in 1815, Maginnis married English immigrant Elizabeth Jane Armstrong in 1839 and moved to New Orleans shortly thereafter. In New Orleans, Maginnis was involved in many lucrative businesses: shipbuilding and lumber, sugar (owning several local plantations), and finally cotton. He was even elected to the legislature in 1875 and 1876.[36]

Maginnis had many children. Two of his sons, Arthur Ambrose Maginnis Jr. (A. A. Maginnis) and John Henry Maginnis, continued the family cotton business and became esteemed local figures themselves. They both married daughters of New York City's "Boss" Tweed. A. A. Maginnis, who married Mary Amelia Tweed, was a member of the Knights of the White Camellia, the White League, the Citizens' League, the Pickwick Club, and Comus; he was a close family friend to Jefferson Davis, donated to orphans, and during bouts of epidemics he funded the pumping apparatus that flushed the city.[37] John Henry Maginnis, "Cotton King" in New Orleans, married Lizzie Tweed and had three children: John Henry Maginnis Jr., William Tweed Maginnis, and Josephine, who was queen in a tableaux society in 1892 while also maid to Winnie Davis on Comus' Nippon court, before becoming Comus queen in 1893.[38] Josephine Maginnis' other family members included an aunt and Rex queen, Margaret Cecelia Maginnis, who married Boston and Pickwick Clubs member Peter Francisco Pescud (whose family includes a Revolutionary War hero); aunt and Rex maid Laura Elizabeth Maginnis, who married the New Orleans city treasurer; and uncle Charles Benjamin Maginnis, who married Susan Karr Bush (sister to Charles Janvier's wife) and whose daughter married famous Mardi Gras historian Arthur Burton La Cour.

Josephine Maginnis herself, after her court reigns, married George M. Rose, a businessman from New York City. Rose's father, "a great leader in American advertising," was the president of Royal Baking Powder Company and had amassed one of the largest fortunes in advertising.[39] Maginnis and Rose had three children and split their time between New York and Paris. The 1917 *New York Social Register,* which documented prominent families, lists them as living at the Plaza Hotel and as members of nine elite social clubs, including the New York Yacht Club.[40]

While the Maginnis family cemented their ultra-elite status with fourteen court appearances, unequivocally the most active dynasty was the Buckner family, who participated in twenty-one courts between 1878 and 1902.[41] These appearances rested on twelve women. The Buckners were featured in all of the old-line courts, and, while most of their roles were as maids, Katie (Catherine), Kate, Edith, and Fannie ruled as queens.[42] Although Minnie Norton Buckner never reigned, she was chosen as maid for three courts in 1894; then, four years later, she served as Momus maid, just one year before marrying William J. Barkley, Princeton graduate and sugar merchant/planter. Minnie, Katie, Edith, and Fannie were sisters and third-generation New Orleans elite.

At the fore of the Buckner dynasty was Henry Sullivan Buckner, a Kentucky-born cotton factor (later, member of the Cotton Exchange) who single-handedly saved the Louisiana bank from folding in 1857 by extending his own personal credit. By 1860, Buckner, who had married Catherine Allan, was worth more than an estimated one hundred thousand dollars, in addition to owning property valued at fifty thousand dollars.[43] Son Newton Buckner also developed a career in cotton, becoming a merchant in both New Orleans and England. Newton Buckner married Parmelia Grand Norton (related to another krewe dynasty, the Richardsons), and together they had four krewe court daughters, mentioned above. After court involvement, Katie went on to marry Daniel Dudley Avery, whose mother was also a Richardson, and whose family lived on Avery Island and was connected to the McIlhenny company that produced Tabasco-brand pepper sauce.

Two of the Buckners' daughters married into another krewe dynasty: the Eustis family. The Buckners' eldest daughter, Ellen, was "a woman of great wit and grace" who married her cousin James Biddle Eustis, descendant of a prominent Massachusetts family that included his great-uncle William Eustis, governor of Massachusetts, President Madison's secretary of war, and minister to the Netherlands. James Biddle Eustis, graduate of Harvard, practiced law in New Orleans before fighting for the Confederate army, then later pursued a political career whose highlights included being a U.S. senator and ambassador to France. In Washington, D.C., and Paris, Ellen Buckner, as was fitting for an old-line family, "shone with brilliancy in the highest social circles."[44] Like sister Ellen, Laura Buckner also married a Eustis. In 1870, Laura married her cousin and lawyer/businessman Cartwright Eustis (James Biddle Eustis' second cousin), who had attended Harvard but dropped out with the factionalism and upheaval of the Civil War. Cartwright Eustis became a partner in A. Baldwin & Company, the oldest and one of the largest mill supply houses in the country.[45] Together, Laura and Cartwright had eleven children, three of whom—Ellen "Nellie," Katharine "Kittie," and Maude Eustis—were krewe court women.

Between the 1870s and the 1910s, these families intermarried and strengthened their social positions by participating in multiple krewe courts. Their dominant presence throughout the Carnival seasons underscores a point that historian Bertram Wyatt-Brown makes about traditions in the Old South: intricate marriage patterns among a handful of prestigious households "not only reinforced positions of honor and wealth but also ensured continuations of custom and demands for conformity," which effectively created "chains of duty" from one generation to the next.[46] Through krewe courts, certain New Orleans families were able to maintain a romantic sense of the honor-bound Old South and translate their appreciation of the past into a hierarchical power system in the present, underscoring the importance of the mock monarchy to krewe traditions.

Historians have somewhat differed in their assessment of female participation in old-line courts. Samuel Kinser, for instance, has argued that the presence of female queens and maids undercut male dominance at krewe parades and balls, but, as scholar Karen Leathem saw it, the "early queens seemed to be afterthoughts, chosen without much ado by kings at the balls and remaining at the periphery of the main ballroom ritual—the maskers' tableaux and the dancing that followed."[47] Following Leathem's perspective, it was true that court women were restricted from participating in the most prevalent activity of the evening (general ballroom dancing), and after their obligatory partaking in the grand march or first dance, krewes relegated queens and maids to the stage, where the women ensconced themselves on thrones and couches for the rest of the evening. Krewesmen still held most of the power, but not all of it. For ball spectators, the first glimpse of queenly power emerged in the grand march dance.

Within the old-line Carnival ball world, the grand march functioned as the core performative element of krewe royalty and acted as the central arena for female participation. After the conclusion of the tableaux, krewes commenced with a grand march in one of two ways: either the krewesmen marched around by themselves and formed geometrical patterns when the captain's whistle blew (after which the king presented his queen and her maids), or the krewe introduced the female court first, and both the court and krewe performed the grand march together. Either way, the grand march was instrumental to krewes' social status. Even though the 1892 Proteus grand march only lasted one turn around the room, for instance, the *Times-Democrat* described that upon Proteus' "God-like arm in bashful dignity leaned his beautiful and gentle queen, Miss Valentine Cassard, one of the most beautiful of New Orleans' dark-eyed daughters," and that the "majestic company" of the krewe court "walked in stately and slow dignity up the stage . . . followed by the whole of the glittering and silken Mystic Krewe."[48]

The grand march was not an original krewe concept; the practice is derived from ancient Roman civic pageantry that spawned the European tradition of ceremonial entries, masques, and court ballets of the fifteenth through seventeenth centuries. During the Middle Ages, royalty and the Church used public grand marches (known as royal entries) to announce their arrival. These propaganda parades, complete with a cavalry entourage, enabled esteemed monarchs to proclaim status and mark important events through opulent pageantry. Likewise, European courts explored the power of pomp indoors through courtly dances like the pavan, a simple and stately processional dance with a slow and dignified countenance, comprised of step-together patterns. The pavan displayed dancing couples in linear or circular patterns and required "walking with decorum and measured gravity," an embodiment of the dancers' eminent nature.[49] Prestige through stately dancing was important—so important, in fact, that the concept traveled from the Renaissance into the baroque court of Louis XIV, where the Sun King—a gifted dancer himself—expected his dancing noblemen to exude a concept of French esprit that drew from a model of Greek gods and goddesses, figures who were greater than everyday mortals but not "possessing unfortunate extremes of exalted spirituality."[50] By the turn of the eighteenth century, French dances were the rage in all European courts, where the dancing masters were predominantly French.[51] From there, the courtly style spread to America.

By the mid-nineteenth century, the grand march (also known as a polonaise) dominated public and society ball scenes. In late nineteenth-century New Orleans, Carnival balls mirrored the practices of most metropolitan balls throughout the United States and in European cultural centers, where grand marches introduced the ballroom dancing portion of evening. Famous dancing master Thomas Hillgrove stipulated: "At the commencement of a ball, it is customary for the band to play a march, while the company make a grand entree and march round the room; at the conclusion of which, the company, or as many as convenient, should be seated."[52] As hinted here, the grand march was a 3/4 time couple line dance that wound its way around the ballroom floor in circuitous and interweaving patterns.[53] Generally, couples lined up together, with the most esteemed pair in the lead.[54] The partners would then promenade around the ballroom, separate and rejoin, all through well-defined geometric patterns. The Krewe of Proteus, for example, performed a single tableau in 1893, and then "the march began when the curtain went up again. It was led by the king, who was followed by his most royal of courtiers. After wheeling into serpentine coils, the train evolved into a march, and Proteus escorted the queen of the ball from her box to the center of the stage. . . . They formed the first set in the lancers, in the centre of the stage. But with marvelous quickness, as though the minstrel-magician had used his power, the floor was covered with maskers and their partners."[55]

Uniquely, krewes used the polonaise's "serpentine coils" to show dignified presentations of regal bodies, which "twined and intertwined in the mazes of an intricate march."[56] While grand marches peppered society dances across the nation, those balls featured social leaders but not, as in New Orleans, kings and queens. Old-line performances proclaimed to New Orleans society that krewesmen, along with their polished women, were natural rulers. Even more, in replicating the embodied display of power evidenced by European kings and queens, the grand march presented the season's court for all guests to admire while not so subtly stating that, even among the cream of society, there were individuals who stood out as the pinnacle of New Orleans style. These krewe participants costumed as mock royalty for Carnival balls, but in everyday life, they still dressed the part as the most prestigious businessmen in town and as their most illustrious daughters. Courtliness and regal promenades inside the Carnival ball signified elite status outside the theater walls.

The emphasis on courtliness and regal promenades increased even further through the Comus/Rex ritual meeting of the courts and a resulting double grand march, which began in 1882. The meeting of the courts quickly developed into a tradition that repeated each year with Rex's just-before-midnight arrival at the Comus ball and his graceful, introductory bow to krewe kin, Comus. Rex, with his queen and courtiers, assumed a place of honor as applause radiated from the audience. At the appointed time, the Comus captain formally introduced Rex and his queen to Comus and *his* queen. Bows and curtsies ensued, Comus and Rex switched partners, and then the entire throng of monarchs and attendants commenced with a double grand march. At the end of this choreographed interaction, Comus and Rex signaled farewell to the crowd, retreated with their party to a private supper, and thus ended another brilliant Carnival.[57] According to historian Samuel Kinser, the meeting of the courts was symbolic of krewe convictions, and it revealed a broader political sentiment—Rex, the semi-public, semi-masked political figure bows to Comus, the mysterious, hidden god of the social underworld. Kinser argued, "Power is a private thing." Comus, after all, is masked, even at his own ball.[58]

The grand march conveyed the krewes' power in very visible terms and expressed krewesmen's desire to elevate their members to a revered status beyond what was capable in the non-Carnival world. Endless danced processions around the room by a krewesman singled out as king marked some men as accomplished enough to attain status in a hierarchy within a hierarchy. They embodied ultimate prestige. Grand marches enhanced this concept through physical parading of the king and his extensive entourage for all guests to admire. But guests also admired the beautiful court women. Since krewe queens and maids were young and unmarried, their presence marked them as actively engaged in an elevated marriage market. To set themselves apart as the best catch, krewe court women had to display polished manners and exemplify the genteel ideal of an accomplished lady. Queens and maids were meticulously scrutinized by krewe, family, and audience: every movement mattered; their bodies were vessels of their character. Since they were not reared from birth in a real court setting, krewe court queens and maids had to somehow convey that they were different from the other daughters. Because of this, krewe court women defined their femininity through everyday but elevated body language, a performance of the polished pedestrian that ensured their reign would be successful.

Pedestrian dance signifies an approach to everydayness and everyday movement, grounded in the concept of walking but also extending to the utilization of "natural" movements, such as folding one's hands and purposeful gestures.[59] Isadora Duncan, a forerunner of modern dance, used skips, runs, sways, and even standing as part of an emerging conversation that fused aesthetic dance, neoclassicism, and high art. For Duncan, dance manifested the connection between humanity and nature. Her organic system was rooted in curvilinear movement; she was inspired by the waves of the ocean, evident even in the ebb and flow of how she took each step. Through examples of pedestrian dance we see that movement is a fundamental human experience, and as such, everyday movement as dance carries with it important indicators of cultural identity. In the grand march and presentation of court to guests, pedestrian tasks like waving and walking assumed cultural meanings and became a kinesthetic index of group values. In this way, pedestrian movement worked to dissolve the "barriers between art and life rather than hyperbolically exaggerate the distance between them."[60] In doing so, courtly presentations referenced possibilities for prestige that might exist in the everyday beyond the Carnival realm, exhibiting a tension between everydayness and sociocultural elevation.

Old-line krewes' use of pedestrianism explored this tension. Krewe courts capitalized on a democratic approach to body language by placing habitual movements in a formal context that accompanied the trappings of high culture, ultimately elevating themselves. This underscored the potency of krewesmen in proclaiming their cultural mastery, even of the everyday (presumably unnoticed) locomotion of social behavior.

In stylizing the trappings of everydayness in order to further set themselves apart, krewesmen polished their style. For Comus and his kin, the polished pedestrian of grand marches (like the tableaux performed before it) harkened to the relevance of old, European courtly ways within a rapidly changing American context. This new theatricality cemented a status quo to which krewesmen had long clung. Elitism reigned, and in the manner of a wave, a curtsy, or a smile, queens and maids in the old-line krewe courts assured their position in this performance of identity, especially in the grand march dance, which operated as a formal introduction of the seasonal mock monarchy to ball guests.

Choreographically, grand marches and court presentations were comprised of five (mainly pedestrian) modes of movement: walking, posing, bowing, curtsying, and waving, all of which had to be mastered. Whenever a queen bowed or wielded her scepter, she had to do so "with exquisite grace."[61] After all, as one exposé on krewe court training explained: "Carnival royalty is not born; it is made."[62] While the "making" of Carnival royalty referenced an American ethos of democratic politics unavailable to countries with real ruling (birthright) monarchies, old-line krewes emulated the European precedent nonetheless. Like the French court dancers of the Sun King's reign, queens-to-be were "required to be completely poised, and no action in everyday life was left to chance."[63] As a result, through a polishing of everyday, pedestrian motion, court queens and maids adhered to intricately choreographed standards of movement and defined themselves as refined, sophisticated, majestic women. Effectively, they used this concept of the polished pedestrian to enhance their status and craft a sense of performative, feminine regality.

Above all other pedestrian movements (except, perhaps, walking), curtsies—symbols of feminine deference—were given the most detailed descriptions in nineteenth-century dance manuals and were the apex of a krewe court grand march. As the court members wound their way through the march, they stopped at key points in the ballroom and either waved their scepters or bowed (or both) for the audience. A queenly bow, of course, is a curtsy. A curtsy, seemingly simple, had seven fundamental components. Frank Leslie Clendenen's 1895 publication, *The Fashionable Quadrille Call*

Book and Guide to Etiquette, stipulated that the "courtesy in dancing is made thusly: step right foot to side and pass left foot in a semi-circle to the back (fourth position) until it rests upon the toe and ball, and at the same time bend the knee of the standing leg, incline the body forward, straighten the standing leg, and gradually draw the advanced foot to its correct normal position."[64]

Masters of the polished pedestrian had to know the steps but perform in an unstudied and natural way. Women were advised not to "attempt to display any scientific movements, so as to lead others to speak of your abilities as professional, but always appear to execute your movements correctly to the time of music, and with the ease and grace of an educated person. Be always attentive to your partners."[65] Unstudied, easy grace was the mark of a "popular" and "radiant" Mardi Gras queen. As *Elements of the Art of Dancing* explained: "It is hardly possible to enumerate the disadvantages that arise from an awkward deportment of the person. It is therefore of the utmost consequence to commence by forming a genteel and elegant carriage or deportment of the body."[66]

Take, for example, Emily Poitevent, 1895 queen of Comus. Poitevent, born in Pearlington, Mississippi, in 1875, hailed from a family known for its Huguenot roots. Her father, John Poitevent, was a wealthy New Orleans businessman who, by 1870, owned the largest lumber mill in Mississippi. He provided materials to build bridges between Mobile and New Orleans and operated steamers that transported his lumber to various Central and South American ports. According to *Munsey's Magazine* (which covered the most important emerging women from around the country, including Vanderbilts, Roosevelts, and other prominent debutantes who later became a Lady or a duchess through marriage), Poitevent "travelled a good deal" with her aunt, Eliza Jane (E. J.) Nicholson, *New Orleans Picayune* owner and poetess. Mentioned in this same source are what we can assume to be Poitevent's "reigning" characteristics: her possession of "wonderful dark eyes and a magnificent carriage." Accordingly, the article reported that "those who met her . . . carried away a brilliant picture of the romantic beauty of Louisiana."[67]

In 1893, Emily Poitevent participated as Rex maid while her father ruled as

Emily Poitevent, 1895 queen of Comus, was revered for her dignified and graceful body language. Courtesy The Historic New Orleans Collection, acc. no. 1977.68.1.

King of Carnival; three years later, Poitevent ascended to her own throne as queen of Comus. As Comus queen, Poitevent represented her family lineage and class status very literally through her body. She "bore herself with royal grace and dignity, and right nobly did she wear the magnificent jewels which Comus presented his lovely queen." Here again, grace and dignity surface as important bodily markers of prestige. Apparently Poitevent was so deft at the art of these refinements that it "was generally conceded that the kingly Comus never chose a more gracious and beautiful queen to share the honors of his throne."[68]

One outgrowth of her success as a perfect emblem of old-line femininity was that Poitevent later married Franklin B. Hayne, New Orleans native, Cotton Exchange member, eventual president of the Poitevent family lumber business, and (possibly most important) Rex 1904. The strategic alliance not only strengthened bonds between two Carnival families, thereby entrenching the Poitevent name further in New Orleans tradition, but also conferred on Emily the rewards of her polished deportment: membership in a family whose men had fought valiantly for their country, all the way back to the American Revolution. The Poitevent/Hayne marriage reflected the ideal of old-line possibilities: a noble heritage that bespoke European ancestry but was firmly planted in American sensibilities—the dual lineage achieved mostly by the krewe family dynasties. Poitevent's "magnificent carriage," it seems, revealed more than a refined education in graceful deportment; it also positioned her to enter the inner sanctum of social power.

Because the stakes were so high, ease and grace were not enough to constitute a truly polished woman. Compliance factored into the scripting of elegant deportment, too. In dancing deferential curtsies, krewe court women acknowledged the power in front of them—kings and possible husbands. Accordingly, the queens and maids physically expressed respect in these moments. But other forms of compliance surfaced, too. When Dorothy Collins Spencer was queen of Oberon in 1915, she had no idea of what to expect. "No matter what happens, appear oblivious," advised Collins' mentor, Tante E. Denegre.[69] A female court member could pull off snags in the "show" as long as she exuded a demure obliviousness—a demonstration of her training in both refinement and subservience and a testament to her support of krewe mores. Denegre's advice, however, also belies a tension inherent in court participation. Just because some women appeared oblivious did not mean that they in fact were unaware of the possible pitfalls associated with krewe rituals—physically and perhaps even ideologically. The appearance of oblivion, therefore, could act as a mask for women who chose to uphold the old-line codes through a tactic of simulated compliance with the masquerade unfolding before her. In this way, the scripted body operated as an instrument of feminine choice for queens and maids.

Often, though, feminine subservience and refinement reflected krewe daughters' support of the old-line system, illustrated through the perfect curtsy or, later, quadrille. The chosen queens and maids were, after all, testaments to their fathers' involvement in the organization. This was a poignant reminder that men sculpted the southern, New Orleanian feminine ideal through scripted body language couched as krewe royalty. As Reid Mitchell asserted: "Reigning as queen or attending a queen as a maid was simultaneously a rite of passage, an act of submission, and a mark of honor. Participation in the Carnival courts was the outward and visible sign that a daughter was conforming to the demands that 'society' placed upon her."[70] Many young women appreciated the old-line values and eagerly anticipated Carnival season as a time when they might carry on their family's traditions within the krewe court arena. These women took their duties very seriously. Mrs. William Seward Allen, on the fiftieth anniversary of her reign, recalled, "I've always felt that being Queen of Carnival was a very impressive honor." She continued: "Perhaps it's imaginary, but I believe there is a tone of deference reserved for queens."[71] Within the realm of polished pedestrian promenades, female krewe court participants signified their acquiescence to their fathers' sociocultural institution and, in turn, were rewarded with esteem from the group.

The deference Allen mentioned permeated the outlook krewesmen bestowed on female family members. Whereas balls previously limited women to the role of spectator, female courts meant that old-line krewes put their daughters on pedestals (literally, thrones) as exemplars of an idyllic past that was perpetuated through debutante daughters. Old-line Carnival queens became symbols that southern culture was defined by beauty, demureness, and purity. This elevation of krewesmen's daughters to a cultural status symbol was, as Karen Leathem explained, integral in restoring krewe families' self-respect after the upheaval of the Civil War. According to Leathem, it was through a "positioning of their women" that New Orleans krewesmen "solidified and constructed their society" after the war. Through this presentation of virginal daughters clad in formal, white gowns, Leathem continued, krewesmen created a symbol of elite society that was grounded in rhetoric of white supremacy and a romanticized, antebellum past.[72]

Women's own ties to this past were complicated. Many affluent southern women rallied behind their husbands and fathers during the first years of the Civil War, but as time dragged on, the war's outcome grew less certain. Gender historian Laura Edwards argues that privileged women were unable to denounce the Confederacy because denouncement meant an abandonment of antebellum life and a rejection of their own privileged position.[73] Moreover, many New Orleans women, like socialite Clara Solomon, were also unhappy at the prospect of reconciling with the North.[74] Solomon's sentiments reflect New Orleans women's opposition to Gen. Benjamin Butler and his Union occupation. New Orleans women loathed Butler and lashed out at Union soldiers on the street by voicing opposition to the occupation or by vacating public spaces once soldiers appeared.[75] Butler's solution: the infamous "Woman Order," General Orders No. 28, which proclaimed that any woman who showed contempt for northern officers or soldiers, through verbal or physical insult, would be held liable and treated accordingly, that is, as a "woman of the town."[76]

Interestingly enough, Butler's order, and the one that followed, Order No. 76 (which demanded that all New Orleans citizens, including women, take an oath of allegiance to the United States), granted women political accountability at the same time that they attempted to subdue refined women under the reign of northern men. New Orleans women, of course, swore the oath, but as Drew Gilpin Faust argues, the women then appealed to southern men and rallied behind traditional notions of womanhood as they accused Butler of launching an "assault on sacred female purity." In doing so, New Orleans women maneuvered themselves further into a problematic position: they were at once empowered by the disruptive ramifications of their actions and at the same time locked back into a subordinate role under the rubric of conventional southern womanhood.[77]

During the years directly following the Civil War, when most old-line organizations formed, many affluent women continued to rely on antebellum southern culture as a springboard for their own agency. In efforts to "reassure defeated Confederates about their honor, courage, and manhood and to bury the pain of failure by redefining it as a noble sacrifice and ultimate moral victory," women turned to the Lost Cause platform.[78] In New Orleans, upper-class women formed the Ladies Memorial Association (LMA), as early as 1861, under the name the Ladies Aid Society.[79] Members of the organization made uniforms, nursed soldiers, paid soldiers' rent, and fed families. After the war they raised money for soldiers' medical care and the erection of monuments, decorated graves, and provided financial support for mourning families and for soldiers to travel home. Uniquely, the group also built on their vibrant New Orleans past and love of dancing as they staged lavish charity balls and tableaux whose proceeds were distributed to widows and orphans.[80]

Most importantly, LMA groups enabled women from krewe families to maintain a sense of independence while honing skills that society traditionally expected of them: deference to father and, later, husband. Maintaining this subservient attitude while branching out into public charity was likewise precarious. Historian Jane Censer observed that, because of this dilemma, "elite southern women would become increasingly polarized between a revived image of the 'southern belle' and that of the emancipated new woman."[81] This schism increased even further when the next generation of southern women—the first to grace the Carnival ball stage—juggled the heightened fervency emanating from both traditionalists and reformists alike when the New Woman movement gained momentum and supporters across the metropolitan South. Krewe daughters (from prominent Carnival families like Richardson, Aldigé, Denegre, Freret, and Farrar) participated in the Junior Confederate Memorial Association while also facing a new era in women's rights.[82]

The coming of age for the first generations of Carnival court women coincided with an idea of "woman" that was in flux.[83] Shifting ideas of womanhood equated to cracks in the consensus of the Carnival ball court. Even within the highest stratum of court families, for instance, potential candidates for queen or maid occasionally used their position to jockey for personal goals. Rebellion took on various guises, including a resistance to

Alice Aldigé, 1907 queen of Proteus, came from a family that was involved in
the Junior Confederate Memorial Association and appeared in six krewe courts.
Courtesy The Historic New Orleans Collection, acc. no. 1987.45.14.

Carnival balls as a marriage market site. Corinne von Meysenbug, for example, donned the Elves of Oberon queen's mantle and doubled as a Rex maid in 1899, but not before becoming secretly engaged to Rathbone DeBuys, thereby asserting her independence in matters of the heart and in securing a future home for herself.[84] Other queens-in-waiting used Carnival as an opportunity to articulate philosophies related to the women's movement. Elizabeth White, whose superkrewe family reared her in the late nineteenth-century Carnival traditions, became a debutante in 1923. White read French and specialized in art and "voice culture." Her newspaper biography revealed that she "recites Creole monologues cleverly" and "adores music." Importantly, the news column noted that White "delights in developing her character by any sacrificial means not too spectacular. By which token, thinks it every woman's duty to vote as often as the law allows."[85]

Accordingly, krewe court membership could be a platform for future forays into more liberating social activities, like the women's movement. As krewesmen's daughters grew older, many became leading social figures who worked to alleviate modern social problems. Carnival women participated in war-relief efforts, organized Christian women's groups, and donated their time to charities, but it appears that these women were more mature in years, already on the fringe of the Carnival court proceedings.[86] The names associated with Carnival court families—Farrar, Walmsley, Grima, and more—can be found in the history books of suffrage and women's rights organizations, and older women from the krewe families of Bisland and Farrar, for instance, were charter members of the Woman's Club.[87] While young, though, the lure of court participation (and thus family tradition over assertive independence) was seductive, as we see with Mary Orme Markle, 1914 Comus queen, 1914 maid for both Momus and a tableaux society, and 1915 Rex maid. In her memoirs, Markle wrote: "To be queen of Comus was my social ambition as a girl, as that was the most elite and oldest social carnival ball in N.O. & I may add still is to-day."[88]

Once older, krewe court women could continue to cultivate their complicated negotiations between tradition and independence by forming their own krewes and staging their own Carnival balls. Early female krewe balls surfaced from the women of old-line families and mostly emulated the men's krewe practices. The Carnival organization Les Mysterieuses staged a leap

BRUNHILDA.   JULIET.   SEMIRAMIS.   POCAHONTAS.

Les Mysterieuses tableau, "Four Types of Fair Women."
New Orleans Daily Picayune, January 4, 1900.

year ball in both 1896 and 1900. For their first ball (January 10, 1896), the
Mysterieuses queen was—like the old-line kings—masked. The ball, which,
according to Perry Young, "quickened the pulse of male society," followed
Comus' and other male krewes' format, including call-outs in which masked
women invited men to the floor for dancing.[89] As the *States-Item* reported,
the krewe performed a grand march, and "then came the clamoring for
partners and much fun was enjoyed by the girls, thinking that turn about
was fair play, and that they would have the fun this time."[90]

Two other groups followed. The first was the Mystic Maids, who disbanded in 1908.[91] Then the Mittens, an uptown krewe comprised of the
season's debutantes, formed in 1901 but folded after 1920.[92] The first female
krewe to substantially last, however, was the Krewe of Iris, which formed
in 1922 and in 1949 actually televised their Carnival ball.[93] Just a few years
earlier, another organization, the Krewe of Venus, had also expanded Mardi
Gras into new terrain. They staged an all-female public parade.[94]

The formation of affluent women's krewes at the turn of the century illustrated that old-line krewesmen no longer solely shaped the preservation

of class identity through Carnival practices. Krewesmen's female family members, drawing on the subtle agency they cultivated in Carnival court and women's rights activities, became even more active in mythologizing their pasts, this time, with power for themselves. At female krewe balls, the men in formal fashions were on display while masked kreweswomen orchestrated regal and romantic interactions on both the stage and the dance floor.

It is interesting that Les Mysterieuses chose the poppy to represent their 1900 ball motif.[95] Poppies have a long-standing, varied symbolic presence. The ancient Greeks, for instance, associated them with both Hypnos (god of sleep) and Morpheus (god of dreams). As such, the flower is associated with visions and death. But the poppy has another side: one of promise and rebirth, especially in its symbolic connection to Demeter (Greek goddess of fertility and agriculture). Like the ancient Greco-Roman texts, Victorians also gave the flower a variety of meanings, based on color. Red poppies, for instance, were linked to death, remembrance, and consolation in the West, but in the East they symbolized success and love.[96] Although the poppy might have referenced the upcoming disintegration of Les Mysterieuses (it was their final ball, after all), there is another possible meaning inherent in this symbolism. The poppy was not a vision of collapse but instead one that signaled a lasting presence as a dream fulfilled, even if the krewes themselves endured only for a moment. In real life (or, at least, the Carnival world), the "strange and silent group" of previous Carnival court queens and maids found their voice and seized control of staging their own desires, no matter how ephemeral.

In this way, participating in the grand march when young and then staging their own balls when older provided space for women to test the limits of both their adherence to and manipulation of old-line values and traditions. Queens and maids learned about and embodied these values as members of the krewe court, first through the grand march and then in the royal maskers' dances that followed.

Like the grand march, the royal maskers' dances defined krewes as inheritors of aristocratic European traditions with an Americanized twist. Though the king and queen did not always participate in this part of the ball, the courts' dukes and maids took to the dance floor and proclaimed

"Emblem of the Mysterious." *New Orleans Daily Picayune*, January 4, 1900.

their distinguished positions by engaging in a dance that most all of the krewesmen and ball guests watched. Like nobles of the Renaissance and the French baroque generations who followed, New Orleans krewesmen used formal dances to further proclaim their lofty status and generate power.[97] By positioning themselves as part of a courtly performance that spectators in balconies watched unfold, krewesmen played out scenes of pomp, aided by an air of romantic sentiment. Guests acknowledged krewesmen's superiority as the masked men and their partners displayed the best dancing skills and manners for their captive audience. Thus, set apart by their eminence, krewe court members emphasized their organization's adherence to hierarchy and stability through the most common of the royal dances, the quadrille.

The quadrille developed from seventeenth-century square dances popular throughout Europe. Whereas British square dances became "longways for as many will" (two lines that extended as far as space allowed, with one partner in each line, facing each other), French square dance formations consisted of only a few couples, usually four or eight.[98] The French-style quadrille emphasized patterned exchanges between partners that remained within the space of the square. English dances, on the other hand, used a "casting off" method wherein dancers began in one spot and moved to the back of the line. The dance ended when dancers regained their original positions. Whether English or French, quadrilles relied on geometrically patterned phrases strung together to make a full dance, similar to the grand march.[99] By the mid-nineteenth century, these patterns settled into a format that included only a handful of phrases—usually a five-pattern series for each dance.[100] Within the next few decades, the movement (once full of complex and constantly changing footwork, mostly turns, jumps, and slides) gave way to easy promenades and interweaving lines of dancers that engaged in a gentle, gliding walk.[101] The quadrille retained its stately air but became more accessible for the growing number of people striving for gentility.

The quadrille was a status symbol. American and European genteel society considered it to be the "most universally approved of all the fashionable dances. . . . Among all the various dances that have been introduced, the Quadrille holds a high position."[102] Status accompanied the quadrille because it allowed the cream of society to stand apart as refined dancers while also creating a space for them to mingle only with each other. Only the highest-

Illustration of initial changes in a first quadrille set, published in an 1822 manual. Most dance manuals published after the mid-nineteenth century provided only text descriptions. From Thomas Wilson's *Quadrille and Cotillion Panorama* (1822), An American Ballroom Companion (online collection), Library of Congress.

ranking guests—for Carnival balls, that meant mock royalty—danced the first quadrille at a ball. Quadrilles were, as one manual pointed out, "always appropriated by the aristocratic element."[103]

Dancers expressed the quadrille's links to status and hierarchy through a formal movement style akin to the regality of the court grand march. Though they often had to memorize the quadrille's geometric "figures," a range of technically sound dancers were able to achieve proficiency as these elements became more fixed through codification. This change accentuated simplicity while retaining a studied air. Essentially, the quadrille's codification disposed of any elements that distracted from its regal overtones. After all, the "peculiar feature of quadrille dancing is simplicity. The dancers should glide through the various figures in a waving, graceful manner."[104] Consequently, through grace and simplicity (defining genteel virtues), the quadrille constructed a space that championed class solidarity through formal, scripted bodily movement.

The quadrille's physical formality complemented the krewe court aesthetic of privilege and emphasized stately community. After all, as one manual reminded dancers, "Do not forget that you belong to the set, and not the set to you."[105] Participation in quadrilles was a symbol of honored status and belonging, an idea further enhanced by the quadrille's overriding ideology: institutionalized stateliness. As *The Dancer's Guide and Ball-Room Companion* affirmed, the quadrille was "the great institution of the ball-room."[106]

The lancers quadrille was especially appropriate for krewe royal maskers' dances because its stateliness was linked to New Orleans' favorite European court. According to *The Royal Ball-Room Guide*: "This quadrille is of a very old date. It was originally danced in the costume of the Polish Lancers, by both ladies and gentlemen, at the Court of Louis, the expensive monarch of France."[107] Drawing on French patterns of nobility was, of course, inherent in old-line krewes' adoption of Creole Carnival customs, but the lancers also fulfilled krewesmen's yearning for courtly ways through its alternate heritage as a dance that, once outside of Louis' courts, found its niche as a decidedly "English" quadrille. As one turn-of-the-century dance manual described it, the lancers quadrille "is full of grace, with its salutes and its bows, its slow and rather solemn movement." Full of "charming figures, in which the cavaliers salute with a graceful ease, and the ladies dip deep in their light skirts to make delightful courtesies," the lancers satisfied krewesmen's desires to follow a lineage that placed them in both English and French realms, thereby embracing the finest qualities that both offered.[108] Furthermore, by dancing the lancers quadrille, krewes physically linked themselves to the most prestigious European courts and consequently associated their own dancing with regal bearing: stateliness, formality, ornamental style, and elegance. Dancing the quadrille likened krewe court members to real-life courtiers and impressed audiences with a projected aura of divine right.

Once the grand march and maskers' dances concluded, the krewe court retired to the stage for the rest of the ball. There they poised themselves on thrones and fashionable couches and surveyed their dominion as the call-outs and general ballroom dancing commenced. In the later hours of the evening, the court sometimes further retreated to a private supper, but while in performance mode via marches and quadrilles, the mock monarchs and their royal retinue emulated the very best of old-line possibilities. They cultivated a new level of esteem, enhancing even further old-line krewes' penchant for illustriousness and clout. Though young, the court's debutantes were instrumental to this exhibition.

Young socialites became Carnival queens when they were essentially still girls; queenhood ended their adolescence and catapulted them into the sphere of adult obligations, including courtship. Society expected a krewe queen (or maid) to become a wife, then a mother; these parts were as scripted as the curtsies, scepter waves, and quadrille patterns. Krewe court roles carried advantages when facing such proscriptions. Among the benefits of being Carnival royalty were social popularity, family approval, and eventually, the sought-after good marriage.[109] Though participating as ball guests and not as court members in subsequent years, previous queens and maids were continually lavished with honors and attention by the krewes. For ex-court members, being set apart from the rest of the audience created notoriety as a member of the ultra-elite. One way or another, then, female court members remained in the spotlight for many years after their reign and, in doing so, cemented a lasting popularity among the krewe clans and a higher potential for being regarded as a suitable wife in ensuing courtship negotiations.

Of course, krewe fathers were also integral to queens' and maids' social success. As part of this interplay, a debutante's reputation not only reflected her father's reputation but also helped shape it through court participation. In turn, fathers' further-increased standing enabled them to wield influence within the krewe in Carnival matters. It also enabled them to reel in the best of the young, single krewesmen as potential mates for their daughters, thereby ensuring a family legacy rooted in old-line traditions. As Bertram Wyatt-Brown observed, antebellum society expected southern, white gentlemen to be charismatic and wealthy and have large, respectable kinship networks; marriage and fatherhood further increased this prestige.[110] Krewesmen continued this tradition in the New South through krewe courts, which effected a "symbolic integration of society" that led "to the actual integration and reintegration of socially prominent families." Fittingly in this integration, queens' gowns were often refashioned into their bridal dresses.[111] The courtship success of krewe court women, then, directly reflected the economic, social, and even biological prestige of the father himself, a prestige that court women helped develop.

Daughters, by nature of their family status, epitomized the best that their fathers could offer the next generation of male leaders. For some postwar families, a respectable, old family name was all that men had left. Daughters symbolized the respectability of these ancient lineages. This was literally a weighty affair, considering that court queens navigated their grand marches and quadrilles wielding heavy scepters and wearing elaborate satin gowns, jeweled crowns and stomachers, and mantles attached to velvet trains. Queens represented the richness of krewe life in a myriad of ways. Perhaps because of instances like this, Karen Leathem asserted that "women were frequent forms of exchange in late nineteenth-century Mardi Gras rituals" and that, in the "protected confines of the ballroom, carnival societies crowned debutantes as queens, advertising the power of their fathers and regulating courtship within defined class limits." According to Leathem, this secured krewesmen's "position in an unsettled society."[112] Underlying this arrangement, though, was their daughters' consent. Krewesmen lost their bargaining tools if their daughters didn't agree to participate in the courtly exchange. Daughters, then, gained respect within their families if they willingly participated in their fathers' plans. Like debutantes in other parts of the country, court women knew that they "were engaged in serious business" because their choice of husband was crucial to their entire family. Scholar Laura Edwards argued that "while allowing daughters some latitude in choosing their husbands, parents depended on highly structured social rituals to nudge them in the right direction."[113] In this manner, the choreographed bodily spectacle of krewe court presentations provided a ritualized outlet for the courtship process.

Bound by family obligations, court women were restricted in many ways, but they were not inert. Their physical presence in grand marches and maskers' dances spoke to a more subtle empowerment that played out in motion. Through the polished pedestrian employed in regal promenades and stately quadrilles, court women were testaments to their fathers' ideals, but they also embodied the potential to overcome the obstacles of their class. Simultaneously restricted and empowered, court women possessed the capability to undo krewesmen's ideals if they refused to fall in line (literally in the grand marches) with old-line pomp and circumstance. By donning the role of queen or maid, krewesmen's daughters not only played a crucial role in the maintenance of class ideology, but were also integral in the evolution of that system. The proper wave or curtsy physically symbolized a sophisticated, strong demonstration of the dependability and continuity of women's contributions to cultured, southern life.

As seen through the krewe courts' grand marches and maskers' dances, old-line femininity's participation in a male-dominated system was a complicated business.[114] Although this "strange and silent group" may have seemingly agreed to enact the female submissiveness of their class ideals (and to be sure, many of them did), "using the bow and the smile" could also operate as a performance of feminine resilience and adaptability. Through the scripted krewe presentations of the grand march and quadrille dances, women both tested and upheld the limits of their femininity within the constraints formulated by their fathers. Adhering to the tradition of the southern belle or scripting a new independence (or embracing both) was an important choice that Carnival court women revealed in the most personal ways—through their moving bodies.

FIVE

"The Very Maddest Whirlpool of Pleasure"

BALLROOM DANCING IN THE PROGRESSIVE ERA

In 1906, a tableaux society named Consus staged one of the most elaborate Mardi Gras balls ever for its theme "The Land of Frontinback and Upondown." The French Opera House was decorated accordingly: forests grew from the ceiling, and clouds littered the floor. As one newspaper noted, "The time of topsy-turvy had really come."[1] Not only were scenery and props inverted, but so were the krewesmen's costumes. The men wore facial masks that covered the back of their heads while wigs with peepholes covered their actual faces. Their clothes were also reversed. Fake buttocks protruded in front while false fronts covered their real derrieres. Henri Schindler explained that "as the tableaux were performed, the effects were stunningly impressive and supremely original; it seemed that Consus had added another triumph to his Carnival glory."[2]

While the cast from "The Land of Frontinback and Upondown" were comically original during tableau performances, they were somewhat less successful with the evening's dancing. Trouble ensued when the krewesmen invited their female partners to the dance floor. Because of their costumes, krewesmen had all the appearance of dancing backward, which meant that they danced with their "backs" to their partners. The "physical impoliteness, which of course was only in appearance,"[3] created an illusion "so well-crafted that many of the ladies were deeply offended" by having to dance with someone's backside.[4] Women's protestation escalated, and the ball turned into a full-blown scandal so intense that "a flood of resignations quickly reduced the fabulous society to a memory."[5]

Consus' demise was a blow to the Carnival community. By the turn of the twentieth century, krewe membership rosters overflowed with gentlemen waiting to join. Prestigious New Orleanians and sons of krewesmen prized participation in the old-line krewes, and the organizations rarely admitted new members. Often, krewesmen willed membership to their sons, and so to join Comus or Momus, Proteus or Rex, men had to wait until their fathers passed away.[6] Unable to contain their love of dancing, the younger generation created nonparading tableaux societies that hosted annual Carnival balls and very often included old-line members.[7] Consus was one such tableaux society generated by old-line stock. Prominent Carnival families graced Consus' courts. Women named Lallande, Eustis, Hinks, Wisdom, Werlein, and Pitot were Consus queen and maids. Even the most exclusive of court families—Richardson and Rainey—appeared on Consus court lists. And though Consus was "resigned to the history books," its lively existence, and the existence of a handful of other tableaux societies, revealed the importance of Carnival balls and dancing to New Orleans krewe families.[8]

Consus, like all other krewes, played with fantasy. Though its reign was brief (1897–1906), Consus was widely appreciated by the old-line krewes for its ability to produce spectacular balls. In fact, Consus held a reputation for staging ten of the most elaborate and beautiful Carnival balls in Mardi Gras history. In 1906, evidently, the krewe's vision failed. Consus' collapse resulted from the fact that it lacked the single most important component of balls and dancing: romance. Carnival balls were realms of fancy and whimsy, yes, but they were spaces that coupled fantasy with flirtation and mysterious allure with the promise of heart-pounding romance, all of which worked to ensure class solidarity through marriages that would continue old-line traditions. These desires manifested primarily in the Carnival ball experience guests craved most: the general dancing that closed the evening, when the ballroom floor was open to krewesman and guest alike.

Like tableaux vivants and court marches, the traditions inherent in ballroom dancing were more than just entertainment. Ballroom dances were scripted performances that enabled old-line krewes to preserve traditional values by adhering to heterosocial conventions that championed propriety and decorum. Thus, like other parts of the ball, general dancing primarily functioned as a paradigm of utopian krewe gender identity. The dance floor was an arena where krewesmen could uphold class distinctiveness and play out the chivalric code of the Old South while also testing the limits of these dictums by embracing the latest national dance crazes. As might be guessed, dancing choices during Reconstruction reflected the traditions of hierarchy and formality via quadrilles, whereas a shift in the Gilded Age moved away from the physically bound style of courtly dancing and into the more expressive terrain of an equally refined cultural bastion, the waltz. Ballroom dancing, then, expressed sociopolitical sentiment in that the favored dances clung to a romantic past steeped in affluent, white, western European traditions while somewhat democratizing the dances to reflect an American underpinning. At least this was the unchanging dance landscape until the beginning of the twentieth century, when younger krewesmen advocated a new krewe identity that embraced both change and a zesty style of dance: ragtime.

The changing nature of old-line dance practices illuminated a desire for old-line krewe culture to remain within the bounds of already established courtship rituals (in-class flirting at krewe events led to marriage and then to children who grew up and joined krewes themselves, therefore bolstering class exclusivity through the continuation of krewe customs) but also provided an unexpected key: the dancing itself encouraged experimentation, freedom, and even individuality. The dance floor provided a safe but titillating arena for class-conscious courtship, especially since women either knew the masked men or were assured of the men's respectable reputations, as evidenced by krewe membership.[9] In these ways, old-line ballroom dancing went beyond custom, even beyond the capabilities of tableaux and marches. General dancing—especially in the 1910s—allowed krewes, their families, and guests to do something previously impossible: adapt. While krewes embraced the past in tableaux and court presentations to solidify a sense of togetherness, the general dancing portion of the ball embraced the present and, through flirtations, possibilities of the future.

General dancing commenced once the royal court retired to their thrones onstage, sometimes after midnight.[10] At this time guests in full dress were allowed on the dancing platform, and even after the court (and many krewes-men) had exited—off to some supper or an even more private soiree—dancers could continue their festivities. As with the royal maskers' dances, whoever participated in general dancing could be seen by the guests who lingered in the balconies to gossip and watch the dancing couples. Ballroom romances, like all other parts of the Carnival ball, were spectacles. Despite this attention to their dancing and flirtation—or perhaps because of it—krewesmen and guests were zealous dancers. Mingling among the remaining maskers, who were often overtaken by guests, dancers crowded the parquet and embraced each other while waltzing until dawn.[11] The *New Orleans Times* remarked about Comus' 1870 ball that "some little anxiety was felt by the owners of the theatre at the immense quarried weight introduced upon the floor, but the timbers managed to stand it without shivering."[12] A few years later, a St. Charles Theatre ball evidenced the same dancing vivacity. Of this, a journalist conceded: "As dance followed dance, and flirtation succeeded flirtation, the thought occurred to this reporter, if such joy and such happiness can be ours now, what would it have been if Eve had not eaten that abominable apple, and the miscreant tenant, Adam, had not been ejected from his residence in Paradise."[13] Ballroom dancing was an immensely popular aspect of the night.

Although only krewesmen could participate in the tableaux, and only a select few women were members of the royal courts, general dancing (in the early balls and into the twentieth century) was open to participation by all; most guests took advantage of the opportunity. As the *New Orleans Times* reported of the 1870 Comus ball, "When the last of the Krewe had retired whence they came, wherever that may be, the ball commenced, and many a fair lady and gallant gentleman left their places in the circles to join in the lively scene on the floor, which was soon covered with dancers, who seemed determined to enjoy themselves in spite of the jam." The column continued, "The music and the merry whirl, were well calculated to draw into the giddy round all those who were capable of participating in the glittering scene, yet it was some time before the throng was sufficiently relieved by departures, to allow of real enjoyment to those who still remained."[14]

Guests partly used ballroom dancing to enhance their own status as ball participants. Being lauded by balcony onlookers carried the weight of social approval. But of course the romantic lure of dancing was thrilling. Guests could finally connect with the men and women they had silently flirted with across the theater during the tableaux and court presentation. As one news column pointed out, during the general dancing of Momus' 1907 ball: "Here indeed was youth and loveliness flowing to ether in an endless stream of gayety. Smile answered smile, and laugh echoed laugh. Tinsel flashed back the light intensified, and for once the world was forgot."[15] The excitement of general dancing, in fact, was so overwhelming that hundreds of couples—four hundred couples in the case of Rex's 1879 ball—vied to occupy the dancing platform.[16]

Dance cards from the Carnival balls reveal much about dancing choices. Not only were there a variety of ballroom styles, but krewes also frequently experimented with dance programming. For generations after their implementation, the maskers' dances began with a quadrille and then proceeded to waltzes, more quadrilles, or polkas (a continuously turning dance form). This portion remained fixed, tied to tradition and prestige. The general dances that followed, however, were a mix. In the early decades of krewe balls, dance styles for this part of the ball widely varied, with waltzes (including galops, a dance comprised of chasing steps in which the couple makes a half turn at the end of each phrase); the polka, which hops and glides as the couple rotates; and mazurkas as the most popular. Mazurkas are usually defined by a smooth, singular motion wherein dancers slide one foot away from themselves as their weight shifts down, then, as they pull the opposite foot crossed behind, the body continues into a gentle heel click jump that lands in a neutral upright position with both feet together. As one dancing manual stated: "The Mazurka seems to express sentiments of sweetness and tenderness. It is full of elegance—of an indolent elegance; it is not a vulgar dance; its slowness has something aristocratic about it, even a little haughtiness. The waltz has more passion, but there is grace also in the undulating and gliding Mazurka."[17] Unsurprisingly, the waltzes, polkas, and mazurkas had endless variations and often intertwined with each other to create new versions of popular ballroom dances. The weaving of ballroom styles together could be confusing since the changes were often slight but offered dancers a comfort in knowing the basic steps and therefore prolif-

Comus dance card, 1881, evidencing a mix of dances, beginning with
a lancers, including waltzes, polkas, and a wide selection for the evening.
Carnival Collection, Louisiana Research Collection, Tulane University.

erated throughout the late nineteenth century, not only in old-line balls but
also in society gatherings throughout the country.

At the Carnival ball, these dances were interspersed with reels (inter-
changing couples dances in long, parallel lines), yorkes (a waltz with mazurka heel clicks), glides (a sliding waltz), heel and toes (a more sedate
polka where the dancers first present a heel out to the side, then dig their
toe behind them), schottisches (a walking mazurka/polka mix), and even
their own lancers—all the main components of a respectable American
nineteenth-century ball.[18] By the 1880s, other dances, such as racquet (a
dance that conjures up images of ice skating), Newport (a galloping, leaping
waltz), and Saratoga (a lancers variation with balances, chasses, and salutes),
appeared, though they were rare.[19]

Proteus dance card, 1906, illustrating the krewe's preference for waltzes and two-steps.
Carnival Collection, Louisiana Research Collection, Tulane University.

In the 1890s, most krewes settled into a handful of their favorites for general dancing: waltzes (including the wildly popular waltz variation, the deux-temps) and polkas remained the most danced, followed by yorkes and glides. By 1900, general dance choices condensed further and included only the basic waltz and a new hybrid dance, the two-step, which was part waltz, part polka, and included many directional shifts and presentational moments.[20] This trend, which was also a national one, continued at least into the 1910s, at which point most dance cards were printed with blank spaces to write in twenty-four dances and partners.[21]

Without a doubt, the waltz was the most popular Carnival ball dance throughout the decades. Waltzing in all of its variations provided whirling, heart-pumping excitement—an obvious reason for its thrill and complementary relationship with romance. One reporter noted of the 1873 Comus ball: "Couples gather quickly on the floor, some fair ladies with the grotesque Krewe of Komus for their partners, while others lean on the arms of 'ye gentlemen' of this nineteenth century. Again the music strikes up and all lose themselves in the whirl of the waltz."[22] The waltz was transportive, liberating, exciting.

Waltzing, which only required stepping with a partner in concentric circles, was a simple frolic, full of momentum. Couples revolved around the dancing platform while spinning in their own circular pattern, using their arm embrace to steady their propulsion. The dance was electrifying, invigorating, flirtatious, and accessible all at once. Absolutely, it was the most popular. In fact, three of the most prevalent ballroom dances at Carnival balls besides the basic waltz were all waltz variations: the deux-temps, polka, and two-step. A deux-temps was a waltz that took two steps within a bar of three notes, and each step was executed as a chassez (a sliding movement in which one leg chases the other, resulting in a little hop).[23] As *The Dancer's Guide and Ball-Room Companion* notes: "This valse has certainly held its position as the autocrat of the ballroom for many years past, and there are few valses more graceful than this when it is really well danced."[24] A polka, on the other hand, is a lively, skipping waltz. Even though there was a range of polkas, the fundamental dance was characterized by a light spring followed by a glide, all while revolving.[25] The last waltz variation, the two-step, was a mix of the deux-temps and the polka; it was also called a Washington two-step.[26]

The waltz was not just a New Orleans favorite. It was a popular social dance throughout Europe and America, especially during the nineteenth century. Its name, derived from the German "walzen," means "to turn," "to revolve," and "to wander," which is exactly the movement quality inherent in waltzing. The waltz formally appeared in dance writing around the mid-eighteenth century, and it constantly transformed in style as it migrated, both geographically and through time.[27] By the nineteenth century, however, the two forms of waltzing that previously existed (a constrained version lauded by the upper-class and a hedonistic version practiced by the working class) had melded into a singular waltz ideology, in large part because of the French Revolution. The Revolution disrupted class hierarchies, and in the rebellion, the waltz—trance-like, individual, universal, passionate—emerged as the symbol of romanticism. Its concentric whirling and the close partnership between the dancers both offered escapism and seemed to express the Revolution's "values of liberty, equality and uncertainty."[28]

These waltzing ideologies reflected vast changes in social structures. Dancers of all social strata eagerly embraced the waltz's assertion of equality and freedom as a means of escapist exploration. Dancers from any class could endlessly revolve around the ballroom and get lost in the tight embrace of their partner's arms. That was all that was involved. There were no rules; just two dancers in a sturdy embrace moving in concentric circles around the dance floor to the sway of 3/4 time music.[29] No one needed formal training to learn how to continually turn, and so the accessibility of the movements spread throughout ballrooms. Moreover, the waltz, unlike its minuet and quadrille predecessors, cast off the geometric formality in favor of improvisational routes. Waltzing created a democratic space; everyone could participate in dancing, and, importantly, women could engage in a freedom of movement otherwise denied them.

Despite the egalitarian, liberated Revolutionary ideals of the waltz, a patriarchal control of bodies still dominated the waltzing landscape.[30] After all, a waltzing man led his partner in the dance. And concerning old-line krewes, as Karen Leathem argued, women still had to adhere to men's rules about the Carnival ballroom. Women, for all of their freedom of movement, were, as Leathem noted, "bound up in the social whirl of upper-class entertainment, [and] they had no choice but to follow the game plan laid out by men."[31] Of course, this gender power structure was not unique to the waltz. Male authority was a defining element of *all* couples dances. One of the central, overriding rules of all nineteenth-century ballroom behavior was, "It is recommended that the lady, when waltzing, leave herself to the direction of her partner, trusting entirely to him, without in any case seeking to follow her own impulse."[32]

Journalist W. G. Bowdoin observed during the 1901 Carnival season that men's embrace of women on the dance floor mirrored the end result of courtship rituals: marriage.

> During my stay here I went, of course to one of the Mardi Gras balls and this particularly entertained and pleased me. In an assemblage of cosmopolites, there is a variety of method and the way in which the Knights of Terpsichore took hold of their ladies was multiform. They grasped their subjects in straight lines and in curves that spoke volumes of which, however, those participating

in the "mazy" were entirely indifferent if not unconscious. They rose and fell in rhythmic and poetic motion in unison with the music and once again Byron's lines were pertinent and opportune.

"And all went merry as a marriage bell!"[33]

Waltzing was, perhaps, not only a space for romance but also a training ground for women to learn their place in marriage. Through waltzing, women practiced engaging in harmonious relationships where men safely guided them through dizzying terrain, or so the romantic ideal went. As one dance manual stated: "Ladies ought to abandon themselves entirely to the guidance of their partners and obey the slightest motion indicating a change of direction; as the success of the dancers depends upon moving in concert."[34] A good waltzing partnership could lead to a successful marriage, but only if women yielded to men's directions.

Despite these limitations, the waltz encouraged a new, public (and liberating) exploration of desire for both men and women. Even though the man led the dance, there were still gains for both partners, who could investigate intimacy and escapism within the established rules of gentility. For once, women could offer themselves up to the intoxicating spin of dance. No longer confined, women could participate in producing their own enjoyment. Furthermore, through ballroom dancing and romance, men actually embodied their ultimate goal of being chivalrous southern gentlemen. They learned how to literally sweep a woman off her feet and how to soften themselves to be more agreeable, for as every man knew, "in Waltzing, a gentleman should exercise the utmost delicacy in holding his lady."[35] Though essentially conservative in its organization, waltzing could also double as a sensual experience accepted within reputable society, even as two dancers whirled around the room in a tight embrace. Holding partners, in fact, was a main attraction of ballroom dancing precisely because it afforded opportunities for close bodily contact. This physical elation through waltzing was especially evident in a news report about the 1877 Comus ball, which explained that female dancers were "whirling like Dervishes in dreamy embraces through the mazes of mysterious terpsichorean figures."[36]

By the 1890s, audiences' love of dancing coupled with watching debutantes enter into society dominated so much that krewes implemented a new section within the ball format—the call-outs. Once their seasonal reign ended, court queens and maids continued to participate in ball events by joining the wives of select krewesmen and debutantes not selected for court in a specially demarcated space on the ballroom floor. This space, reserved for call-out honorees, enabled krewes to extend their formal adulation of feminine beauty and accomplishment by designating certain women to dance with krewesmen after the royal maskers' dances but before the floor opened up to guests.[37] The system of call-outs first appeared in Proteus' 1893 ball, when krewesmen selected a number of special dance partners for the evening *in advance* instead of waiting until the general dancing to ask for a partner's hand. Krewesmen submitted their choices to the organization, which then created ordered lists of partners for each interested member.[38] On the night of the ball, committeemen adhered to the predetermined lists and escorted the honored ladies from their special seating area to the dancing platform, where they could whirl around the room with their designated costumed partner. The system became instantly popular, and quickly every krewe began to implement call-outs after the royal quadrilles, thus extending debutante possibilities and traditions and creating a transition between the regal maskers' dances and the open, general dancing available to everyone.

Because call-out ladies sat in a special, reserved section of the parquet, the honor bestowed upon them and the prestige of their status conveyed that they, like the court women, encompassed a femininity encouraged by the old-line krewes. In their roped-off arena, enveloped by "waving strands of silken ribbons, tied with lovers' knots," call-out women were protected by admiration. Like castle-bound damsels of fairy tales, call-out women rested safely within their confines while chivalrous committeemen patrolled the area, making sure that "none might enter but the fortunate fair who bore the special call-out invitations."[39] By the twentieth century, call-out seating occupied the entire ground floor (outside of the dancing platform and stage space). But while the seating area and numbers of call-out women grew, dancing during this part of the ball remained a mark of respect. Ultimately, call-out women came to represent the success of gendered expectations. That so many wives and daughters created "an assemblage of female loveliness of unapproachable perfection" and the "most beautiful and brilliant spectacle possible" in that corner of the theater meant that old-line gender values flourished within their class bounds.[40]

Despite the honor, Carnival historian Perry Young revealed that women chosen for some of the earliest call-outs were hesitant to occupy the special seats; the conspicuousness of their displayed presence led to a fear of seeming to lack social propriety.[41] Soon, however, ladies overcame this hesitation, and call-out sections filled with women who represented the cream of society. Their placement in the seating hierarchy was honor enough, but their turns on the dance floor as others looked on signified that call-out women occupied a class all their own.

The realm of the dance floor was a tightly guarded space. Barriers around the dancing platform meant that anyone who wished to gain admittance had to successfully pass strategically placed committeemen who took their jobs seriously. Gentlemen of the floor committee retrieved call-out women and escorted them to designated masked partners. No dance could begin until every couple, paired up and in place, was on the dance floor ready to begin. Members of the floor committee, or "black-coats," were the ultimate guardians of the dancing realm; they regulated who could or could not enter.[42]

As balcony guests looked on, call-out dancers partook in various waltzes, quadrilles, and polkas. At the end of each dance, maskers presented their call-out partners with keepsake souvenirs. Krewesmen could be very generous, even "appalling," with the number of souvenirs given away, sometimes to the point of making the most popular ladies "fairly laden down with trophies."[43] Krewesmen even gave away parts of their costumes, such as spears or hat plumes.[44] Other favors included decorated boxes or paperweights. Most often, krewesmen lavished their dance partners with hairpins, brooches, or bracelets that depicted the season's theme. These elegant offerings further bequeathed status on call-out ladies, who also gained recognition through their reception by ball spectators. And ball spectators paid attention.

The audience scrutinized the dance floor and took note of how often particular ladies received call-outs. A woman's popularity was clearly enhanced if she won the approval of spectators in the balcony. Guests in the upper tiers often cheered on call-outs with applause and "ejaculations of pride and praise." Those who looked on from the balcony also made known their disapproval of call-out choices by gossiping and making "loud and uninhibited statements" about who was on the dance floor.[45] The krewe, it seems, bestowed women's status, but ultimately, it was the guests who upheld or challenged call-out ladies' reputations.

Still a third tier of status emerged from the call-out practice. The society section of local newspapers began to publish call-out names in the 1890s, but not until the day after the ball. This timely pause protected ladies from the impropriety of having their names revealed before they participated in the honor. After the night was finished, however, the names appeared as a glorious reflection of the ball rather than as improper public attention. Within the safety of their own drawing rooms, queens, maids, and call-out women from the night before could pore over the newspaper and reaffirm themselves as select members of a tightly knit group. Perry Young argued that the standing of these women was ultimately even more prestigious than a queen's status. After all, a lady was only queen once, but call-outs could occur yearly.[46]

Of course, everyone at the ball enjoyed an elevated status to some degree. Attendance at a private, old-line event in itself conferred esteem. But a privileged position in society was not the sole perk of dancing at Carnival balls. Waltzing, even quadrilles, furnished couples a rare opportunity to flirt away from the ears of others and allowed the dancers to come into close physical contact with each other, all with the sanction of their chaperones. These brief encounters of gloved hands or coy glances over the shoulder held a tantalizing power. Because courtship codes of the Gilded Age and the Progressive Era remained formal for the upper class, couples had little private time and certainly few chances for physical contact. Under the ever-present gaze of parents and chaperones, beaus and their sweethearts had limited opportunities for intimate moments. The dance floor filled this void.

In large part, ballroom dancing maintained its popularity, even into the mid-twentieth century, precisely because of this conundrum. In fact, the intertwining of courtship, intimacy, and dancing was an entrenched facet of good society in both America and Europe, attested to by discussions of physical proximity and "proper embraces" in dancing manuals but also appearing in another text: fiction. Even a century before the Carnival balls, one of the ballroom's greatest admirers, Jane Austen, explored the connections between romance and dance.[47] Austen, who documented real-life Georgian ballroom environments in her novels, was deft at portraying how important ballroom dancing was to English courtship. Her writing contained ballroom scenes in which plot moments critical to character development unfolded through flirting and social dance. The ballroom stood as a microcosm of both society and marriage.

For gentry in Georgian England, private balls held at respectable mansions were the primary vehicle for securing marriage partners. Because a person's dancing defined their character (and their character defined their marriageable qualities), the rules of dancing were codified and complex.[48] Partners could dance only after being formally introduced by the host. Each couple was expected to "stand up" (dance) for an entire "set," which included two dances (about thirty minutes). Physical contact between partners was rare during dance time, except when they came together in weaving patterns, much like a modern-day do-si-do. Most dances were "longways for as many will," which meant that long lines of couples filled the dance floor, and movement consisted of facing off with your partner as you both negotiated the line. During these dances, partners were expected to freely converse about socially appropriate topics without being too personal and without missing a step.[49] Yet these exceptional moments were relished for their privacy. Audiences flanked the walls, watching the dancing couples interact, but the dancers themselves were usually out of earshot of the guests. This time was important because even if the dancing couple was engaged, they never spent time unchaperoned and they never called each other by their first names. Dancing provided secluded moments, even chances for intimate touching (especially hand holding), within a realm of formal dos and don'ts. Stringent rules defined genteel manners and the performance of courtship in the ballroom.[50] Dancing created a space for cherished personal contact despite these restrictions.

Carnival organizations saw themselves as American aristocracy, and so they looked to European aristocracy to formulate their own social rules. In nineteenth-century America, as in Georgian England, ballroom dances were rare moments for flirtation away from the ears of chaperones. Though Jane Austen's time was arguably more severe in its courtship limitations, krewesmen and their families adhered to the same rules of romance and social behavior as their English predecessors. Chaperones, formal introductions, similar rules of engagement, refined character, and impeccable dancing style all coalesced as prerequisites for an evening of partner dancing. In turn, the couples' compatibility on the dance floor mirrored their possible future compatibility as man and wife, strengthening the interconnectedness of krewe families. Not surprisingly, such contacts could be sexually charged. The touch of a gloved hand or a man's embrace was thrilling. The ball was "more than just a dance; it was a prime area for young ladies and gentlemen to get to know each other."[51] Moving through patterns, in view of one's partner, added excitement to this interaction as suspended gratification instilled an anticipation of when the partners would next meet, even touch.

Sexually enticing encounters on the dance floor were enhanced by the trancelike abandon of the waltz in particular. Men and women were drawn to each other through the sheer centrifugal force of their dancing. This close proximity between dancing partners developed into a moral issue that agitated the older generation. Of course, rules developed to impose standards of decency on waltzers. Often, these stipulations were couched in terms that avoided the entire issue of sexual cuddling, as seen in this snippet from *The Art of Dancing, Historically Illustrated:* "The dancers should observe a suitable distance between them, as it is not only necessary to the execution of the steps, but is demanded by a proper respect for themselves and those around them. We would particularly urge this, as the practice of leaning too heavily on the gentleman is a fault which is common to the generality of waltzers."[52]

Dance manuals emphasized the rules pertaining to decorous waltz embraces that chaperones enforced on the dance floor. Even in the 1910s, the closeness of dancers continued to worry parents and chaperones. The waltz embrace rule was so widespread, it became known as the "gas light rule," meaning that "when the dancers pass upon the floor the members of the committee must be able to see gas light between them."[53] The rule was at the forefront of all middle- and upper-class social dancing in the 1910s. As the waltz and other social dances evolved into more modern forms, like the one-step, dancers got closer and closer together, much to the chagrin of chaperones. In New Orleans, the debate swirling around dancing and decency surfaced when police superintendent James W. Reynolds issued an order to cease and desist the "demoralizing practices" of vulgar, suggestive "tango" styles. "Daylight Must Show Between Dancers of One-Step: Improper Steps in Orleans to be Met with Arrest, Says Reynolds," read the January 14, 1914, *New Orleans Item* headline.[54] "The tango can be danced without the introduction of suggestive steps," he argued, continuing: "When danced properly it is very pretty and I have not the slightest objection to it. As a matter of fact I like the tango better than any dance I know." Still, the police threatened to drag anyone from the dance floor of local cabarets, "regardless of who they may be," if body language became too vulgar, too intimate while dancing.[55] Despite these strictures, however, romances (as in Austen's novels) developed in real life through *respectable* dancing in genteel society, even within the krewe court setting.

In a rare but true case, one king of Carnival married his queen. Rex of 1895 Frank T. Howard, whose wealth was derived from the Louisiana lottery, spent a small fortune on gifts for his family, court, and queen Lydia Fairchild during the season of his reign. This was before krewes implemented limits on monarchs' spending. As journalist Thomas Griffin made clear, "While there's no official record of how much Mr. Howard spent, a high Carnival authority reported his generosity was overwhelming. His gifts to his queen alone ran into the thousands."[56] Carnival sovereigns were customarily married men, but for the bachelors, a triumphant reign could also be used to find a suitable wife. While marriages between old-line krewe monarchs were uncommon, they did occur—not only between kings and their queens but also among the other court roles. Carnival historian Robert Tallant revealed that kings have married maids, dukes have married maids and queens, and "lesser kings" have married their royal counterparts.[57]

For the guests, the ballroom dancing provided the most space for courtship. Romance was open to everyone. Myra Semmes, for example, was introduced to krewe legend S. P. Walmsley at the 1884 TNR ball, "The Kingdom of Flowers." Six weeks later, Semmes and Walmsley met at the same theater, the French Opera House. This time, they attended the Momus ball, appropriately titled "The Passions." This was not a second meeting for these two lovers; it marked the sweethearts' formal entrance into society as an engaged couple. Moreover, Semmes and Walmsley not only joined two krewe families together through their union, but they also had thirteen children, many of whom became prominent krewe captains, kings, and queens.[58] What began at a Carnival ball resulted in the creation of one of Mardi Gras' most esteemed families.

The romantic allure and fantasy of Carnival ball dancing revolved around not only physical contact but also a core element of Mardi Gras: masking. After all, women danced with masked men who costumed as knights in satin armor and dashing heroes from other lands. An 1893 Proteus ball description elucidated this point by noting that, amid "dreamy, swaying music" and colored lights that surveyed the space, dancers entered a realm that was a "kaleidoscopic maze of fantasy and fact, where the real and unreal were interwoven until the spectator was bewildered with the unending whirl."[59] Masking was central to this "kaleidoscopic maze," and, as journalist W. G. Bowdoin remarked about the 1901 Momus ball: "One of the fancied reasons for the extreme popularity of these carnivals lies in the fact that a veil of secrecy is persistently thrown around the personality of those taking part in the festival sacred to Momus. (All the participants are masked.)"[60]

Masking allowed men to titillate their partners with an allure of the unknown. Protected by anonymity, krewesmen were free to pursue flirtations in a manner otherwise forbidden in everyday life. In the "real world," etiquette scripted every move and compliment to a lady, but costumed as a knight (or even as an elf or seven-foot-tall pelican), a krewesman escaped the confines of everydayness and joined his female partner in a romantic fantasy. This escape was possible because masking simultaneously hid a person while it created a new personality. To protect their "secret" identity, masked men often resorted to nonverbal exchanges that, when exercised with ladies (especially since krewesmen knew their dancing partners), created an imaginative, interactive realm.[61]

This interactive realm was also one of testing limits. Under the veil of secret identity, unattached krewesmen could use dancing time to explore compatibility with several women. Sometimes, when krewesmen had exhausted their call-out list, they broke the rules and called out a lady (who was not on the list) from the upper tiers. During these improvised moments, maskers chose partners based solely on good looks and used the dance floor as a flirtatious introduction to a possible girlfriend.[62] Likewise, krewesmen who doubled as committeemen were also clever. Arthur LaCour explained:

"Not a few committeemen who are members of the krewe of the evening go back stage to don costumes and call out ladies with whom they have conversed during the concert. This strategy bewilders their partners and glorifies jesting maskers in their fanciful conceit."[63]

The "fanciful conceit," however, was not all on the maskers' side. Women also participated in the sport. As fiction writer Napier Bartlett explained: "One never talks to a masked figure as he does to any other companion. The most ordinary mask somewhat appeals to the imagination."[64] Women understood this and kept up the mystery and intrigue, even when they knew which man was beneath which costume. Florence Dymond recalls receiving her notice for a ball call-out and how much fun was inherent in masking: "As we grew older there came the delights of getting a mysterious document saying that 'Masker No. so and so, desired the pleasure of Miss —— company for the first maskers' dance (or maybe the second or third dance) at such and such ball.' They really tried to keep their identity secret, and it was great fun."[65] According to a March 1869 edition of *DeBow's Review* that covered that season's Comus ball, "Several wives knew, yes, just knew, that they saw their husbands, notwithstanding that the said husband had that very evening pleaded the necessity of setting up with a sick friend as a reason for not escorting them to the ball." Continuing in this manner, the magazine reported that "many young ladies affirmed most strongly that some of the Krewe danced strangely like Fritz Poodle or Smith, both of whom, however, had asserted a thousand times most vehemently that they had never even the most distant idea of becoming a Mistick."[66]

Even when wives and female family members suspected their men of being krewe members, the women were not always aware of the extent to which their men were involved or honored by the krewe.[67] While some women were happy when they realized that their husbands were masked courtiers (or even king), not all wives were happy to dance with their masked men. When it didn't adhere to romantic notions (recall Consus' 1906 "The Land of Frontinback and Upondown" debacle), masking could have disastrous effects. Take, for instance, Comus' 1873 "The Missing Links to Darwin's Origin of Species," which had a variety of grotesque costumes: sponge, polyp, flying fish, whale, flies, moths, rat, hippo, hyena, and lobster. It was the lobster who caused problems. After the grand march, the lobster approached the area where his wife was seated and gestured for her to join him in a dance. The wife broke out into a fit. As Perry Young recounted:

> The tableaux had so vividly impressed her that when the big green claws waved their seductive invitation she screamed and made a frantic effort to leave the box. Her friends sought to explain that the Lobster, gesticulating his affection and harmlessness, was one of her friends. But in the deadly hush that followed her first cry, she shrilled, "*I know who he is, but that Lobster can't touch me!*" Such a scene at a Comus ball almost transcends possibilities—but the events that never could occur are the breath of Carnival.[68]

Although the green lobster was not so fortunate in wooing his wife, most krewesmen were happy to masquerade as flirtatious animals of whimsy, and most women were all too happy to participate in the game. And while amorous exchanges littered this segment of the evening, like a good roux (the culinary foundation of New Orleans' prized gumbo dish), dancing incorporated distinct elements that melded together to produce a certain flavor. At their best, old-line ballroom experiences provided a mix of dance and flirtation, romance and reality.

The Carnival ball dance floor, then, had the power to cement class solidarity through romantic encounters. One can only guess how many old-line marriages grew out of enchanted dance-floor meetings. This courtship system continued to work well for the old-line krewes, supporting the southern gentility evidenced through tableaux vivants and the mock court displays while also enhancing the whimsy and fantasy inherent in Mardi Gras revelry. All remained calm until the emergence of ragtime era dances in the early years of the twentieth century, when a new generation of Americans broke with the traditions of their parents' time.

At the center of the nationwide generational shift was heart-pumping jazz, a cultural style that ignited a dance fever throughout the country. Incredibly popular, most ragtime dances involved a syncopated, fast style of movement, and among the ragtime forms, the iconic tango was actually less popular than the reigning champion: animal dances. Animal dances included the turkey trot, bunny hug, and grizzly bear, among others. These couple dances incorporated one-step movements and periodic jumps, interspersed with arm flailing and full-body jerks. Animal dances ignited a craze as they spread across the country from pleasure-seeking neighborhoods in hot nightlife spots like New York City and San Francisco. Their style was raw, fast, improvisational, and hardy.

Obviously, this dancing style was radically different from the refined dances that the rulers of New Orleans Carnival preferred. In fact, Comus member and Carnival historian Perry Young denied that ragtime dances even existed within Carnival balls. Young implied that rag dances remained a lower-class activity, appropriate to the unbridled street dancing that occurred far away from the civility of krewe events. For Young, "the dancing fads known as 'bunny hug,' 'bear,' 'turkey trot,' and similar varieties of modern contact were squelched when they appeared in 1912 and 1913, and found no place in carnival except as street phenomenon."[69] Yet another Carnival historian, Arthur La Cour, directly disputed Young, stating: "Prior to World War I dancing became a strenuous exercise with the introduction of the turkey trot, bunny hug, grizzly bear, and Argentine tango. The maxixe and hesitation waltz proved more restful and dignified. The dances that suggested close contacts of partners were frowned upon by elders and at first were prohibited at the dignified balls at the French Opera House, but to no avail as youth prevailed and modern dances replaced the steps of long ago."[70] La Cour's description attests to the popularity of ragtime dancing. It was thrilling. It was infectious. And for the older generations, it was dangerous. Ragtime's appearance in the Carnival ball exposed a growing difference between older krewesmen and their children, threatening old-line cohesion.

Young's hesitation about—even dismissal of—rag dances reflected the traditional values of the old-line krewesmen and also echoed the apprehensions of a larger reform effort concerning working-class leisure. This reform impulse targeted the drinking, gambling, prostitution, and dances of Progressive Era dance halls (the equivalent of modern-day nightclubs) as the ultimate degradation of American society.[71] The unpolished nature of the dancing style alone was enough to elicit the disapproval of reformers, who drew from a mix of Social Gospel and nativist attitudes in their attempts to replace new social dances with much tamer and traditional forms of ballroom dancing.[72] Reformers sought respectability above all else, and for them, ragtime culture raised serious concerns over race, sexuality, and class. For krewesmen, it threatened the homogeneity of the Carnival ballroom floor. Ragtime's presence during their Mardi Gras events signaled an infiltration.

According to the reformers and respectable society, a contentious aspect of ragtime dances was the movement's animalistic traits. Bent knees, bodies that dipped and crouched close to the floor, individuality and asymmetrical positions (all elements of the African American aesthetic) defied genteel standards.[73] Because of this, reformers considered the dancers to be out of control and sexually suggestive. Countless old-guard WASP reformers denounced animal dances, which emerged from black neighborhoods, as "improper." Like waltzing, these dances involved repetitious turns and spinning. Shoulder shimmies, hip shakes, and quick steps were also characteristic, with specific animal dances mimicking the movements particular to the animal for which the dance was named. The fast-paced dancing outwardly challenged the grace and refinement of middle- and upper-class ideals.[74] Moreover, since animal dances were easy to learn and didn't take up much physical space, they were wildly popular in the turn-of-the-century dance halls that began to multiply in cities as a leisure outlet for working-class Americans.

Even in New Orleans, an area dominated by dance halls surfaced. Called the Tango Belt, it was located at the back end of the French Quarter, across from the legal red-light district, Storyville. The handful of blocks boasted dozens of cabarets, cafés, saloons, and nightclubs, plus three theaters. Places like the Oasis Cabaret, the Elite, Butzie Fernandez, the Haymarket and Ringside cafés, and the Black Orchid were prime spots for listening to live music and dancing the latest crazes. "At its peak, the area had one of the highest concentrations of commercial jazz venues in the city," and all classes of people visited.[75]

The district was dubbed the "Tango Belt" by local newspapers, presumably for the dancing that pervaded the area. But since the area was a hotbed of jazz, it is apt to suggest that (like other cabarets and clubs around the nation) the tango was one of the many fashionably current dances enjoyed, very likely accompanied by animal dances and other ragtime variants. It was also a site of crime: prostitution and robbery ran rampant, and the Tango Belt often encountered police raids. "The wholesale arrests of women who go from cabaret to cabaret to dance the tango and other steps is the beginning of a crusade just instituted by Police Superintendent Reynolds," a news article stated. "I have received several complaints about men being 'touched' by these women who frequent cabarets," Reynolds explained, "and as the holiday season is approaching I am taking this step to rid the city of the dangerous ones."[76] Campaigns against the district were couched in terms of opposing lascivious dancing, but in reality the police chief was trying to clean up the streets and cut down on crime (tango women "touching" men alluded to both sexy dancing and pickpocketing), even going so far as to require employees of Tango Belt establishments to register with the police.[77]

As we can see, ragtime dances brought up more than racial or even generational issues; they ignited concern about modern sexuality and morality. These dances were wildly popular because they afforded dancers an opportunity to openly explore sexuality on the dance floor, and just like the waltz, ragtime dances created social scandal. What was especially imprudent was the close contact between partners of the opposite sex; unlike the formal, largely separated physical stance of quadrilles, ragtime dancing brought men and women together in sexually explicit arrangements. Whirling and turning fast, getting sweaty, and dancing with partners of the opposite sex became morally tricky, especially for women. Yet, chances to intermingle became increasingly popular as women began to test the limits of social acceptability through their bodies. This experimentation became a prime outlet for defining new heterosocial relations while challenging socially pervasive, restrictive gender codes.[78]

Even more disturbing than racial and sexual concerns was that animal dances seeped out of working-class dance halls and into middle- and upper-class social functions. Animal dances infiltrated society circles across America through leisure-loving youth, including Carnival balls. This evidenced the need for an escape from constraining Victorian mores. Historian Lewis A. Erenberg explained that by "turning to the animal world, black culture, and the red-light district for the sources of their cultural regeneration, well-to-do urbanites were searching for a way to liberate some of the repressed wilder elements, the more natural elements contained by gentility."[79] For old-line youth, the search may have also revealed a new luxury: with traditions and rituals firmly entrenched and identity not only established but also lauded, younger krewesmen were able to branch out and experiment with the new, tweaking the ball formula for added excitement.

Gentility was still the rule in Carnival balls, however, and despite the vast national appeal of ragtime dances, krewes demanded conformity to their ideals of decency. Because genteel propriety still reigned, younger ball participants turned to another outlet in their exploration of ragtime liberation—the dance instructions offered by the famous New York City dancing duo Vernon and Irene Castle. The Castles were a married, professional ballroom team who performed in vaudeville and in cabarets across the country until Vernon Castle entered into service in the First World War (he died in a plane crash a few years later).[80] They showed America that the new social dances and romance could go hand in hand while adhering to traditional standards of gentility. Through the Castles' training, New Orleans socialites could still delve into ragtime fun and enjoy modern romance without the accompanying scandal.

The Castles adapted "inappropriate" vernacular dances and, drawing on the dances' popularity, shaped the movements into acceptable frolics for middle- and upper-class settings. The ungainly arm flaps and awkward, jerky movements of the animal dances were, under the creative supervision of the Castles, "tamed" into elegant and streamlined couple dances, all the while maintaining the dignity that prominent New Orleanians held dear. The Castles' refiguring of social dances created an image of respectability that assuaged lingering fears that contemporary social dances might be uncouth.[81]

The Castles' restagings not only allayed upper-class fears but also fell in line with the regality that krewe Carnival balls sought. According to Irene Castle: "To be truly graceful in dancing presupposes a certain stateliness, a dignity of movement that has charm rather than gymnastic skill behind it. The charming dips and turns, the long, slow steps, and the various artistic measures of our dances of to-day all have a certain dignity." Mrs. Castle was quick to point out that the "contortions of the Turkey Trot" naturally faded "because something finer" replaced them.[82]

That "finer" replacement came, of course, from the Castles themselves. Vernon and Irene Castle published manuals that instructed the public on dancing fashions, deportment, etiquette, beauty, and "proper" dancing. This ensured that their reworkings survived, even proliferated, in American society. One aspect of their popularity was their continued championing of

The Castles demonstrate the proper way to begin the Castle Walk.
From the Castles' *Modern Dancing* (1914), An American Ballroom
Companion (online collection), Library of Congress.

modern dances as morally sound. Their focus on social dance's respectability stemmed from their philosophy that all dances were socially acceptable. The Castles stated that the applied dancing style was what made it suitable or offensive: "Objections to dancing have been made on the ground that it is wrong, immoral, and vulgar. This it is certainly not—when the dancers regard propriety. It is possible to make anything immoral and vulgar; all depends on how it is done."[83]

In ensuring that the American populace turned to them to see "how it is done," the Castles created an empire of social dance instruction. Even in New Orleans, their advice to dancers, including how-to photographs, was published in Sunday spreads in the *Times-Picayune,* the city's biggest newspaper.[84] Dancing teams, in imitation of the Castles, performed in local circuits across the country, furthering the Castles' influence. In New Orleans, Flora Ascott Sander, a "dancer who has won her way into popular favor," entertained audiences with dances learned from the Castles themselves. Sander and her partner, Mr. Fernandez, even invented the "Kolb Flower Waltz," presumably a Castle-style riff, in celebration of their venue, the tearoom in the famous Kolb's restaurant on St. Charles Street.[85] Additional access to the Castles came through movies. Charles "Pie" Dufour, New Orleans historian, said that during his high school years he and his friends would go to the Dauphine Theater downtown, pay twenty-five cents admission, and sit in the balcony. Even decades later, Dufour vividly recalled that the Castles frequently appeared in dancing serials before the main film began.[86] Thus, linked to Hollywood, Vernon and Irene Castle's glamorous dancing grew even more appealing to the eager youth who crowded the movie theaters in New Orleans and across the nation.

Beyond newspapers and movies, the Castles also offered actual dance classes in a studio environment. In at least one documented case, an old-line krewe family sent their daughter to New York City to train directly under the Castles' tutelage. Carnival debutante Maud Fox's newspaper biography pointed out that Fox "has [a] wonderful talent for esthetic dancing."[87] In fact, Fox studied dance in New York with Irene Castle. The Fox family's decision to have their daughter work directly with Castle reveals the seriousness of dance training to a Carnival debutante's identity. Dancing was an integral part of a Carnival debutante's role in krewe events and therefore figured prominently in the courtship life of krewesmen's daughters.

But a tension remained for old-line families: the younger generation wanted to express themselves through ragtime's animal dances while parents adhered to the nineteenth-century waltz convention. The Castles' approach provided a manageable compromise. Because of the Castles' influence, polite versions of social dances spread to urbane ballrooms, debutante events, and prestigious Carnival balls, gratifying middle- and upper-class American youths' zest for modern romantic encounters. The taming of modern dances even appeared in classes offered at Newcomb College (the women's college of Tulane University) in 1914. In a playful turn of events, seven accomplished Newcomb students—one of whom was Gladys Eustis, TNR maid that same year—offered instruction in the polite forms of modern dancing to the college faculty. Lessons included the hesitation and the one-step (a tangoesque ragtime dance), which, as the group argued, was "simply the waltz with a little ginger in it."[88] Through this linkage, even krewe dances could imbibe the zest and modernity that ragtime sparked while remaining within the confines of proper society.

Soon, though, across the nation the hard-studied gentility of the steps reverted to the gritty, raw quality of the dance halls by way of rebellious middle- and upper-class American youth who embraced the animal dances' wild energy. Though the krewes did their best to contain the unattractive elements of these dances, they could not restrain the allure of dancing itself. Younger krewesmen and sons branched off to form their own splinter krewes—tableaux societies whose primary focus was the opulent display of class status through condensed court tableaux paired with extended ballroom dancing. The new tableaux organizations surfaced predominantly to meet krewes' demands for masked dancing. Five new krewes formed before 1900: Atlanteans, Elves of Oberon, Nereus, Consus, and the High Priests of Mithras.[89] They did not parade but rather saved all their money and time for the real Carnival event—the ball—and there, ragtime had a sizable presence.

A popular ragtime dance, the one-step, made its way into Carnival balls, both of the old-line and tableaux societies, during the early 1910s. The one-step became very popular across New Orleans social circles, important enough, in fact, that at a 1915 grand masked ball hosted by the Southern Hardware Jobbers Association (a professional gathering of businessmen in hardware, steel, wire, etc.), the one-step outnumbered the waltz three to one.[90] The one-step was a quick-tempo walk with swaying hips and occasional glides, interspersed with waltz-like turns.[91] For the older krewesmen who exalted tradition and the younger ones engaged in change, the one-step offered the perfect physical and ideological compromise: it moved to the fast-paced tempo of rag dancing that thrilled the youth while employing the more modest movement vocabulary that the older generation sought.

The foxtrot (a rag version of the two-step) was also popular in Carnival balls, but not until 1916.[92] Legend goes that vaudeville performer Harry Fox danced his new two-step version in a Ziegfeld *Follies* performance in 1913 or 1914. The trot broke the beat of the two-step into a slow-slow-quick-quick pattern, though after traveling to England and gaining popularity there (then subsequently being tamed by the Castles in America), the foxtrot evolved into a smoother, more elegant, walking style of dance akin to a swaying, walking waltz.[93] The increased appearance of rag variations like the one-step and foxtrot demonstrated that old-line identity at the turn of the century was shifting. Coupled with romance, though, ballroom dancing had a steady foundation upon which to experiment, ensuring that any changes would unfold within the parameters of what the old-line krewes held dear.

Once unsettled by the Civil War, old-line krewesmen used tableaux vivants to proclaim high-status masculinity during a time of political and social reconstruction. Then, in the Gilded Age, krewes focused on femininity and cementing court traditions in order to continue to solidify their status quo, despite the growing political movement of women's rights. Now, in the first decades of the twentieth century, romance and krewe courtship became even more important as modernity's pace quickened and some of the Progressive Era reforms (like limiting weekly work hours or the emergence of unionization) threatened entrepreneurial krewesmen's businesses, while other reform movements (such as with dance halls) promoted a more conservative cultural landscape. Krewes were once again caught between the past and present, and the younger generation—who would continue the old-line traditions well into the twentieth century—advocated for more identity experimentation, at least when it came to dancing. While the tableaux and court components of the old-line Carnival balls remained intact and touted privileged Mardi Gras traditions, in the years before the First World War, young krewesmen realized that if courting and romance were to flourish, the physically arresting tableaux and courts admired on thrones would not suffice. Modern dances appealed to the young krewesmen and their belles, and the lively bodily interactions that dances like the one-step and foxtrot offered encouraged old-line krewes' customary courting traditions to live on. Ragtime breathed new life into krewe romances.

Interestingly, it was through ballroom dancing that old-line krewesmen were able to more readily adapt to the changing world around them. As krewes embraced tamed rag dances, they found ways to appease the elders' penchant for pomp and circumstance while gratifying the youth's zest for new, charged personal connections on the dance floor. This shift was reflected in one of the most important material items of the Carnival ball: dance cards.

Around 1916, some krewes changed their dance-card format. Instead of printing the dance order, there were blank spaces for women to write in the names of dances or the blackcoats they danced with. La Cour recounted: "As the dance programs disappeared the multitudinous experimental movements were indulged in by the younger generation while the older and more conservative leaders continued the more formal dances even when the orchestra played half-time and syncopated melodies."[94] Thus, at Progressive Era balls, dancing opened up ways of expressing class solidarity, not through conformity, but by being flexible enough to create individual breathing space where new love could flourish according to each dancer's desires. Whether waltzing or ragging, ballroom dancing revealed that old-line krewes had finally learned how to marry tradition with modernity, thereby retaining the social power that made them elite.

As the last element of the evening, dancing at balls ended early in the morning, sometimes at dawn. For Comus (whose ball was on Mardi Gras night), dancing had special significance because when it finished, so, too, did that year's Carnival season. Lent had arrived. Despite the end of another Mardi Gras and the dawn of Lent, however, krewesmen and their guests had spent their evenings at Carnival balls, in the throes of delight. On the dance floor, masked men and beautiful women waltzed away the night, embracing their class values of southern gentility and testing those mores through adventurous flirting and intimate ragtime dance encounters.

The vitality of dancing as the center of private krewe practices illustrates the importance of dance to krewe identity. Dancing was the heart of krewe activities, and as krewesmen adapted to the world around them, the dances changed. Dance was so important to krewe life, in fact, that when a fire broke out onstage during the 1898 Mithras ball, couples continued dancing once it was extinguished, despite the ruined scenery and watery floor.[95] For the Mithras krewe and guests, it seemed, the connections made on the dance floor overrode all else. Crucial to the success of Carnival balls as a site of identity, dancing created a krewe courtship foundation—a roux of romance—and generated a space where dancers embraced each other on the parquet while they whirled in and out of fantasy and reality. To the world around them, Carnival ball dancers and romancers slipped into a "sheer metamorphosis through space into the very maddest whirlpool of pleasure."[96] Through dancing, even in the syncopated styles of ragtime, krewesmen and their guests were finally in sync.

Conclusion

Satisfied that they had firmly proclaimed class status through tableaux vivants, mock court pomp, and ballroom dancing, krewesmen concluded each ball with a renewed sense of group bonding. At the end of the ball, high-ranking (or reigning) krewe officials retired to a private supper at a posh restaurant or a member's home while carriages delivered their female guests to uptown mansions. But for some krewesmen, the night was not over; they flocked to Storyville for after-parties at infamous "French balls"—provocative, private masked dances, complete with female tableau performances and mock courts where prostitutes were crowned queen.[1] Located next to the Tango Belt, Storyville offered krewesmen enticing alternatives to the formality of their Carnival ball. The district was a hotbed of jazz, prostitution, and crime. Entertainment at French balls existed well outside of proper ballroom behavior and refinement.

According to Samuel Kinser, French balls began as an antebellum Creole response to Americans' appropriation of Creole Carnival activities. Originally, French balls were elegant affairs for the best of Creole society, but after the Civil War (when Creoles had already retreated to their homes for private dances), American proprietors seized the name for their own public dances that encouraged masking and sexual expression.[2] By the 1880s, one of the most famous French balls was the Ball of the Two Well-Known Gentlemen. Journalist James Gill points out that police chief David Hennessy initially controlled this dance and its sponsor, the Red Light Club. In turn, Hennessy answered to the man who appointed him: old-line krewesman and New Orleans mayor Joseph Shakespeare. Such arrangements ensured that attendance at the Ball of the Two Well-Known Gentlemen was comprised of influential men, who, according to the *Mascot,* were "generally recognized . . . as the lovers of women notoriously lewd and abandoned."[3]

By the late 1890s, French balls took place at Odd Fellows Hall (on Camp Street) or in Storyville, the notorious (and legal) red-light district.[4] Public French balls catered to men of all classes, tourists and New Orleanians alike. Private French balls were the domain of old-line men and their friends and, though no less ribald than the public events, were considered to be more refined in taste (only the choicest prostitutes attended). The two-dollar ticket price, which rose to three dollars in 1906, was an attempt to ensure exclusivity at the private events.[5] However, when men from nonelite classes still tried to get in, the entrepreneurs quickly developed a strict invitation system, remarkably similar to the one previously used by the old-line krewes. Even women were kept out unless they could furnish written proof (registration cards) that they were professional prostitutes in good standing.[6] This practice was intended to deter undesirable prostitutes but also wealthy wives masquerading as women of the night in order to see for themselves what drew their husbands from home.[7]

Advertisements in the famous blue and red books—catalogs of Storyville brothels—provide clues about possible French ball companions.[8] Bertha Golden, for instance, was known as a "first-class" octoroon who "also has the distinction of being the only classical Singer and Salome dancer in the Southern States."[9] Another "mademoiselle," Rita Walker, supposedly once a Chicago Salome, was reportedly "one of the first women in America to dance in her bare feet."[10] Entries like these in the tenderloin directories touted the titillating talents of the most expensive prostitutes, intriguing men who hoped to meet these professionals (and possibly sample their expertise) at the French balls. Moreover, once at the party, men could continue to build upon the traditional gender codes they instituted at the tableaux balls as they exercised their masculine privilege over women's bodies through flirting, carousing, and even sex.

Although Karen Leathem argued that men's visits to French balls were extensions of upper-class male privileges in sexual license, not "a longing for disorder," it seems that French balls fulfilled both needs—sexual and rebellious.[11] Of course, men visited these "sporting" events to explore extramarital pleasures long enjoyed by prestigious New Orleans men, but French balls also allowed old-liners to mock themselves while simultaneously reinforcing the boundaries they constructed at their own private balls. The events were comical in their crowning of a queen, their tableau performances, and their grand march (the "Grand Shadow Dance") that unfolded in the early hours of the morning.[12] But even though this play on old-line rituals was entertaining, first-class French balls were also very serious in their iteration of strict class and racial lines; only prominent white men visited, and only white prostitutes reigned as queen in a role that genteel women had occupied just hours earlier.[13] According to Alecia P. Long, French balls "simultaneously replicated and ridiculed the ideas about respectability that shaped the culture beyond the boundaries of the vice district."[14]

Though French balls were part of New Orleans' Carnival festivities from the 1880s through the first decades of the twentieth century, American involvement in World War I led to Storyville's closure on November 12, 1917.[15] The French balls soon faded, but more than just krewesmen's after-parties were affected by the First World War and the changes wrought by the new century. Old-line traditions as a whole were deeply altered. Carnival historian Henri Schindler argued that "World War I swept away many of the older social hierarchies throughout Europe, but in New Orleans the position of the elite remained intact and unchallenged. The old ruling class had not lost a sequin."[16] Despite Schindler's romantic view, there *were* challenges and disruptions to the old-line system that altered the krewesmen's grasp on Mardi Gras, perhaps the most visible symbol of their upper-class prestige.

The war itself terminated Mardi Gras festivities until 1920. After that, krewes were slow to return to the Carnival scene.[17] One obstacle was that the French Opera House burned down in 1919.[18] With the loss of this jewel, old-line krewes relocated their balls, ending the importance of the French Quarter to krewe festivities.[19] After the war, young krewes established a new masking tradition—kings and dukes were masked only by faux facial hair and makeup. This signaled a major separation between nineteenth-century old-line krewes and twentieth-century societies where the seriousness of kingly secrecy, even at the ball, disappeared.[20] Other shifts signaled changes to old-line traditions, as well. The war was one event within an era of national transformation. Unsurprisingly, perhaps, the unraveling of old-line sovereignty came along gender, race, and class lines—the very fronts that old-line

Carnival pageants sought to control through scripted bodily performances of krewe rhetoric.

One stride was that women gained universal suffrage by 1920. Connected to Mardi Gras, this created an enlivened sense of female, public Carnival participation, and for kreweswomen in particular, suffrage publicly expanded the agency that they had gained in private when they generated their own krewes and staged their own balls. In New Orleans, women engaged in Carnival behavior that was once acceptable only for men and prostitutes. During the first decades of the twentieth century, middle- and upper-class women visited bars; by the 1920s, they also masked in public and danced in the streets.[21] Old-line krewe gender codes were publicly disrupted even if they were still enforced in the private Carnival tableaux balls. But even courts saw shifts: in 1923, married women gained acceptance as Carnival queens in some krewes.[22]

While old-line women staged Carnival balls that played with gender expectations or took to the streets for dancing and revelry, New Orleans' African American neighborhoods continued to evolve established ambulatory parading traditions through the Mardi Gras Indians that first appeared in the 1880s, explored emerging practices through the advent of the Baby Dolls in 1912, and developed what arguably began as a spoof on old-line practices but came to (also arguably) embrace old-line tactics through organizations like the Zulu Social Aid and Pleasure Club. Though the krewe of Zulu emerged in the early years of the twentieth century—they first marched as "Zulus" in 1909, rode on floats in 1915, and were incorporated as an organization in 1916—they didn't create a Carnival ball ritual until well into the twentieth century, perhaps signifying their reluctance to incorporate old-line practices into their own rituals.

The Original Illinois Club (OIC), on the other hand, was founded more than a decade before Zulu and focused predominantly on dancing. Furthermore, the OIC emulated, rather than mocked, old-line practices. Wiley Knight, a Tennessee native who lived in Chicago and worked as a train conductor, moved to New Orleans in 1894 and opened a dancing school uptown. "When I came to New Orleans," Knight said, "there were no carnival balls for Negroes. The only entertainments were square dances and quadrilles. I saw a need for introducing dancing and the social graces to the

Negro community. So I opened a dancing school which I conducted during my spare time."[23]

The OIC originated in Knight's dancing school, which championed standards of respectability in New Orleans' middle- and upper-class black communities. OIC members were some of New Orleans' most wealthy black citizens (it quickly became an all-male organization), and its balls included grand marches, krewe courts comprised of debutantes, and ballroom dancing. The club also became known for a unique tradition: fathers partnered their debutante daughters in the "Chicago Glide," a waltz variation introduced by Knight and still performed at OIC balls.[24]

Most importantly, the OIC did not employ masking, and it blurred the performative participant/observer line.[25] A particular feature was that women could ask men to dance. In this way, the OIC utilized old-line krewe traditions but implemented variations for the purpose of enlarging a community that, while exclusive, didn't create divisive hierarchies within its own social traditions. Community underscored every element of the OIC ball, including the "serving of an elaborate buffet supper, which consisted of everything from 'soup to nuts.'"[26]

Finally, class and economics affected krewesmen's domination over Mardi Gras. Middle-class revelers challenged the old order by creating their own parade and marching group traditions. The Jefferson City Buzzards, for instance, formed in 1890, took to uptown streets on Mardi Gras day with their own walking parades. The transformation of trucks into floats for neighborhood "truck parades" was another middle-class development that gained popularity across the city. "These mobile cabarets, complete with jazz bands and dancing," Leathem argued, "offered an alternative to formal, male-dominated parades."[27] As Schindler noted, some krewes that formed between 1900 and World War I disappeared while others flourished; the ones that survived fostered diverse participation in what had once been the realm of urbane, white men.

As for those urbane, white men, Prohibition put a damper on drinking habits while new income taxes curtailed krewe expenditures. Accordingly, old-line krewes, once nouveau-riche, were now "old money" and avoided anything that might suggest vulgar ostentation.[28] The days of Parisian gown designers were gone.[29] Gowns, invitations, floats, and costumes were American made after World War I, and thus material culture links to European luxury were at an end. The era from 1884 to World War I—which Schindler termed the "Golden Age" of Mardi Gras—full of otherworldly empires and comical themes, defined by grand, artistic traditions, had passed.[30]

By this time, however, old-line krewes had codified their Carnival rituals. Generations after the emergence of the first Comus parade and ball, moneyed Americans and Creoles had intermarried and coalesced into a powerful New Orleans group—the Mardi Gras monarchy.[31] Despite any contestations of their power and politics in everyday life, old-line krewes created a realm for themselves where white elitism and conservative politics combined to produce a romantic ideal on which they modeled their identity. Krewesmen kept the forces that encroached on their territory (the government, radical politicians, immigrants, and women's rights) from usurping the cultural power established through their Mardi Gras traditions. Carnival play was a serious matter. Through seasonal themes, parades, masking, and especially balls, old-line krewesmen cast themselves as gods, kings, and conquerors—heroes across the millennia (and presumably for millennia to come). Krewesmen established themselves as the patriarchal rulers of New Orleans society. Victor Turner conceptualized such actions as reflexive rituals, epitomized by a "critique, direct or veiled, of the social life it grows out of, an evaluation (with lively possibilities of rejection) of the way society handles history."[32] Carnival balls grounded this process.

As outsiders in a Creole city, American immigrants in nineteenth-century New Orleans settled in their own neighborhoods and began to either dictate or discard the French and Spanish customs of the city.[33] Through their manipulation or rejection of these traditions, subsequent generations of Americans—the men who formed old-line krewes (most of them northerners)—came to dominate New Orleans culture.[34] Krewe parades through the streets sculpted the loose Creole tradition of street parties into a more codified and exaggerated expression of social hierarchy. Old-line krewes brought order to what they viewed as a chaotic system, and, in the process, processions emerged as a new and uniquely American tradition. Positioned on floats, krewesmen literally towered above spectators and asserted their claim to high social standing. Moreover, Mardi Gras themes consistently referenced an Anglo-Saxon past, emphasizing monarchy, imperialism, and refined high-art culture.[35] Thematically masked krewe members paraded through public space as arbiters of New Orleans culture and then retreated to private balls that affirmed their privilege and collective identity through bodily performances. Alienation as a previously "foreign" group faded as tableaux vivants, mock royalty, and ballroom dancing reinforced group bonds.

These same Americans ruled nineteenth-century New Orleans business life.[36] They became prominent cotton merchants, lawyers, and other business leaders. When the Civil War threatened their economic prosperity, krewesmen joined the Confederacy and defended their interests.[37] After the war, they slowly regained a financial foothold, and eventually the extravagant expenditures on krewe parades were rivaled, even surpassed, by the amount of money old-line krewes invested in their private Carnival balls.

Every element of the balls and krewe pageants reflected class-consciousness, steeped in ostentatious displays of luxury and social superiority. Krewe families' Carnival festivities, far beyond the means of middle- and working-class New Orleanians, required enormous investments of time and money. Lavish parade floats, seasonal costumes, tableau sets, and expensive ball gowns demonstrated economic power and status. Invitations, dress codes, theater decorations, call-out favors, and court jewels all alluded to affluence, thereby situating krewes as a prosperous and prestigious group that set discriminating standards of taste and refinement. Even dancing styles, especially related to the court, relied on pomp and circumstance that was modeled after spectacles of European royalty. Old-line krewes, like European monarchs, used these displays (the art of courtliness) as a tool of power.

The interconnectedness between power, identity, and performance emerged from the start of old-line Carnival balls, which began with a staple of Renaissance court spectacle, "the moving emblematic tableau."[38] Through choreographed tableaux vivants, krewesmen became a reflection of their figurehead, Comus, Proteus, or Momus himself, and embodied an elevated status within their self-ordained monarchy. They further refined their identity through alignment with Renaissance ideals: they presented themselves as educated, courtly, artistic, moral, and just. Krewesmen (costumed as knights and mythological heroes) proclaimed themselves the defenders of women, their land, and their privileged standing as natural leaders—all articulated through a romantic reworking of their Lost Cause involvement. Accordingly, krewesmen championed their women as a mixed representation of delicate debutantes who needed protection, and supportive goddess-like beauties who wholeheartedly defended their men's causes. Early krewe tableaux centered on the political ideas that threatened them most (Radical Reconstruction and, later, women's rights), and by embodying their class ideals through posing and scripted scenes, krewesmen simultaneously alleviated their sociopolitical anxieties, reconstructed a sense of community, and decreed themselves to be kingly, even godly.

These re/constructions of identity also took shape on the Carnival ballroom dance floor. In the Gilded Age, krewe courts took center stage. Regal and elegant, krewe court participants performed stately grand marches and formal royal masked dances. As polished pedestrians, even the simplest of moves, such as walking, became physical statements of refinement and class virtue. Added to this, their roles as court members set kings and dukes, queens and maids, apart as elevated within an already elevated social circuit. Empowerment, then, became a defining aspect of court appearances, which commanded guests' attention and respect. Within this realm, select krewesmen masqueraded as kings and gods while they put their debutante daughters on display as queens and maids. But daughters were not simply pawns; their performances were important elements in shaping and reflecting krewe ideals and in maintaining order amid a world in flux. As tableau performances waned in the last years of the nineteenth century and krewe courts began to govern the Carnival ball agenda, the illustration of power and regality that the mock monarchy and grand marches exemplified became a defining factor in old-line identity. The implication was clear: krewe courts reigned over other krewesmen and, by implication, the rest of society.

While choreographed promenades instilled regality, even conformity, ballroom dancing provided space for excitement and romance while maintaining class distinctiveness. Through quadrilles, krewes further linked themselves to the formality of European aristocracy, emulating the structure and social hierarchy implicit in the quadrille's history. And although quadrilles remained a staple of ball etiquette for the first few decades of Carnival balls, waltzing became immensely more popular by the end of the nineteenth century, as dance cards reveal. With waltzes, krewesmen embraced a dance steeped in revolution and passion but ultimately tamed by refined society. This distinction is important. A "refined pleasure" allowed krewes to participate in a potentially rebellious dance while maintaining a sense of class propriety, just as they did at the beginning of the twentieth century with ragtime dancing. Even though both the waltz and ragtime became associated with female liberation and sensuality, male partners continued to dictate floor patterns, physical touching, and romantic interactions, thus enabling kreweswomen to embrace romantic explorations while krewesmen continued to act as both protectors and southern gentlemen. Ultimately, old-line krewes offered female participants chances to explore personal desires through dancing, but the men tightly regulated those explorations. Jurisdiction over image, bodies, and relationships was key to krewe identity formation. Despite the entrenched gender codes, what did loosen was individuality. With the introduction of ragtime into the Carnival ball repertoire, krewesmen began to make choices about what they would dance and when. Multiple styles reigned concurrently alongside one another, revealing a new flexibility. Krewesmen were finally able to adapt to the world around them.

The prominence of the body—and of the body in motion—is vital to understanding old-line krewes. While historians recognize the three-pronged characteristics of Mardi Gras—parading, masking, and balls—no Carnival practice changed as radically as the old-line Carnival ball ritual. Krewe parades maintained their general routes, organization, and use of floats. Masking remained a social commentary on current events but always worked in tandem with parading (however loosely) or dancing. The balls themselves, however, changed to meet the needs and identity of old-line krewesmen. While seasonal themes usually dictated all three elements of parading, masking, and balls, and the format of the ball remained virtually unaltered, the focus of balls gradually shifted from male tableau performances to courtly demonstrations of power to class cohesion through romantic ballroom dancing. Throughout Reconstruction, men occupied the spotlight. They defended their past and values through imposing tableaux that praised whiteness and southern masculinity, tailoring a cohesive sense of selfhood that embodied their ideals. By the 1880s, mock kings and, more visibly, queens ruled the evening and reassured krewesmen and guests alike that they were all a part of a distinctive New Orleans population, a regal class, whose attention to traditional gender codes signified a prevailing Gilded Age gentility and glamour. By the dawn of the twentieth century, however, these concerns were distilled into a single ball element: ballroom dancing, which simultaneously underscored krewesmen's anxieties and ideals on every front. Moreover, the general dancing kept pace with current national trends, adapting more readily than other more rigid components of the ball format. Dancing was the old-line krewes' key to the future.

Old-line krewe bonds were strong but not indestructible; they could not completely evade encroaching outside forces. Europe (ironically, the seedbed of Mardi Gras' royal pageantry) disturbed the domain of New Orleans' monarchs. World War I interrupted Carnival celebrations, and by 1920, power shifted. The younger krewes that formed around the turn of the century began inscribing Mardi Gras in their own way, and by the late 1960s, gay and lesbian groups added their own performances into the mix of krewe, parade, and ball possibilities. In response to exclusion from membership in the older krewes, or in mockery of these exclusionist policies, today's krewes continue to negotiate traditions of their own and have transformed Mardi Gras into an experience based in large part on diverse identities, including the use of satirical drag and other performative approaches in order to generate and solidify a sense of community on their own terms. Yet, even the most idiosyncratic and progressive krewes draw from the elite recipe of pageantry. They continue to practice the established conventions of tableaux, courtly processions, and social dancing—the conventions established by the old-line krewes whose secret side set the stage for Mardi Gras in the twentieth century and into the new millennium.

APPENDIX

TABLE 1. Popular Carnival Court Families, 1870–1920

FAMILY NAME	FIRST NAME	KREWE	YEAR	COURT ROLE[a]
Aldigé	Alice	Rex	1883	
	Amelie	Comus	1890	
	Amelie	Momus	1891	Q
	Amelie	Atlanteans	1891	
	Louise	Proteus	1892	
	Alice	Proteus	1907	Q
	Alice	Nereus	1907	
	Marie	Atlanteans	1909	
Buckner	Katie (Catherine)	TNR	1878	Q
	Kate	Comus	1890	Q
	Kate	Proteus	1891	
	Helen	Momus	1891	
	Laura	Argonauts	1893	
	Minnie	Rex	1894	
	Minnie	TNR (IV)	1894	
	Minnie	Atlanteans	1894	
	Minnie	Momus	1898	
	Alice	Rex	1896	
	Alice	Momus	1896	
	Edith	Elves of Oberon	1897	Q
	Edith	TNR (IV)	1897	
	Hettie	Atlanteans	1898	
	Frances	Rex	1899	

TABLE 1. Popular Carnival Court Families (*continued*)

FAMILY NAME	FIRST NAME	KREWE	YEAR	COURT ROLE[a]
Buckner	Frances	Atlanteans	1899	
(*continued*)	Julia	Momus	1901	
	Julia	TNR (IV)	1901	
	Fannie	Momus	1902	Q
	Fannie	Comus	1902	
	Christine	Nereus	1902	
Claiborne	Lulu	Momus	1896	
	Amélie	Elves of Oberon	1902	Q
	Amélie	TNR (IV)	1902	
	Amélie	Nereus	1902	
	Lucie	Atlanteans	1907	Q
	Lucy	Rex	1908	
	Lucy	Rex	1909	
	Lucy	Momus	1909	
	Clarisse	Atlanteans	1914	
	Clarissa	Rex	1916	
Dunbar	Louise	Comus	1891	
	Louise	Momus	1893	
	Louise	Momus	1894	Q
	Olga	Momus	1903	
	Olga	Proteus	1908	Q
Eustis	Anita	Rex	1881	
	Kate	Rex	1882	
	Nellie	Atlanteans	1897	
	Kittie	TNR (IV)	1898	
	Kittie	Momus	1898	
	Kittie	Consus	1898	
	Maud	Atlanteans	1907	
	Maud	Rex	1908	
	Maud	Comus	1909	
	Maud	Atlanteans	1909	Q
	Gladys	TNR (IV)	1914	

TABLE 1. Popular Carnival Court Families (*continued*)

FAMILY NAME	FIRST NAME	KREWE	YEAR	COURT ROLE[a]
Farrar	Mary	Comus	1905	
	Mildred	Comus	1909	
	Jane	TNR (IV)	1909	
	Jane	Mithras	1909	
	Jane	Comus	1914	
Fenner	Clarice	Rex	1888	
	Ms. (generic)	Mithras	1898	
	Clarisse	Comus	1903	
	Gladys	Momus	1903	
	Gladys	TNR (IV)	1904	
	Gladys	Atlanteans	1908	Q
	Elizabeth	Mithras	1920	
	Elizabeth	TNR (IV)	1920	
Grima	Emma	Atlanteans	1906	Q
	Emma	Rex	1907	
	Emma	Atlanteans	1907	
	Marcelle	Momus	1916	Q
	Marcelle	TNR (IV)	1916	
	Marcelle	Atlanteans	1916	
Hardie	Isabel	Comus	1898	Q
	Isabel	TNR (IV)	1898	
	Alice	Momus	1904	
	Alice	Comus	1906	
	Alice	Momus	1910	Q
	Ella	Comus	1907	
Hincks	Annette	Elves of Oberon	1895	
	Emily	Mithras	1900	
	Emma	Consus	1901	
	Emma	Falstaffians	1901	
	Léda	Proteus	1907	

TABLE 1. Popular Carnival Court Families (*continued*)

FAMILY NAME	FIRST NAME	KREWE	YEAR	COURT ROLE[a]
Janvier	Celeste	TNR (IV)	1905	
	Celeste	Comus	1906	Q
	Celeste	Rex	1908	
	Lois	Elves of Oberon	1911	
	Lois	TNR (IV)	1911	
	Lois	Rex	1912	Q
	Josephine	Rex	1913	
	Josephine	Proteus	1913	Q
	Josephine	TNR (IV)	1913	Q
	Josephine	Rex	1914	
	Regina	Rex	1917	
	Regina	TNR (IV)	1917	
Lallande	Juanita	Comus	1895	
	Juanita	Proteus	1897	Q
	Ethelyn	Rex	1895	
	Ethelyn	Rex	1897	Q
	Ruby	Comus	1900	
Legendre	Lillian	Rex	1877	
	Lilian	Atlanteans	1905	
	Ms. (generic)	Rex	1905	
	Anaïs	Rex	1907	
	Anaïs	Proteus	1907	
	Virgie	Rex	1908	
	Virgie	Atlanteans	1910	
	Anina	Atlanteans	1909	
	Katherine	Atlanteans	1911	Q
	Katherine	Comus	1912	
	Katherine	Rex	1913	
	Ethelyn	Momus	1915	
	Edith	Momus	1917	
	Edith	Mithras	1917	

TABLE 1. Popular Carnival Court Families (*continued*)

FAMILY NAME	FIRST NAME	KREWE	YEAR	COURT ROLE[a]
Levert	Mathilde	Comus	1894	Q
	Stephanie	Elves of Oberon	1895	
	Beatrice	Mithras	1902	
	Ella	Proteus	1906	Q
	Ella	Elves of Oberon	1906	
Maginnis	Margaret	Rex	1874	Q
	Laura	Rex	1880	
	Laura	Rex	1884	
	Josephine	Comus	1892	
	Josephine	Argonauts	1892	Q
	Josephine	Comus	1893	Q
	Josephine	Momus	1895	
	Marguerite	Comus	1907	
	Margaret	Mithras	1907	Q
	Elizabeth	Rex	1907	
	Elizabeth	TNR (IV)	1907	
	Elizabeth	Rex	1908	Q
	Josephine	Momus	1914	
	Josephine	Mithras	1914	
Merrick	Bessie	Rex	1899	
	Bessie	Rex	1901	Q
	Caroline	Rex	1900	
	Caroline	Rex	1901	
	Laura	Elves of Oberon	1909	Q
	Laura	Rex	1909	
	Laura	Momus	1910	
	Caroline	Rex	1900	
	Caroline	Rex	1901	
	Laura	Elves of Oberon	1909	Q
	Laura	Rex	1909	
	Laura	Momus	1910	
	Susan	Momus	1912	Q
	Susan	Comus	1912	

TABLE 1. Popular Carnival Court Families (*continued*)

FAMILY NAME	FIRST NAME	KREWE	YEAR	COURT ROLE[a]
Merrick	Susan	TNR (IV)	1912	
(*continued*)	Susan	Rex	1913	
	Susan	Rex	1914	
Minor	Louise	Argonauts	1893	Q
	Amélie	Atlanteans	1905	
	Amélie	Nereus	1906	
	Charlotte	Falstaffians	1906	
	Mary	Atlanteans	1908	
Orme	Mary	Comus	1914	Q
	Mary	Momus	1914	
	Mary	Mithras	1914	
	Mary	Rex	1915	
	Abbie	Rex	1916	
	Abbie	Mithras	1916	
	Abbie	Momus	1917	
	Isabel	Rex	1920	
	Isabel	TNR (IV)	1920	
Rainey	Kate	TNR (IV)	1898	
	Kate	Consus	1898	
	Kate	Rex	1902	
	Maud	TNR (IV)	1899	
	Louise	Comus	1901	
	Louise	Elves of Oberon	1901	Q
	Louise	Proteus	1901	
	Maude	Momus	1902	
	Helen	Comus	1905	Q
	Katherine	Momus	1912	
	Katherine	Mithras	1912	
	Katherine	Momus	1913	Q
Richardson	Susie	Rex	1883	Q
	Susie	Proteus	1883	Q
	Susie	TNR (II)	1884	

TABLE 1. Popular Carnival Court Families (*continued*)

FAMILY NAME	FIRST NAME	KREWE	YEAR	COURT ROLE[a]
	Cora	Rex	1887	
	Cora	Rex	1889	Q
	Cora	Comus	1893	
	Ada	Rex	1889	
	Ada	Rex	1893	Q
	Genevieve	Rex	1889	
	Sadie	Comus	1894	
	Sadie	Elves of Oberon	1896	
	Corinne	Consus	1898	
	Elise	TNR (IV)	1901	Q
	Margaret	Comus	1901	Q
Van Benthuysen	May	Nereus	1896	Q
	May	Comus	1897	
	May	Rex	1896	
	May	TNR (IV)	1896	
	May	Momus	1897	
	May	Nereus	1898	
	May	Rex	1901	
	May	Rex	1902	Q
	Maytie	Momus	1900	
Villeré	Corinne	Atlanteans	1900	
	Corinne	Nereus	1900	
	Omer	Rex	1900	(matron of honor)
	Alma	Momus	1913	
	Alma	Elves of Oberon	1913	
	Alma	Rex	1914	
	Celeste	Elves of Oberon	1914	
	Celeste	Rex	1916	
Walmsley	Carrie	Rex	1882	
	Gratia	Comus	1903	
	Myra	TNR (IV)	1907	
	Myra	Mithras	1907	
	Myra	Comus	1908	

TABLE 1. Popular Carnival Court Families (*continued*)

FAMILY NAME	FIRST NAME	KREWE	YEAR	COURT ROLE[a]
Walmsley	Carrie	TNR (IV)	1910	Q
(*continued*)	Carrie	Momus	1913	
	Byrd	TNR (IV)	1914	
	Byrd	Momus	1915	
Wisdom	Jessie	Rex	1903	
	Jessie	TNR (IV)	1903	
	Jessie	Consus	1903	
	Jessie	Comus	1904	
	Jessie	TNR (IV)	1905	Q
	Eliza	Mithras	1911	

[a] Court roles noted only for queens (Q); unless otherwise specified, the women listed served as court maids.

Source: Compiled from Perry Young, *The Mistick Krewe: Chronicles of Comus and His Kin* (New Orleans: Carnival, 1931), "Table of Displays," 219–68. Families represented here had at least five carnival court appearances from 1870 to 1920.

TABLE 2. Carnival Court Family Dynasties in Old-Line Krewes
and Tableaux Societies, 1870–1920

FAMILY NAME	AFFILIATED KREWES	YEAR SPAN	COURT APPEARANCES	# OF COURT WOMEN
Buckner	Comus, Momus, Rex, Proteus, TNR (I), TNR (IV), Elves, Atlanteans, Argonauts	1878–1902	21	12
Legendre	Comus, Momus, Rex, Proteus, Atlanteans, Mithras	1877–1917	14	9
Richardson	Comus, Rex, Proteus, TNR (II), TNR (IV), Consus, Elves	1883–1901	14	8
Maginnis	Comus, Momus, Rex, TNR (IV), Mithras, Argonauts	1874–1914	14	7
Rainey	Comus, Momus, Rex, Proteus, TNR (IV), Elves, Consus, Mithras	1898–1913	12	6
Claiborne	Comus, Momus, Rex, TNR (IV), Atlanteans, Elves, Nereus	1896–1916	10	4

Source: Derived from Perry Young, *The Mistick Krewe: Chronicles of Comus and His Kin* (New Orleans: Carnival, 1931), "Table of Displays," 219–68. Old-line krewes include Comus, Momus, Proteus, Rex, and the Original Twelfth Night Revelers (TNR). The tableaux societies are the second, third, and fourth incarnations of TNR, Atlanteans, Elves of Oberon, Nereus, and High Priests of Mithras. Secondary tableaux societies (formed between 1900 and 1916) include the Falstaffians, the Olympians, Athenians, and Krewe of Nippon. Other families who had a respectable number of appearances in Carnival courts from 1870 to 1920 emerged as additional Carnival family dynasties in the 1920s. They are Fenner, White, Levert, Hardie, Fox, Grima, Villeré, and Plauche (1930s).

TABLE 3. Old-Line Krewe Seasonal Themes, 1870–1916

KREWE	YEAR	THEME	CATEGORY[a]
Comus	1857	The Demon Actors in Milton's *Paradise Lost*	G/A
	1858	The Classic Pantheon	G
	1859	The English Holidays	F
	1860	Statues of the Great Men of Our Country	G
	1861	The Four Ages of Life	M
	1866	The Past, the Present, and the Future	M
	1867	Triumph of Epicurus	A
	1868	The Departure of Lalla Rookh from Delhi	F/E
	1869	The Five Senses	A/G
	1870	The History of Louisiana from 1539 to 1815	G
	1871	Spen[s]er's Faerie Queen	A
	1872	Dreams of Homer	G/A
	1873	The Missing Links to Darwin's Origin of Species	M
	1874	The Visit of Envoys from the Old World and New to the Court of Comus	G/F
	1876	Four Thousand Years of Sacred History	G
	1877	The Aryan Race	M
	1878	Scenes from the *Metamorphoses* of Ovid	G
	1880	The Aztec People and Their Conquest by Cortez	G/E
	1881	The Myths of Norland	F
	1882	The Worships of the World	F
	1884	Illustrated Ireland	F/G
	1890	The Palingenesis of the Mistick Krewe	M
	1891	Demonology	F
	1892	Nippon, the Land of the Rising Sun	F/E
	1893	Salammbo (Flaubert)	A
	1894	Once Upon a Time	F
	1895	The Songs of Long Ago	A/F
	1896	The Month and Seasons of the Year	M
	1897	Homer's Odyssey	G/A
	1898	Scenes from Shakespeare	L
	1899	Josephus	G
	1900	Stories of the Golden Age	G
	1901	Selections from the Operas	A
	1902	The Fairy Kingdom	F

TABLE 3. Old-Line Krewe Seasonal Themes (*continued*)

KREWE	YEAR	THEME	CATEGORY[a]
	1903	A Leaf from the Mahabarata	F
	1904	Izdubar	F
	1905	The Lost Pleiad	G
	1906	The Masque of Comus	G/F
	1907	Tennyson	F/G/A
	1908	Gods and Goddesses	G
	1909	Flights of Fancy	F/G
	1910	Mahomet	F/E
	1911	Familiar Quotations	M
	1912	Cathay	F
	1913	Time's Mysteries	F
	1914	Tales from Chaucer	A
	1915	Lore and Legends of Childhood	F
	1916	Glimpses of the Modern World of Art	A/G
	1917	Romantic Legends	F
TNR	1870	A Twelfth Night Revel	G
	1871	Mother Goose's Tea Party	F
	1872	English Humor	A
	1873	The World of Audubon	A
	1874	Dolliana and Her Kingdom	F
	1876	The March of Ages	G
	1878	A Twelfth Night Revel	F
TNR (II)	1884	The Kingdom of Flowers	F
	1885	Domino	M
	1886	(No theme mentioned)	M
TNR (III)	1887	Domino	M
TNR (IV)	1894	A Twelfth Night Revel	F
	1895	Les Incroyables (1795–99—The Directory)	M
	1896	"That Orbed Maiden with White Fir Laden"	F
	1897	The Chrysanthemum	M
	1898	Minstrels of the Olden Time	A
	1899	The Realm of the Butterflies	A

TABLE 3. Old-Line Krewe Seasonal Themes (*continued*)

KREWE	YEAR	THEME	CATEGORY[a]
TNR (IV)	1900	The Four Seasons	A
(*continued*)	1901	The Palace of the Water Nymphs	F
	1902	The Birthnight of the Hummingbird (Goodrich)	M
	1903	Pierrot Domino	M
	1904	Harlequin	M
	1905	A Night in Japan	F/E
	1906	The Cave of Magic	F
	1907	The Realm of Peace	M
	1908	Court of Misrule	M
	1909	The Revels of the Gems	M
	1910	The Garden of the Gods	G
	1911	The Battle of the Flowers	M
	1912	The Butterfly (Jean Ingelow)	A
	1913	The Origin and Quaint Customs of Twelfth Night	M
	1914	Peer Gynt	A
	1915	The Great Chan and the Fairy Se Wang Moo	F/E
	1916	The Myth of the Gilded Man (Indian Legend)	F
	1917	Sheik-al-Jabal	E
	1920	Scraps	M
Rex	1872	Triumphal Entry	M
	1873	Egyptian	F
	1874	Persian	F
	1876	Persian and Egyptian	F
	1877	Military Progress of the World	G
	1878	The Gods Modernized	G
	1879	The History of the World	F
	1880	The Four Elements	M
	1881	Arabian Nights Tales	F/A
	1882	The Pursuit of Pleasure	A
	1883	Atlantis—The Antediluvian World	F
	1884	The Semitic Races	F/G
	1885	Ivanhoe	A/F
	1886	The Triumph of Aurelian/Grand Historical Scenes	G
	1887	Music and Drama/Odds and Ends/Washington	F/G
	1888	The Realm of Flowers	M

TABLE 3. Old-Line Krewe Seasonal Themes (*continued*)

KREWE	YEAR	THEME	CATEGORY[a]
	1889	The Treasures of the Earth	M
	1890	Rules of Ancient Times	G
	1891	Visions	M
	1892	Symbolism of Colors	M
	1893	Fantasies	F
	1894	Illustrations from Literature	A/G
	1895	Chronicles of Fairyland—Fantastic Tales for Young and Old (Fergus Hume)	A/G
	1896	Heavenly Bodies	G
	1897	On the Water—Real and Fanciful	M
	1898	Harvest Queens	M
	1899	Reveries of Rex	F
	1900	Terpsichore	M
	1901	Human Passions and Characteristics	M
	1902	Quotations from Literature	A
	1903	Feasts and Fetes	F
	1904	In the Realm of Imagination	F
	1905	Idealistic Queens	M
	1906	In Utopia	F
	1907	Visions of the Nations	F
	1908	The Classics of Childhood	F
	1909	The Treasures of the King	M
	1910	The Freaks of Fable	F
	1911	Arts and Sciences	A
	1912	Faces of Nature	M
	1913	Enchantments and Transformations	F
	1914	The Drama of the Year	M
	1915	Fragments from Song and Story	A/G/F
	1916	Visions from the Poets	A F
	1917	The Gifts of the Gods to Louisiana	G
	1920	Life's Pilgrimage	M
Momus	1872	The Talisman	G
	1873	The Coming Races (Entwicklungsgeschichte)	A
	1876	Louisiana and Her Seasons	G
	1877	Hades—A Dream of Momus	G

TABLE 3. Old-Line Krewe Seasonal Themes (*continued*)

KREWE	YEAR	THEME	CATEGORY[a]
Momus	1878	The Realms of Fancy	F
(*continued*)	1880	A Dream of Fair Women	G
	1881	Scenes from Popular Subjects	A
	1882	The Rama Yama	F
	1883	The Moors in Spain	F
	1884	The Passions	M
	1885	The Legends Beautiful	F
	1887	Myths of the New World	F
	1889	The Culprit Fay (Joseph Rodman Drake)	A/F
	1890	Paradise and the Peri	F
	1891	Palmer Cox's Brownies	F
	1892	Aladdin or the Wonderful Lamp	F
	1893	The Legend of the Four Leaf Clover	M
	1894	The Fairies and the Fiddler	F
	1895	Mahabarata	F
	1896	Comic History of Rome	G
	1897	Domino	M
	1898	Bals Masques	A
	1899	Cinderella, Or the Little Glass Slipper	F
	1900	Legends from the Court of King Arthur	F/A
	1901	Our Festivals	M
	1902	Bryon's Poems	A/F
	1903	Myths of the Red Men	F/E
	1904	Visions of the World's Vanities	F
	1905	Vathek, Ninth Caliph of the Abassides	F/E
	1906	Leaves from Oriental Literature	F/E
	1907	The Quest of the Fountain of Youth	F
	1908	Aesop's Fables	F
	1909	Signs and Superstitions	F
	1910	The Winged World	M
	1911	The Language of Flowers	M
	1912	Chronicles of Momus	M
	1913	Above the Clouds	M
	1914	Odds and Ends of Nonsense	F
	1915	Tales of the How and Why	F

TABLE 3. Old-Line Krewe Seasonal Themes (*continued*)

KREWE	YEAR	THEME	CATEGORY[a]
	1916	Pinocchio	F
	1917	Ventures of Baron Munchausen	A/F
	1920	A Pierrot Ball	A
Proteus	1882	Ancient Egyptian Theology	E/F
	1883	The History of France	G
	1884	The Aeneid	G
	1885	The Myths and Worships of the Chinese	E
	1886	Visions of Other Worlds	G
	1887	Anderson's Fairy Tales	F
	1888	Legends of the Middle Ages	F
	1889	The Hindoo Heavens	E
	1890	Elfland	F
	1891	Tales of the Genii	E
	1892	A Dream of the Vegetable Kingdom	A
	1893	Kalevala (Myths of Finland)	F
	1894	Shah Nameh, The Epic of the Kings	E
	1895	Asgard and the Gods	G
	1896	Dumb Society	A/F
	1897	Orlando Furioso (Ariosto)	F
	1898	A Trip to Wonderland	F
	1899	E Pluribus Unum	G
	1900	Tales of Childhood	F
	1901	Al Kyris the Magnificent (From Ardath—Corelli)	A/F
	1902	Flora's Feast	M
	1903	Cleopatra	G
	1904	The Alphabet	M
	1905	The Rubaiyat	E/G
	1906	The Inspirations of Proteus (Silver Anniversary)	F
	1907	The Queen of the Serpents (From the Thousand and One Nights)	F/E/A
	1908	The Light of Asia (Sir Edwin Arnold)	A/F
	1909	Romances of Wales	F
	1910	Astrology	M
	1911	The Last Days of Pompeii (Bulwer-Lytton)	A

TABLE 3. Old-Line Krewe Seasonal Themes (*continued*)

KREWE	YEAR	THEME	CATEGORY[a]
Proteus	1912	Zoroaster	G
(*continued*)	1913	Adventures of Telemachus	F
	1914	Gerusalemme Liberata (Tasso)	A
	1915	Famous Lovers of the World	G
	1916	Sherwood	F
	1917	The Earthly Paradise	F

[a] These categories, created by the author, were used to determine the popularity of krewe themes. "G" stands for "Gods and Great Men," including classical mythology, history, and stories from the Bible. "F" denotes "Fairy Tales and Folklore," including literature and loose narratives based on legends, fables, general myths, and nursery rhymes (usually romantic in aesthetic presentation). "E" represents "The Exotic 'Other,'" fantasies of world travel and literature related to those places. "A" indicates "Arts & Nature," including visual and performing arts, leisurely pursuits, and animals. The final category, "M," represents "Miscellaneous" and encompasses any remaining themes.

Source: The seasonal themes (and spellings) were taken from Perry Young, *The Mistick Krewe: Chronicles of Comus and His Kin* (New Orleans: Carnival, 1931), "Table of Displays," 219–68.

NOTES

INTRODUCTION

1. The Mardi Gras, or Carnival, season is one of celebration, marking a festive period before Lent (when revelers are supposed to turn toward fasting and penitence in the weeks before Easter). Traditionally, the Carnival season begins on January 6, the Epiphany, also known as Twelfth Night, and culminates on Mardi Gras Day, the day before Ash Wednesday.

2. Scholarship does address Carnival balls as instrumental in Mardi Gras, but no work deals in depth with the actual dancing itself. Besides Karen Trahan Leathem's 1994 dissertation, "'A Carnival According to Their Own Desires': Gender and Mardi Gras in New Orleans, 1870–1941" (Ph.D. diss., University of North Carolina at Chapel Hill, 1994), which provides a compelling argument about elite gender in Mardi Gras, other works that peripherally deal with Carnival balls include Phyllis Hutton Raabe, "Status and Its Impact: New Orleans Carnival, the Social Upper Class and Upper-Class Power" (Ph.D. diss., Pennsylvania State University, 1973); Karen Luanne Williams, "Images of Uneasy Hybrids: Carnival and New Orleans" (Ph.D. diss., Emory University, 1992); Benton Jay Komis, "A Reading of Cultural Diversity: The Island New Orleans" (Ph.D. diss., Harvard University, 1998); and Henry Arnold Kmen, "Singing and Dancing in New Orleans: A Social History of the Birth and Growth of Balls and Opera, 1791–1841" (Ph.D. diss., Tulane University, 1961).

3. For the purposes of this book, "old-line" refers to the oldest, most exclusive Mardi Gras organizations, all of which were formed between 1857 and 1890 as predominantly elite, white, Protestant, American, all-male clubs: the Mistick Krewe of Comus, Knights of Momus, Rex, Proteus, and the original Twelfth Night Revelers (TNR). As a side note, many of the younger men from Comus, Momus, Proteus, and Rex families formed additional, ball-only organizations in the 1890s. Though equally prestigious, these organizations are not fully characteristic of old-line krewes. They are called "tableaux societies," further discussed in chapter 5.

4. "Dreams of Homer" was Comus' 1872 theme; "The World of Audubon" was the 1873 theme for TNR.

5. The seriousness of play is a theory explored in depth by anthropologist/theorist Victor Turner in his seminal collection of essays *From Ritual to Theatre: The Human Seriousness of Play* (New York: PAJ, 1982). In this work, Turner argues that "play" constitutes symbolic action with multiple meanings and the possibility of maintaining social order, introducing new modes of "portraying or embellishing old models for living" and the potential for "cultural innovation, as well as the means of effective structural transformations within a relatively stable sociocultural system" (85).

6. None of Comus' six founders were New Orleanians. Some of Rex's founders were northerners, too (see Errol Laborde, *Krewe: The Early New Orleans Carnival, Comus to Zulu* [New Orleans: Carnival, 2007], 15–23, 51–55; and Errol Laborde, *Marched the Day God: A History of the Rex Organization* [Metairie, La.: School of Design, 1999], 7).

7. For Confederate army participation, see *Report of Historical Committee M.K.C. 1857 to 1894,* Comus ball booklet (New Orleans, December 1897), 8, in 1894 Comus folder, box 6, Carnival Collection, Louisiana Research Collection (LaRC), Tulane University; Laborde, *Marched the Day God,* 6; and James Gill, *Lords of Misrule: Mardi Gras and the Politics of Race in New Orleans* (Jackson: University Press of Mississippi, 1997), 59–77. For discussion of the old-line krewes' support of nativist, conservative Democrat ideas, see Reid Mitchell, "Comus," in *All on a Mardi Gras Day: Episodes in the History of New Orleans Carnival* (Cambridge: Harvard University Press, 1995), 65–81; and Gill, *Lords of Misrule,* 77–143.

8. William E. Greene, "Dancing and Deportment, Salutations," in *The Terpsichorean Monitor* (E. A. Johnson & Co., Printers, 1889), 4.

9. Perry Young, Comus chronicler, writes that the Mistick Krewe of Comus faced "financial strain" in the late 1880s because its social club counterpart, the Pickwick Club, resided in "palatial new quarters on Canal Street." To offset the strain, Comus did not parade between 1885 and 1890. During this time, however, Comus continued its dedicated tradition of balls: "The Pickwick Club gave carnival balls each year, of a lavishness and elegance never surpassed in the city. These were held in the spacious and luxuriously furnished home of the club. In 1885 it is said that there were 2000 guests at the ball. In 1886—the greatest ball ever given in New Orleans—there were bands and dancing on each of the four floors" (Perry Young, *The Mistick Krewe: Chronicles of Comus and His Kin* [New Orleans: Carnival, 1931], 168).

10. *New Orleans Times-Democrat,* January 12, 1890, 4, col. 1.

11. Perry Young's version of this decision differs from other accounts in that Young states the Rex organization decided to visit only Proteus. Upon hearing the news, that year's Rex (impersonating Urukh, king of Chaldea) displayed his unhappiness with the decision and announced that he would first visit Comus. This decree, according to Young, was part of the fuel for the fight on Canal Street (Young, *The Mistick Krewe,* 175).

12. Judith Lynne Hanna, *To Dance Is Human: A Theory of Nonverbal Communication* (Chicago: University of Chicago Press, 1987), 3.

13. Cynthia Jean Cohen Bull, "Sense, Meaning, and Perception in Three Dance Cultures," in *Meaning in Motion: New Cultural Studies in Dance,* ed. Jane C. Desmond (Durham, N.C.: Duke University Press, 1997), 270.

14. Deidre Sklar, "Five Premises for a Culturally Sensitive Approach to Dance," in *Moving History/Dancing Cultures: A Dance History Reader,* ed. Ann Dils and Ann Cooper Albright (Middletown, Conn: Wesleyan University Press, 2001), 30.

15. Gerald Jonas, *Dancing: The Pleasure, Power, and Art of Movement* (New York: Abrams, 1998), 164.

16. François Delsarte (1811–1871) was a French music teacher and aesthetic theorist who developed a system of elocution. The Delsarte System of Expression was grounded in a fixed relationship between physical and spiritual expression and sought to find the correlation between movement and meaning. James Steele Mackaye, Delsarte's only known American student, incorporated Delsartean methods into American physical culture from 1870 on, and Mackaye's students after him (notably Genevieve Stebbins) continued to draw on Delsartean principles in American performances and contexts, including in tableaux, gymnastics, breathing techniques (as a part of oration and wealthy parlor classes on deportment), and, eventually, as inspiration for the emergence of modern dance. Chapter 3 will discuss Delsartism, especially in its connection to tableau performance, in more detail.

1. "VIVE LA DANSE!": BALLS AND MARDI GRAS IN NEW ORLEANS HISTORY

1. Perry Young, *The Mistick Krewe: Chronicles of Comus and His Kin* (New Orleans: Carnival, 1931), 60–61.

2. *Report of Historical Committee M.K.C. 1857 to 1894,* Comus ball booklet (New Orleans, December 1897), 8, in 1894 Comus folder, box 6, Carnival Collection, Louisiana Research Collection (LaRC), Tulane University.

3. *New Orleans Daily Picayune,* February 26, 1857, 1, col. 7.

4. See *Mardi Gras in New Orleans and the Mistick Krewe of Comus, MCMXXIV* (New Orleans: Mistick Krewe of Comus, 1924), PAM F 379. N5 M948 1924, Historic New Orleans Collection.

5. Henri Schindler, *Mardi Gras Treasures: Invitations of the Golden Age* (Gretna, La.: Pelican, 2000), 9.

6. Samuel Kinser, *Carnival, American Style: Mardi Gras at New Orleans and Mobile* (Chicago: University of Chicago Press, 1990), 17.

7. Arthur Burton La Cour, *New Orleans Masquerade: Chronicles of a Carnival* (New Orleans: Pelican, 1952), 10.

8. The two dances from this list most pertinent to old-line Carnival balls, the quadrille and waltz, will be discussed in chapter 5. For a thorough explanation and recorded video reconstructions of the remaining dance forms, see Elizabeth Aldrich's "Western Social Dance: An Overview of the Collection," especially the pages on baroque, late eighteenth-century, and nineteenth-century dance (Aldrich, "Western Social Dance: An Overview of the Collection," part of the American Ballroom Companion Collection within the American Memory project of the Library of Congress, http://memory.loc.gov/ammem/dihtml/diessay6.html).

9. Samuel Kinser, *Carnival, American Style: Mardi Gras at New Orleans and Mobile* (Chicago: University of Chicago Press, 1990), 24.

10. Reid Mitchell, *All on a Mardi Gras Day: Episodes in the History of New Orleans Carnival* (Cambridge: Harvard University Press, 1995), 12.

11. See Arthur Hardy, *Mardi Gras in New Orleans: An Illustrated History,* 2nd ed. (Metairie, La.: Arthur Hardy Enterprises, 2003), 6; Young, *The Mistick Krewe,* 17; and R. Randall Couch, "The Public Masked Balls of Antebellum New Orleans: A Custom of Masque Outside the Mardi Gras Tradition," *Louisiana History* 35, no. 4 (1994): 407. After the Spanish left, masks returned to the Carnival season, though Americans also intermittently banned them during the first two decades of the nineteenth century. For American bans, see Schindler, *Mardi Gras: New Orleans* (New York: Flammarion, 1997), 19; and Kinser, *Carnival, American Style,* 63. The elite never adhered to the masking prohibitions, though, and under American rule the general population also disregarded the laws. Penalties for masking and public masked balls were infrequent, and by 1835 the legal period for masking was extended from the original limitations of January 1 to Mardi Gras and embraced all of the time between November 1 to May Day (see La Cour, *New Orleans Masquerade,* 10; and Schindler, *Mardi Gras,* 19–22; although Henry Kmen notes that the year was 1836 in Henry Arnold Kmen, "Singing and Dancing in New Orleans: A Social History of the Birth and Growth of Balls and Opera, 1791–1841" [Ph.D. diss., Tulane University, 1961], 34–35).

12. "Carnival," January 19, 1781, p. 47, bk. 2, in *Digest of the Acts of Deliberations of the Cabildo, 1769–1803,* compiled by the WPA, http://nutrias.org/~nopl/inv/digest/digest17.htm.

13. New Orleans' population included 2,751 black people in 1791. Of this population, 1,147 were free people of color. By 1810, 4,950 free people of color resided in the city, and by 1830, "free blacks numbered 11,477 persons in a total population, black and white, of 46,082" (Kinser, *Carnival, American Style,* 23).

14. Ibid., 25.

15. The dances themselves, however, were likely less censored in New Orleans than in other parts of the United States, where (especially in the Northeast) dancing and religion frequently battled, each gaining ground now and then. Economic prosperity during the early eighteenth century led to more leisure time, including the cultural pursuit of dance as well as opera and music. Simultaneously, religious revivals, especially the First Great Awakening, spread throughout the colonies and often attempted to stamp out social "wickedness," including dancing. Especially famous was Puritan minister Increase Mather's 1684 *An Arrow Against Profane and Promiscuous Dancing Drawn out of the Quiver of the Scriptures,* in which he outlined the reasons why mixed-sex dancing was sinful (men and women dancing separately, or leaping—a natural expression of joy—were allowable as long as they were performed in moderation). Of mixed, or "promiscuous," dancing, Mather argued that the "unchaste Touches and Gesticulations used by *Dancers,* have a palpable tendency to that which is evil" (Increase Mather, *An Arrow Against Profane and Promiscuous Dancing Drawn out of the Quiver of the Scriptures; By the Ministers of Christ at Boston in New England* [Boston: Printed by Samuel

Green, 1684], 3, Early English Books Online Database, http://gateway.proquest.com.proxy .lib.fsu.edu/openurl?ctx_ver=Z39.88–2003&res_id=xri:eebo&rft_id=xri:eebo:image:40571).

16. Joseph E. Marks III, *America Learns to Dance: A Historical Study of Dance Education in America before 1900* (New York: Exposition, 1957), 37.

17. For workers, servants, and slaves, impromptu dancing in communal areas on holidays was most common.

18. Mederic Louis Ellie Moreau de St. Mery, *Moreau de St. Mery's American Journey (1793–1798),* trans. and ed. Kenneth Roberts and Anna M. Roberts (New York: Doubleday, 1947), ix, xvi, 333.

19. A note about the term "Creole": most krewe histories use "Creole" in reference to New Orleanians of European descent (mainly French but sometimes also Spanish), most of whom spoke French. Historian Reid Mitchell, whose view I follow, explains the complexity of the label:

> In antebellum Louisiana, Creole meant native-born. As Joseph G. Tregle has shown, a Creole could be "white, black, colored, French, Spanish, or Anglo-American." But in 1804, the Creole community was overwhelmingly French-speaking. Furthermore, the Creole political community was composed of French-speaking white people native to the state of Louisiana—black people in antebellum Louisiana had no political rights. If a politician was a "leader of the Creoles," he represented the native-born, French-speaking white community, the so-called *ancienne population.* In political terms, then, Creole was sometimes used as a form of shorthand for the French-speaking white community. In cultural terms, Creole might be used to designate values and practices indigenous to Louisiana at the time of American annexation. (*All on a Mardi Gras Day,* 11)

See also Joseph G. Tregle, "Creoles and Americans," in *Creole New Orleans: Race and Americanization,* ed. Arnold R. Hirsch and Joseph Logsdon (Baton Rouge: Louisiana State University Press, 1992), 131–85.

20. Kmen, "Singing and Dancing in New Orleans," 6.

21. Henri Schindler, *Mardi Gras: New Orleans* (New York: Flammarion, 1997), 17; Robert C. Reinders, *End of an Era: New Orleans, 1850–1860* (New Orleans: American Printing, 1964), 154.

22. Young, *The Mistick Krewe,* 19.

23. See C. C. Robin, *Voyage to Louisiana, 1803–1806,* trans. Stuart O. Landry Jr. (New Orleans: Pelican, 1966), 56–57; W. C. C. Claiborne to James Madison, January 10, 1804, in *Official Letter Books of W. C. C. Claiborne (1801–1816),* ed. Dunbar Rowland (Jackson, MS: Printed for the State Department of Archives and History, 1917), 331; and Kmen, "Singing and Dancing in New Orleans," 13–14.

24. W. C. C. Claiborne to James Madison, January 31, 1804, in *Official Letter Books of W. C. C. Claiborne,* 354–55.

25. John H. B. Latrobe, *Impressions Respecting New Orleans: Diary and Sketches, 1818–1820* (New York: Columbia University Press, 1951), 34.

26. Kmen, "Singing and Dancing in New Orleans," 12. For a thorough description of the *bals de bouquet,* see Sir James Edward Alexander's 1833 travelogue, *Transatlantic Sketches:*

Comprising Visits to the Most Interesting Scenes in North and South American and the West Indes, with Notes on Negro Slavery and Canadian Emigration (Philadelphia: Key and Biddle, 1833), 237.

27. Mardi Gras historian Samuel Kinser suggests that the *bals de roi* might have even been the initial method for selecting the king, who would set off the slew of *bals de bouquet* (Kinser, *Carnival, American Style*, 59).

28. Robert Tallant, *Mardi Gras... As It Was* (repr., Gretna, La.: Pelican, 1989), 103.

29. Young, *The Mistick Krewe*, 45.

30. The entire five-act opera appeared infrequently after November 1835, at which point the ball scene was either presented alone or as a finale for a varied program. For more about the role of dance in Auber's opera and about the star dancers who performed in it (such as Marie Taglioni and Fanny Essler), see Maribeth Clark, "Understanding French Grand Opera through Dance" (1998), Publicly Accessible Penn Dissertations, Paper 955, http://repository .upenn.edu/cgi/viewcontent.cgi?article=2114&context=edissertations. See also Robert Ignatius Letellier, who further explains: "According to Louis Véron, the work was less successful than it might have been because the conception of the costumes and sets in the style of Louis XV in the first four acts hampered the actors from expressing their emotions with the necessary ardour and freedom required. After the 41st performance (27 April 1834), all stagings were of individual acts or scenes. Thus act 5 was given 57 times, the closing tableau alone 17 times" (introduction to *The Ballets of Daniel-Francois-Esprit Auber*, ed. Robert Ignatius Letellier [Newcastle upon Tyne: Cambridge Scholars Publishing, 2011], xx).

31. There is some discrepancy in source materials about what constitutes a galopade. Many dance manuals from the late nineteenth century (a time of prolific manual publication) record galops rather than galopades. Most manuals either list a galop dance as a quadrille variant of waltz-like nature, or a galop step as a maneuver within a quadrille dance, often in a double quadrille and used as an exciting finale for a ball. In any case, whether a distinct dance, a name for the style with which a quadrille was danced, or even as a general country dance done to a galop piece of music, galop descriptions usually denoted a lively manner and depicted a scene where couples performed chasing steps. Simply, "galop" is likely the shortened name of "galopade."

32. Schindler, *Mardi Gras*, 27.

33. Edward Ferrero, *The Art of Dancing, Historically Illustrated. To Which Is Added a Few Hints on Etiquette; Also, The Figures, Music, and Necessary Instruction for the Performance of the Most Modern and Approved Dances...* (New York: Edward Ferrero, 1859), 151.

34. "Court and Fashionable Life," in *Court Journal: Court Circular & Fashionable Gazette*, vol. 5 (Alabaster, Pasemore & Sons, 1833), 788, col. 3.

35. Tallant, *Mardi Gras*, 112.

36. Mitchell, *All on a Mardi Gras Day*, 25–26.

37. Karen Trahan Leathem, "'A Carnival According to Their Own Desires': Gender and Mardi Gras in New Orleans, 1870–1941" (Ph.D. diss., University of North Carolina at Chapel Hill, 1994), 132.

38. Another old-line krewe, the Krewe of Proteus (established in 1881), was the first to admit Creole members. One of their founding fathers (and first captain), Judge George Theard, was

Creole. Eventually, Proteus and the other old-line krewes admitted prestigious Creole men to their membership and, through intermarriage, their families (see Charles L. Dufour, *Krewe of Proteus: The First Hundred Years* [New Orleans: Krewe of Proteus, 1981], 39; Leonard V. Huber, *A Pictorial History of Carnival in New Orleans* [Gretna, La.: Pelican, 2003], 48; and Tallant, *Mardi Gras*, 155).

39. Michelle Ferrari, "American Experience: New Orleans," transcript, webpage created on December 1, 2006, www.pbs.org/wgbh/amex/neworleans/filmmore/pt.html.

40. Mitchell, *All on a Mardi Gras Day*, 108.

41. Young, *The Mistick Krewe*, 65.

42. In the 1850s, New Orleans was the leading cotton port in the nation (Reinders, *End of an Era*, 37).

43. Augusto P. Miceli, *The Pickwick Club of New Orleans*, 2nd ed. (New Orleans: Pickwick, 1964), 3.

44. Reinders, *End of an Era*, 5–7.

45. Miceli, *The Pickwick Club of New Orleans*, 2; Errol Laborde, *Krewe: The Early New Orleans Carnival, Comus to Zulu* (New Orleans: Carnival, 2007), 15.

46. Laborde, *Krewe*, 15–16. Pope was also Roman Catholic, an extreme rarity in early krewe membership. Perhaps his religion was overlooked, or at least tolerated, because, as Miceli notes, "Dr. Pope was one of the most respected and influential members of the original group" (Miceli, *The Pickwick Club of New Orleans*, 16).

47. *New Orleans Daily Picayune*, April 28, 1868, 4, col. 1; Laborde, *Krewe*, 14, 20–21.

48. Laborde, *Krewe*, 18–19.

49. Arthur W. Bergeron Jr., *Guide to Louisiana Confederate Military Units, 1861–1865* (Baton Rouge: Louisiana State University Press, 1989), 184.

50. Laborde, *Krewe*, 22–23.

51. Ibid., 19; Augusto P. Miceli notes that, of the 231 members of Comus' "public face," the Pickwick Club, 140 served in the Confederate army; a few individuals, "inspired by a desire to preserve the Union, did not participate in the war," surmising that "it took moral and physical courage to maintain their conviction and opposition in such an emotionally-charged climate." Other abstainers were either too old to fight or physically infirm (Miceli, *The Pickwick Club of New Orleans*, 33).

52. Laborde, *Krewe*, 17.

53. Bergeron, *Guide to Louisiana Confederate Military Units*, 184.

54. Tallant, *Mardi Gras*, 113–14; Young, *The Mistick Krewe*, 65–66. Each krewe was associated with a private gentlemen's club that hosted social events throughout the year. Comus was initially tied to the Pickwick Club; Momus to the Louisiana Club; and even Rex had the Boston Club. Of course, clubs and krewes had overlapping membership. Some Comus men were also a part of Rex; other men belonged to both Momus and Proteus, and so on. Club headquarters were stately and often had their own lounges and ballrooms. They usually served as krewe business meeting places and eventually, as parade-route stops where the queens and maids of that year's court could watch the affiliated parade and toast their male monarch.

55. The original TNR lasted only seven Carnival seasons, but various groups have reappeared under their name since their demise in 1878 (there was no TNR activity in 1877). See La Cour, *New Orleans Masquerade*, 31–32, for subsequent incarnations of the TNR, including the second group, which emerged in 1884, became the King's Own Royal Guard, held jousting tournaments at the fairgrounds, and championed a queen who decided on the winning knight.

56. An interesting description of Proteus by Mardi Gras New Orleans (a popular online website for Mardi Gras history, parade routes, photos, videos, etc.): "Proteus was the son of Poseidon, herded Poseidon's seals, the great bull seal at the center of the harem. He can tell the future, change his shape and will only answer to someone who can capture him." This description speaks to the nuances of krewe names. Proteus can shape-shift, beholden only to someone superior enough to catch him. Moreover, he is a single male amid a harem, implying virility (see "Krewe of Proteus Parade Route," www.mardigrasneworleans.com/schedule/parade-info/parades-proteus.html).

57. Dufour, *Krewe of Proteus*, 8.

58. Tallant, *Mardi Gras*, 139.

59. Laborde, *Krewe*, 77.

60. Since Rex was only partially masked instead of fully (like Comus, Momus, and Proteus), the seasonal Rex monarch's identity could be guessed by spectators and even began to be published in newspapers in the late nineteenth century.

61. Although many Rex histories credit the krewe's creation as honoring the Grand Duke Alexis of Russia (who was visiting Mardi Gras at the time), Reid Mitchell disagrees. Mitchell sees Alexis as passive aspect of the krewe's emergence and the parade as a mockery (see Mitchell, *All on a Mardi Gras Day*, 55). Additionally, Errol Laborde tackles the Alexis element as creation story and instead focuses on Rex's purpose for forming as a unifier intent on reinvigorating the local economy (see Laborde, *Krewe*, esp. chap. 3, "Myth Busting: The Real Reasons for Rex," 43–49).

62. Schindler, *Mardi Gras*, 71.

63. Rosary Hartel O'Brien, "New Orleans Carnival Organizations: Theatre of Prestige" (Ph.D. diss., University of California, Los Angeles, 1973), 128.

64. Mitchell, *All on a Mardi Gras Day*, 72, 83.

65. Leathem, "A Carnival According to Their Own Desires," 21–23.

66. Kmen, "Singing and Dancing in New Orleans," 8.

67. Huber, *Mardi Gras*, 44.

2. "A MOST BRILLIANT ASSEMBLY": PREPARING FOR THE BALL AND CHOREOGRAPHING CLASS

1. Robert Tallant, *Mardi Gras . . . As It Was* (repr., Gretna, La.: Pelican, 1989), 148.

2. For the most part, if someone was invited to one ball, they were most likely on the guest list for other balls of the same status, though this wasn't a formal rule. For example, see Rex

1889 admit card, fol. 21, St. Martin Family Papers, 1732–1950, MSS 68, Louisiana Research Collection (LaRC), Tulane University. Both Rex and Proteus invitations were administered to this family, a common feature among the archival collections I perused.

3. *New Orleans Daily Picayune,* February 13, 1877, 4. Two thousand dollars in 1877 is roughly equivalent to $45,000 in 2016.

4. Comus member and Mardi Gras historian Perry Young maintains a sizable connection between Comus and Parisian designers into the 1910s, whereas the krewe account in the *One Hundred Years of Comus* booklet states: "The parade of 1873 was the first parade to be designed and constructed in New Orleans. Before that time Comus used to order his costumes and parts of the floats from France. Since then New Orleans has built its own floats and made its own *papier maché* figures. Most of the costumes are made in New Orleans, but the masks come from abroad" (*One Hundred Years of Comus,* Comus ball booklet, p. 22, box 10, Dorothy Spencer Collins Papers, LaRC, Tulane University). George Janvier, leader of Comus since the mid-1930s, also wrote in 1956 that Robert D'Adrien in Paris still makes queens' jewels (tiara, necklace, and scepter) (Janvier, *What I Have Learned in Twenty Years as Captain of Comus* [1956], 28, box 9, fol. 45a, William O. Rogers Collection, 1859–1900, MSS 648).

5. Tableau cars were elaborately painted floats used in the parades and then sometimes deconstructed so that the sides of the floats (the scenic tableaux) could be used as set designs for the balls.

6. Perry Young, *The Mistick Krewe: Chronicles of Comus and His Kin* (New Orleans: Carnival, 1931), 215.

7. The monetary equivalent in the year 2016 is roughly $175,500.

8. Charles L. Dufour and Leonard V. Huber, *If Ever I Cease to Love: One Hundred Years of Rex, 1872–1971* (New Orleans: School of Design, 1970), 33.

9. See, for example, *New Orleans Times-Democrat,* February 27, 1900; and *New Orleans Daily Picayune,* March 8, 1905, 10.

10. Henri Schindler, *Mardi Gras Treasures: Invitations of the Golden Age* (Gretna, La.: Pelican, 2000), 9.

11. See John T. Magill, "Carnival Leftovers: The Ephemera of New Orleans Mardi Gras," Ephemera Society of America, www.ephemerasociety.org/articles/lla-magill.html.

12. Leonard V. Huber, *A Pictorial History of Carnival in New Orleans* (Gretna, La.: Pelican, 2003), 29. With the departure of many New Orleanians to aid in the war effort and the diversion of money to the same entity, many of the most opulent Mardi Gras traditions faded. After the war, new Carnival organizations emerged and old-line groups resurfaced, but the *extreme* grandiose nature of old-line practices remained in the past.

13. Young, *The Mistick Krewe,* 212.

14. Janvier, *What I Have Learned in Twenty Years as Captain of Comus,* 3.

15. Article from 1859 *New Orleans Daily Picayune* 1859 qtd. in Leonard Huber, *Mardi Gras Invitations of the Gilded Age* (New Orleans: Upton Printing, 1970), 1.

16. Dated March 8, 1859, as noted in "Excerpts from "Reminiscences of the First Balls of the Mystic Krewe of Comus by a Founding Member," in *One Hundred Years of Comus,* 11.

17. Young, *The Mistick Krewe,* 213.

18. Ibid., 214.

19. "1891 or 1949, Carnival Queens Make Excited [rest cut off]: The Oldest Queen Watches Changes," news clipping, Brown Scrapbook, box 2, Queens of Carnival Scrapbook Collection, 1953–1982, UC MSS 318, 83-21-L, Historic New Orleans Collection.

20. According to George Janvier, the old tradition of members calling on each season's court was abandoned; instead, the family now informs the queen of her being chosen, and on Christmas morning, the krewes send orchid corsages to ladies of the court, white for queen and purple for maids (Janvier, *What I Have Learned in Twenty Years as Captain of Comus,* 22).

21. "1891 or 1949, Carnival Queens Make Excited [cut off]."

22. The Revelers determined their queen by handing out cake to selected young women. One slice contained a golden bean that conferred queenly status upon whoever ate it, akin to eighteenth-century *gâteau des roi.* For the Momus ball, krewesmen selected a group of maids who then had enough time to get white ball gowns. At the ball, Momus himself designated the queen from among these women when he handed the captain's scroll to her and then led her to the dance floor for the grand march (see Leonard V. Huber, *Mardi Gras: A Pictorial History of Carnival in New Orleans* [Gretna, La.: Pelican, 1977], 51).

23. Dorothy Spencer Collins memoirs, "Rambling through the Years to 1977," p. 2, box 10, Collins Papers, LaRC, Tulane University.

24. Ibid., 31. Since Collins identifies Walmsley's eldest daughter as Myra Loker, we can deduce that "Buzz"—"the King and Queen maker"—is Sylvester Pierce Walmsley, born in Dubuque, Iowa, in 1858. S. P. Walmsley, a prominent cotton merchant whose father was the president of the Louisiana National Bank for many years, was Rex in 1890 and a Comus captain for more than twenty-five years (see "Administrations of the Mayors of New Orleans" T. Semmes Walmsley [1889–]," Louisiana Division of the New Orleans Public Library, http://nutrias.org/info/louinfo/admins/walmsley.htm; and "Sylvester Pierce Walmsley," Find a Grave, www.findagrave.com/cgi-bin/fg.cgi?page=gr&GRid=101211333).

25. Tableaux societies are discussed further in chapter 5. Many tableaux society rosters share membership with the old-line krewes.

26. Collins, "Rambling through the Years to 1977," 40–41.

27. Janvier, *What I Have Learned in Twenty Years as Captain of Comus,* 18.

28. Ibid., 19–20.

29. It is interesting that Halliday references Cinderella, a character notorious for her forced servitude, although Halliday seems not to be referring to this aspect but rather to Cinderella having led an enchanted life, one from a fairy tale, in which she got all her heart desired (her dreams came true).

30. Rose Kahn, "Carnival Queen of 1904 Returns Each [rest cut off]," news clipping, box 1, Queens of Carnival Scrapbook Collection, Historic New Orleans Collection.

31. Collins, "Rambling through the Years to 1977," 1.

32. Miss Tharp was an uptown dancing teacher during the early twentieth century. For a reference to her dance lessons for elite children, see William West interview, March 25, 1975,

transcript, p. 15, side 2, Friends of the Cabildo Interview Transcripts, LaRC, Tulane University. For queens turning to training future krewe courts during the 1950s and onward, see "Lessons for a Queen" in the Green Scrapbook, box 2, Queens of Carnival Scrapbook Collection, Historic New Orleans Collection. This article emphasizes the importance of learning how to walk, hold a scepter and bow, as well as hold a partner's hand and bow. The main difference between the leading instructors was whether they taught a French court bow or an English one.

33. For the popularity of dance manuals and their relationship to other etiquette and "how-to" manuals in American culture, see Gretchen Schneider, "Using Nineteenth-Century American Social Dance Manuals," *Dance Research Journal*, 14, nos. 1 & 2 (1981–82): 39–42.

34. See Elizabeth Aldrich, "Book Publishers, Manuals, and Their Audience," in *From the Ballroom to Hell: Grace and Folly in Nineteenth-Century Dance* (Evanston: Northwestern University Press, 1991), 9–13. For more about the relationship between new dances and dance manuals, see Aldrich "Nineteenth Century Social Dance."

35. Aldrich, *From the Ballroom to Hell*, xvii.

36. *The Ball-Room Guide. With Coloured Plates* (London: Frederick Warne and Co., 1866), iv.

37. The ball was the Falstaffians' 1913 ball. The Pitot family was also associated with the krewes of Consus and Proteus. Henry Pitot, interview by Dorothy Schlesinger, August 27, 1974, pp. 8–9, Friends of the Cabildo Interview Transcripts, LaRC, Tulane University.

38. See "Mistick Krewe of Comus," *DeBow's Review* 6 (March 1869): 226, for a description of Comus' 1869 ball.

39. See Janvier, *What I Have Learned in Twenty Years as Captain of Comus.*

40. Arthur Burton La Cour, *New Orleans Masquerade: Chronicles of a Carnival* (New Orleans: Pelican, 1952), 216.

41. See, for instance, *New Orleans Times-Picayune*, February 17, 1915, 7.

42. See, for instance, Janvier, *What I Have Learned in Twenty Years as Captain of Comus,* 17; and *New Orleans Daily Picayune*, March 2, 1870, 1. Most sources that deal with Mardi Gras balls discuss the "flying wedge" and similar tactics at some point.

43. "Mistick Krewe of Comus," *DeBow's Review,* 225.

44. See, for instance, an early Comus newspaper notice in *New Orleans Times*, March 1, 1870.

45. *New Orleans Daily Picayune*, February 28, 1897, 7.

46. *New Orleans Times-Picayune*, February 17, 1915, 7.

47. Lily Jackson, "French Opera House," *New Orleans Times-Picayune*, February 5, 1984, 1, *Vieux Carre Survey*, binder for Square 71, Historic New Orleans Collection.

48. John M. Parker Jr. and Mrs. Edith Parker, interview by W. B. Carlin, November 13, 1976, p. 14, Friends of the Cabildo Interview Transcripts, LaRC, Tulane University.

49. Mr. William G. Nott, March 3, 1975, p. 10, Friends of the Cabildo Interview Transcripts, LaRC, Tulane University. When Nott eventually had his own family, his daughter was honored several times over. She was queen of Twelfth Night Revelers, a maid in Rex, a youth in Pirouettes, and maid at Apollo. (ibid., 8).

50. A quirky kink in the seating hierarchy also emerged with an undercover component of the Carnival ball scene—prostitutes in the third balcony "masking" as ladies, though

these occurrences may have been more myth than reality. In *Mardi Gras ... As It Was*, Robert Tallant writes: "Not too many years ago a coterie of prostitutes were ejected by the police from a balcony during a ball, an event that seriously disturbed the entire evening. They had been invited by a whimsical member of the krewe, who was further delighted that the girls did not go quietly, but loudly denounced the entire affair as the officers dragged them down the aisles" (177).

51. *New Orleans Daily Picayune*, February 27, 1900, 2.

52. For a sample description of women at the 1869 Comus ball, see "Mistick Krewe of Comus," in *DeBow's Review* 6 (March 1869): 221.

53. Maureen E. Montgomery, *Displaying Women: Spectacles of Leisure in Edith Wharton's New York* (New York: Routledge, 1998), 31.

54. Valerie Steele, *Fashion and Eroticism: Ideals of Feminine Beauty from the Victorian Era to the Jazz Age* (New York: Oxford University Press, 1985), 132.

55. Thorstein Veblen argued not only that the overt luxuriousness of moneyed fashion denoted a financial ability on the spender's part to be able to purchase costly goods (an indulgence in surrounding oneself with more than just the essentials for survival) but also that the type of high fashion consumed restricted people's ability to move freely, to "work." Thus, clothing operated as visible conformation that the wearer was "not under the necessity of earning a livelihood," therefore the "evidence of social worth is enhanced in a very considerable degree" (Veblen, *The Theory of the Leisure Class* [Boston: Houghton Mifflin, 1973], 120).

56. Marianne Thesander, *The Feminine Ideal*, trans. Nicholas Hill (London: Reaktion, 1997), 43.

57. Prosper Jacotot, *Voyage d'un Ouvrier dans la Vallée du Mississippi: De Saint Louis a la Nouvelle-Orleans (Scenes de Moeurs), 1877*, trans. S. Fucich and F. Peterson (New Orleans: Federal Writers' Project, 1939), 13, in M1065, LaRC, Tulane University.

58. *New Orleans Daily Picayune*, February 28, 1897, 7.

59. "Mystick Krewe of Comus," clipping in ledger about February 22 ball, Walmsley Family Papers, UC MSS 548, 86-57-L, Historic New Orleans Collection.

60. Janvier, *What I Have Learned in Twenty Years as Captain of Comus*, 9–10.

61. Young, *The Mistick Krewe*, 215.

62. A hair rat is a mesh form that women use to style their hair. A donut-shaped hair rat, for instance, allows women to pull their hair through the center hole and then wrap the hair around the rat to form a full bun.

63. Kahn, "Carnival Queen of 1904 Returns Each [rest cut off]," news clipping.

64. 1910 debutante queen Amelia Baldwin of Rex had her royal gown created by a Parisian designer ("Mrs. West Reigned in 1910; She Notes Many Changes," *New Orleans Times-Picayune*, February 4, 1975, 2).

65. "1891 or 1949, Carnival Queens Make Excited [cut off]: The Oldest Queen Watches Changes."

66. Marjorie Roehl, "A Parade of Royal Robes," *New Orleans Times-Picayune*, February 14, 1988, Clippings Collection, box 1: "Balls," LaRC, Tulane University.

67. "Momus Holds Its Glorious Court," *New Orleans Daily Picayune*, February 26, 1897, 10.

68. *New Orleans Daily Picayune*, March 3, 1897, 8. See also Von Meysenbug Diary, p. 86, fol. 82, Von Meysenbug-Lyons Papers, MSS 293, Historic New Orleans Collection, which describes Corrine Von Meysenbug's Elves of Oberon 1899 queenly garb.

3. "THE AGE OF CHIVALRY IS NOT PASSED AND GONE": TABLEAUX VIVANTS DURING RECONSTRUCTION

1. *New Orleans Times-Democrat*, February 23, 1900, 3

2. Momus box 11, 1900 fol., Carnival Collection, Louisiana Research Collection (LaRC), Tulane University.

3. *New Orleans Daily Picayune*, February 23, 1900, 1.

4. Qtd. in *New Orleans Times-Democrat*, February 23, 1900, 3.

5. Ibid.

6. Rex, though old-line, did not produce tableaux balls. Instead, it chose a more traditional ball format for after-parade dancing and participated in the tradition of the Rex court, visiting the Comus ball shortly before midnight on Mardi Gras. This choice reflected the semi-civic nature of the krewe and enabled them to invite guests from outside the krewe ranks (mostly prosperous northerners), thereby operating as a public face of unification during Reconstruction.

7. For a history of tableaux vivants, see Jack W. McCullough, *Living Pictures on the New York Stage* (Ann Arbor: UMI Research Press, 1983), esp. chap. 1; Kirsten Gram Holmstrom, *Monodrama, Attitudes, Tableaux Vivants: Studies on Some Trends of Theatrical Fashion, 1770–1815* (Stockholm: Almquist and Wiksell [Almqvist], 1967); and Robert M. Lewis, "Tableaux Vivants: Parlor Theatricals in Victorian America," *Revue Française D'Etudes Amercaines* 36 (April 1988): 280–91.

8. Mary Chapman, "'Living Pictures': Women and *Tableaux Vivants* in Nineteenth-Century American Fiction and Culture," *Wide Angle* 18, no. 3 (1996): 28–29; John Kasson, *Rudeness and Civility: Manners in Nineteenth-Century Urban America* (New York: Hill and Wang 1990), 2.

9. For more about American Delsartism, see Nancy Lee Chalfa Ruyter, *The Cultivation of Body and Mind in Nineteenth-Century American Delsartism* (Westport, Conn: Greenwood, 1999); Nancy Lee Chalfa Ruyter, "Antique Longings: Genevieve Stebbins and American Delsartean Performance," in *Corporealities: Dancing Knowledge, Culture and Power,* ed. Susan Leigh Foster (New York: Routledge, 1995), 70–89; and Nancy Lee Chalfa Ruyter, "The Genteel Transition: American Delsartism," in *Reformers and Visionaries: The Americanization of the Art of Dance* (New York: Dance Horizons, 1979), 17–30; as well as Genevieve Stebbins, *Delsarte System of Expression* (New York: Werner, 1902).

10. For suffrage parade tableaux, see chapter 3, "On Stage: Personality, the Performing Self, and the Representation of Woman Suffragists," in Margaret Finnegan, *Selling Suffrage: Consumer Culture and Votes for Women* (New York: Columbia University Press, 1999); and Linda G. Ford, *Iron-Jawed Angels: The Suffrage Militancy of the National Woman's Party, 1912–1920* (New

York: University Press of America, 1991), 47–53. For more about tableaux in pageantry and their subsequent shaping of the modern dance movement, see chapter 7 in Naima Prevots, *American Pageantry: A Movement for Art & Democracy,* Theatre and Dramatic Studies Series, No. 61 (Ann Arbor: UMI Research Press, 1990), 131–52.

11. For more about Delsartism and American physical culture, as well as American Delsartism in settlement houses, see Linda J. Tomko, *Dancing Class: Gender, Ethnicity and Social Divides in American Dance, 1890–1920* (Bloomington: Indiana University Press, 1999). For tableaux's relationship to other parlor entertainments, see Robert Lewis, "Domestic Theater: Parlor Entertainments as Spectacle, 1840–1880," in *Ceremonies and Spectacles: Performing American Culture,* ed. Teresa Alves, Teresa Cid, and Heinz Ickstadt (Amsterdam: VU University Press, 2000), 48–62. For middle-class consumption of tableaux and parlor games, see Karen Halttunen, *Confidence Men and Painted Women: A Study of Middle-Class Culture in America, 1830–1870* (New Haven: Yale University Press, 1982), 175–90.

12. McCullough, *Living Pictures on the New York Stage,* 1–6. For more about tableaux vivants as narrative devices in fiction, see Chapman, "Living Pictures"; and Grace Ann Hovet and Theodore R. Hovet, *"Tableaux Vivants:* Masculine Vision and Feminine Reflections in Novels by Warner, Alcott, Stowe, and Wharton," *American Transcendental Quarterly* 7, no. 4 (December 1993): 336–56. For children's tableaux and fiction, see Nina Auerbach, *Private Theatricals: The Lives of the Victorians* (Cambridge: Harvard University Press, 1990).

13. Ann Severance Akins, "Dancing in Dixie's Land: Theatrical Dance in New Orleans, 1860–1870" (Ph.D. diss., Texas Woman's University, 1991), 347.

14. William West interview, March 25, 1975, transcript, p. 15, side 2, Friends of the Cabildo Interview Transcripts, LaRC, Tulane University.

15. See, for example, Philip Hone, *The Diary of Philip Hone, 1828–1851,* vol. 2, ed. Bayard Tuckerman (New York: Dodd, Mead, 1889), 117.

16. Marilyn Mayer Culpepper, *All Things Altered: Women in the Wake of the Civil War and Reconstruction* (Jefferson, N.C.: McFarland, 2002), 231.

17. Monika M. Elbert, "Striking a Historical Pose: Antebellum Tableaux Vivants, *Godey's* Illustrations, and Margaret Fuller's Heroines," *New England Quarterly* 75, no. 2 (June 2002): 237. For more about women's role in tableaux vivants, see Elbert, "Striking a Historical Pose"; Hovet and Hovet, *"Tableaux Vivants";* and Chapman, "Living Pictures." See also Jane Turner Censer, *The Reconstruction of White Southern Womanhood, 1865–1895* (Baton Rouge: Louisiana State University Press, 2003), 24.

18. "Reminiscences of the First Balls of the Mystic Krewe of Comus and Two Previous Affairs," 4, "Author Unknown (Copied from an Old Manuscript found in the Archives of the Pickwick Club by C.R.C)," New Orleans: Mardi Gras, Tuesday, February 12, 1929, 1985.19.7, Historic New Orleans Collection; *New Orleans Daily Crescent,* February 26, 1857, qtd. in the pamphlet *Opinions of the Press on the First Appearance of the Mistick Krewe of Comus* (New Orleans: The Mistick Krewe of Comus, March 1, 1927), 3.

19. Qtd. in *Opinions of the Press on the First Appearance of the Mistick Krewe of Comus,* 3.

20. See "Art VII—Mardi Gras," *DeBow's Review* 6, no. 3 (March 1869): 227–31.

21. "Reminiscences of the First Balls of the Mystic Krewe of Comus and Two Previous Affairs," 8–9.

22. *New Orleans Daily Crescent,* February 23, 1860, 1.

23. See *New Orleans Times-Democrat,* February 6, 1891.

24. See Comus 1878 folder, Carnival Collection, LaRC, Tulane University, in which the thick program booklet describes the punishment of Midas, triumph of Bacchus, Hercules' adventures, and other tales from Ovid.

25. Still other seasons of enchantment relied on general myths and literature from other countries.

26. *New Orleans Times-Democrat,* March 2, 1892, 3.

27. See, for instance, "Art VII—Mardi-Gras," *DeBow's Review,* which talks about Comus' "The Five Senses"; and "Comus Creates a Garland of Glory," *Daily Picayune,* February 19, 1896, 2, which describes Comus' "The Months and Seasons of the Year."

28. For more about the krewe costume designers, see Henri Schindler, *Mardi Gras Treasures: Costumes from the Golden Age* (Gretna, La.: Pelican, 2002). Additionally, many archives now have online catalogues with excellent digital images that can be accessed easily for research viewing (see the Carnival Collection at the Tulane University Digital Library, https://digitallibrary.tulane.edu/islandora/object/tulane:p15140co1140; The Carnival Collection of the Louisiana Division of the New Orleans Public Library, http://nutrias.org/~nopl/carnival/main.htm; and a general catalog search of Carnival, Mardi Gras, balls, or any of the krewes discussed in this work via the online catalog of the Historic New Orleans Collection, http://hnoc.minisisinc.com/THNOC/scripts/MWIMAIN.DLL?get&file=%5bWWW_THNOC%5dsimple_search_all.htm).

29. Karen Trahan Leathem, "'A Carnival According to Their Own Desires': Gender and Mardi Gras in New Orleans, 1870–1941" (Ph.D. diss., University of Carolina at Chapel Hill, 1994), 88–89.

30. Steven Swann Jones, *The Fairy Tale: The Magic Mirror of Imagination* (New York: Twayne, 1995), 20.

31. Examples of romantic tales and courtly love include "The Middle Ages" (Proteus 1888); "Legends from King Arthur's Court" (Momus 1900); and "Sherwood Forest" (Proteus 1916); themes around romantic poetry: "Spenser's *Faerie Queen*" (Comus 1871); "Lord Byron" (Momus 1902); and "Tennyson" (Comus 1907).

32. *Mardi Gras in New Orleans and the Mistick Krewe of Comus, MCMXXIV* (New Orleans: Mistick Krewe of Comus, 1924), 16, PAM F 379. N5 M948 1924, Historic New Orleans Collection.

33. Jones, *The Fairy Tale,* 25.

34. For more about America's return to chivalry in art, see *King Arthur's Modern Return,* ed. Debra N. Mancoff (New York: Garland, 1998); and Tison Pugh, *Queer Chivalry: Medievalism and the Myth of White Masculinity in Southern Literature* (Baton Rouge: Louisiana State University Press, 2013).

35. For a discussion of changing southern masculinity, see Craig Thompson Friend, "From Southern Manhood to Southern Masculinities: An Introduction," in *Southern Masculinities:*

Perspectives on Manhood in the South since Reconstruction, ed. Friend (Athens: University of Georgia Press, 2009), vii–xxvi.

36. *Report of Historical Committee M.K.C. 1857 to 1894,* Comus ball booklet (New Orleans, December 1897), 13, in 1894 Comus folder, box 6, Carnival Collection, LaRC, Tulane University.

37. Bertram Wyatt-Brown, *Southern Honor: Ethics and Behavior in the Old South* (New York: Oxford University Press, 1982), 41. For more about male bonding in war, see ibid., 35–60; Mary Ann Clawson, *Constructing Brotherhood: Class, Gender, and Fraternalism* (Princeton, N.J.: Princeton University Press, 1989), 124; and Samuel Kinser, *Carnival, American Style: Mardi Gras at New Orleans and Mobile* (Chicago: University of Chicago Press, 1990), 312.

38. "Editor's Drawer," *Harper's New Monthly Magazine* 19, no. 111 (August 1859): 427.

39. *New Orleans Daily Crescent,* February 23, 1860, 1.

40. See James Gill, *Lords of Misrule: Mardi Gras and the Politics of Race in New Orleans* (Jackson: University Press of Mississippi, 1997).

41. Frank L. Loomis, *A History of the Carnival and New Orleans Illustrated* (New Orleans: American Printing, 1905), 5.

42. "Municipal Reform in Typical American Cities: X.—The Struggle to Rehabilitate New Orleans," *New York Times,* September 6, 1903. The Hennessy investigation refers to the events that ensued after Chief of Police David Hennessy was fatally shot in 1890. Flower, Janvier, and other krewe leaders spearheaded efforts to find Hennessy's killer, resulting in the lynching/murders of eleven Italian men. For more about krewe involvement in the Hennessy trial lynchings, race riots, and secret political organizations, see Samuel Kinser, *Carnival, American Style;* Reid Mitchell, *All on a Mardi Gras Day: Episodes in the History of New Orleans Carnival* (Cambridge: Harvard University Press, 1995); Stephen Ives, *American Experience: New Orleans,* Public Broadcasting System series, 2007, online transcript at www .pbs.org/wgbh/amex/neworleans/filmmore/pt.html; James Gill, *Lords of Misrule,* esp. chap. 7, "Who Killa da Chief?," and p. 160; and Rosary Hartel O'Brien, "New Orleans Carnival Organizations: Theatre of Prestige" (Ph.D. diss, University of California, Los Angeles, 1973), which also discusses the devolution of krewes from aristocracies to castes, esp. 136–58.

43. For an excellent, succinct description of the political turmoil that ensnared New Orleans in the 1880s, see "Municipal Reform in Typical American Cities: X." "The Ring" had devastated the city's economy and even its physical appearance through corruption in the municipal, police, and fire departments. According to the *New York Times,* New Orleanians were close to anarchy. With no real Republican Party in place after Reconstruction's end, a group of Democrats surfaced to fight corruption and repair New Orleans. This Municipal Reform League began by entrusting the city's debt to its most prominent bankers, who sat on the New Orleans Board of Liquidation. Unsurprisingly, old-line family names pepper the list of board members: Janvier, of course, as well as Hardie, Walmsley, Shakespeare, and Theard. See a historical spreadsheet of the New Orleans Board of Liquidation, City Debt Board Members, at www.boardofliquidation.com/ PDF/BLCD%20Member%20Lineage.pdf. Other reform ideologies included "taking the police out of politics"; selecting municipal officials based on merit, not party line; and rebuilding levees and wharves.

44. O'Brien, "New Orleans Carnival Organizations," 18–19, 156–58.

45. E. Digby Baltzell, *The Protestant Establishment: Aristocracy and Caste in America* (New York: Random House, 1964), 7–9.

46. Diana Kendall, *Members Only: Elite Clubs and the Process of Exclusion* (Lanham, Md.: Rowman and Littlefield, 2008), 13, 85, 101–5.

47. Baltzell, *The Protestant Establishment*, 136, 139.

48. Old-line krewes admitted elite Catholic Creoles to their ranks by the late 1870s. These groups merged in efforts to combine a new threat—carpetbaggers and immigrants. Both Americans and Creoles united in their dislike of the carpetbag regime, and somehow, the Catholicism of the new immigrants (presumably not as relaxed as that practiced by the Creoles), was more distasteful than that of the rich and lax Creole population already established in New Orleans. For more about this merger between Creole Catholics and Anglo-Saxon Protestants, see Henri Schindler, *Mardi Gras: New Orleans* (New York: Flammarion, 1997), 43. For more about the nuances of Catholicism in New Orleans, see Mitchell, *All on a Mardi Gras Day*, 43. Proteus is a great example of the American-Creole merger. Comus' captain suggested that a new krewe form from Comus' overflow, and thus emerged Proteus, the first krewe with a Creole captain and a sizable Creole population, indicative of the intermarrying between elite Americans and elite Creoles (see Arthur Hardy, *Mardi Gras in New Orleans: An Illustrated History*, 2nd ed. [Metairie, La.: Arthur Hardy Enterprises, 2003], 36).

49. Mitchell, *All on a Mardi Gras Day*, 57.

50. For connections between Reconstruction parades/tableaux and political sentiment, see Thomas Ruys Smith, "'Oh, Weep for New Orleans!': Civil War and Reconstruction," chap. 4 of *Southern Queen: New Orleans in the Nineteenth Century* (London: Continuum, 2011), 103–32.

51. For early tableaux vivants, krewes deconstructed their parade floats for the ballroom stage. Krewes removed the sides of the floats—which were painted murals—so that the art doubled as scenery for the tableau presentations.

52. Young, *The Mistick Krewe: Chronicles of Comus and His Kin* (New Orleans: Carnival, 1931), 109.

53. Mitchell, *All on a Mardi Gras Day*, 68–70.

54. Young, *The Mistick Krewe*, 242–43. *Entwicklungsgeschichte* translates as "history of the development."

55. Schindler, *Mardi Gras*, 51–52.

56. Mitchell, *All on a Mardi Gras Day*, 65.

57. Young, *The Mistick Krewe*, 125.

58. *Daily Picayune*, February 26, 1873.

59. Thomas Nast, *Pardon. Franchise Columbia.—"Shall I trust these men, and not this man?"* // Th. Nast., digital image original published in *Harper's Magazine Co*, August 5, 1865, retrieved from the Library of Congress, www.loc.gov/item/2010644408.

60. See Kaye DeMetz, "Theatrical Dancing in Nineteenth-Century New Orleans," *Louisiana History* 21, no. 1 (Winter 1980): 23–42.

61. For more about minstrelsy and dance, see Lynne Fauley Emery, *Black Dance: From 1619 to Today* (Princeton, N.J.: Princeton Book, 1988); Marian Hannah Winter, "Juba and American Minstrelsy," in *Chronicles of the American Dance*, ed. Paul Magriel (New York: Henry Holt, 1948), 39–63; and Marshall Stearns and Jean Stearns, *Jazz Dance: The Story of American Vernacular Dance*, updated ed. (New York: DaCapo, 1994).

62. Young, *The Mistick Krewe*, 141–46. This is not to say, however, that krewe themes and performances were acceptable to everyone. Momus' "Hades" set off a wave of dissatisfaction. Local military troops refused to escort ensuing parades until the old-line krewes apologized. The Oval Office even sent telegrams to New Orleans, "concerned that Rex or Comus processions would parade similar contempt." In reaction, the ever-present public-face Rex (in the most general terms) was forced to publicly denounce Momus' antics. Rex's words brought peace, and the rest of the 1877 Carnival proceeded without further complications. This was crucial to the city's well-being, especially since additional public, military, and governmental outrages against the old-line krewes could have destabilized the vital tourism industry that New Orleans built around Mardi Gras. Such disturbance could have also led to additional street violence (see Mitchell, *All on a Mardi Gras Day*, 74–75; and Schindler, *Mardi Gras*, 58–59).

63. Mary Russo, *The Female Grotesque: Risk, Excess and Modernity* (New York: Routledge, 1995), 14.

64. Judy Hilkey, *Character Is Capital: Success Manuals and Manhood in Gilded Age America* (Chapel Hill: University of North Carolina Press, 1997), 154.

65. *New Orleans Daily Picayune*, February 14, 1877, 3.

66. 1877 Comus folder, box 10, Carnival Collection, LaRC, Tulane University.

67. *New Orleans Daily Picayune*, February 14, 1877, 3.

68. See *Tableaux, Charades, and Pantomimes: Adapted Alike to Parlor Entertainments, School and Church Exhibitions and for Use on the Amateur Stage* (1889; repr., Freeport, N.Y.: Books for Libraries Press, 1971), 26.

69. W. G. Bowdoin, "The Mardi Gras Is On," news clipping from February 20, 1901, F 379. N5 B6, 73-408-L, Historic New Orleans Collection.

70. Schindler, *Mardi Gras*, 67.

71. Qtd. in Young, *The Mistick Krewe*, 154–55. For pictures of Rex's presentation of "brawny men who hid their beards and moustaches behind false faces," see the pictures from the 1906 pageant "In Utopia," which contains at least three photographs of manly "females" on floats (Photographs box 1, Carnival Collection, LaRC, Tulane University).

72. *New Orleans Daily Democrat*, February 6, 1880.

73. George Augustus Sala, *America Revisited: From the Bay of New York to the Gulf of Mexico, and from Lake Michigan to the Pacific*, 4th ed. (London: Viztelly, 1883), 340.

74. Chapman, "Living Pictures," 11, 13.

75. Ibid., 38–41. For more about "virtue gone awry" immortalized in tableaux vivants, see "Naomi and Her Daughters-In-Law" and "Joan of Arc at the Stake," in *Tableaux, Charades, and Pantomimes*, 22–23.

76. I came to this deduction after looking at each krewe's seasonal themes, from the krewe's inception to World War I.

77. Bailey Van Hook, *Angels of Art: Women and Art in American Society, 1876–1914* (University Park: Pennsylvania State University Press, 1996), 84, 189.

78. Lake Pontchartrain is a large estuary at the city's north boundary. It was named for the French politician and minister of marine during the reign of King Louis XIV, Louis Phélypeaux, Count of the estate Pontchartrain.

79. McCullough, *Living Pictures on the New York Stage*, 144. See Leathem, "A Carnival According to Their Own Desires," 64–66; and Kinser, *Carnival, American Style*, 276.

80. Wyatt-Brown, *Southern Honor*, 92–93.

81. "Reminiscences of the First Balls of the Mystic Krewe of Comus and Two Previous Affairs," 11.

82. *New Orleans Daily Picayune*, March 2, 1870, 8.

83. Ramsay Burt, *The Male Dancer: Bodies, Spectacle, Sexualities*, 2nd ed. (New York: Routledge, 2007), 33–34. Burt draws on and extends theories presented in Michael Fried, *Absorption and Theatricality: Painting and the Beholder in the Age of Diderot* (Chicago: University of Chicago Press, 1980).

84. For scholarship exploring Lee as the "Marble Man," see Emory M. Thomas, *Robert E. Lee: A Biography* (New York: Random House, 2000); and Thomas L. Connelly, *The Marble Man: Robert E. Lee and His Image in American Society* (Baton Rouge: Louisiana State University Press, 1977).

85. Nina Sibler, "When Charles Francis Adams Met Robert E. Lee: A Southern Gentleman in History and Memory," in *Inside the Confederate Nation: Essays in Honor of Emory M. Thomas*, ed. Lesley J. Gordon and John C. Inscoe (Baton Rouge: Louisiana State University Press, 2005), 349–50.

86. John J. MacAloon, introduction to *Rite, Drama, Festival, Spectacle: Rehearsals toward a Theory of Cultural Performance*, ed. MacAloon (Philadelphia: Institute for the Study of Human Issues, 1984), 1.

87. Marina Warner, *Monuments and Maidens: The Allegory of the Female Form* (London: Weidenfeld and Nicholson, 1985), xx. Warner also writes on the same page: "Often the recognition of a difference between the symbolic order, inhabited by ideal, allegorical figures, and the actual order, of judges, statesmen, soldiers, philosophers, inventors, depends on the unlikelihood of women practicing the concepts they represent."

88. Laura Edwards, *Gendered Strife and Confusion: The Political Culture of Reconstruction* (Chicago: University of Illinois Press, 1997), 129.

89. Wyatt-Brown, *Southern Honor*, 234.

90. Kasson, *Rudeness and Civility*, 3.

91. Leathem, "A Carnival According to Their Own Desires," 70.

92. Warner, *Monuments and Maidens*, xxi. Warner argues: "Armour is worn by so many imaginary women, projections of the ideal, visual and literary, in our civilization today in order to demonstrate by deep association their law-abiding chastity, their virtuous consent to patriarchal monogamy as the system by which descent is traced and properly transmitted." She continues: "Their bodies are made masculine through buckler, breastplate, helmet, and spear, often directly recalling representations of Athena, to manifest their good behaviour in recognizing male precedence in kinship, or male authority in society and the home" (124–25).

93. Russo, *The Female Grotesque,* 63.

94. Looking to Ancient Greek ideals as the embodiment of feminine beauty and virtue was popular in the late nineteenth century. For krewes, this link underscores their attempts at displaying a Renaissance intellect, but for dance, utilizing Greek ideals was a method of female liberation. See chapter 3 for sources on Delsartism, which was grounded in classical Greek aesthetics.

95. "Art VII—Mardi-Gras," 228.

96. The Mistick Krewe of Comus 1924, 5.

97. Leathem, "A Carnival According to Their Own Desires," 71–75.

98. Van Hook, *Angels of Art,* 1–3, 15–17, 90–93, 97–101.

99. See *New Orleans Daily Picayune,* March 2, 1870.

100. "The Mistick Krewe of Comus" 1870, 261.

101. Young, *The Mistick Krewe,* 222.

102. Van Hook, *Angels of Art,* 124.

103. Warner, *Monuments and Maidens,* 149.

104. Young, *The Mistick Krewe,* 215.

105. See Napier Bartlett, *Stories of the Crescent City* (New Orleans: Steel & Company's Times Job Print, 1869).

106. *New Orleans Times-Democrat,* February 14, 1893.

107. *New Orleans Daily Picayune,* February 14, 1893.

108. *New Orleans Times-Democrat,* February 8, 1894.

109. See, for instance, the Comus throne set for 1902 (1987.2.52 Curatorial, Historic New Orleans Collection).

110. The heyday of theatrical tableaux vivants on American stages had also passed by this time, eclipsed by the rising popularity and affordability of movies (McCullough, *Living Pictures on the New York Stage,* 131).

111. *New Orleans Times-Picayune,* March 7, 1916, 1, 5.

112. Tableaux vivants as political theater were also popular during the Renaissance (see George R. Kernodle, "Renaissance Artists in Service of the People: Political Tableaux and Street Theaters in France, Flanders, and England," *Art Bulletin* 25, no. 1 [March 1943]: 59–64).

113. Mitchell, *All on a Mardi Gras Day,* 67–72.

4. "A STRANGE AND SILENT GROUP": COURTLY GRAND MARCHES AND QUADRILLES IN THE GILDED AGE

1. *New Orleans Times-Democrat,* February 27, 1884, 6.

2. Reid Mitchell, *All on a Mardi Gras Day: Episodes in the History of New Orleans Carnival* (Cambridge: Harvard University Press, 1995), 102.

3. *New Orleans Times-Democrat,* February 27, 1884, 6.

4. Perry Young, *The Mistick Krewe: Chronicles of Comus and His Kin* (New Orleans: Carnival, 1931), 167.

5. *Mistick Krewe of Comus, 1857–1924,* Comus souvenir booklet published by the krewe in 1924, Carnival Collection, Historic New Orleans Collection.

6. Mitchell, *All on a Mardi Gras Day,* 102.

7. *One Hundred Years of Comus,* Comus ball booklet, p. 22, box 10, Dorothy Spencer Collins Papers, Louisiana Research Collection (LaRC), Tulane University; Young, *The Mistick Krewe,* 166–67; Leonard V. Huber, *A Pictorial History of Carnival in New Orleans* (Gretna, La.: Pelican, 2003), 44; Mitchell, *All on a Mardi Gras Day,* 102; Robert Tallant, *Mardi Gras . . . As It Was* (repr., Gretna, La.: Pelican, 1989), 150.

8. Souvenir ball booklet for Comus, 1926, Carnival Collection, Historic New Orleans Collection.

9. See letters of introduction for Susan Richardson, written by both Winnie Davis and Jefferson Davis, June 30, 1888, box 1, Bright/Richardson Family Papers, 1888–1947, 89-42-L, Historic New Orleans Collection.

10. Cita Cook, "Women's Role in the Transformation of Winnie Davis into the Daughter of the Confederacy," in *Searching for Their Places: Women in the South across Four Centuries,* ed. Thomas H. Appleton Jr. and Angela Boswell (Columbia: University of Missouri Press, 2003), 144.

11. By 1898, old-line krewes habitually furnished their queens with a mantle, crown, and jewelry (see *One Hundred Years of Comus*). Queens were also outfitted with stomachers and scepters. For a description of Davis' jewels, see Henri Schindler, *Mardi Gras: New Orleans* (New York: Flammarion, 1997), 121.

12. *New Orleans Times-Democrat,* March 2, 1892, 3, cols. 1–4.

13. D. R. McGuire, "So the Rebels Yelled: When Darling of the South Ruled Comus," *New Orleans Times-Picayune,* February 25, 1938, 38.

14. *New Orleans Times-Democrat,* March 2, 1892, 3, cols. 1–4.

15. "Polished pedestrian" is a term unique to this work. It surfaced as a concise way to approach the scripted, cultivated (elegant) sense that can emerge from everyday body language during ritualistic or milestone events. The smooth walk of a bride down the aisle of her wedding, people standing at attention for the Pledge of Allegiance or when a judge enters a courtroom, applauding a performance, or removing hats and bowing heads in sacred places are examples of this in action.

16. The public image of the suffragist was a theme of ridicule by krewes in their Mardi Gras parades, such as with the last float in Comus' 1877 parade, "The Aryan Race," where a futuristic picture of women's rights and voting privileges was seen as leading to a flip-flopped reality of empowered women and emasculated men. Likewise, tableaux that followed the parade "Woman's Election in 1976" revealed krewe misgivings about the public voice of women, satirically staging women in the government and men in the nursery. Clearly, the krewe thought this to be a nonsensical, improbable outcome. Comus' performance not so subtly used humor to remind their own women where the sexes belonged—men at work and women in the home. Thus, the alternative image created (the old-line krewe queen) presented the ideal womanly image—a conservative one tied to marriage, youth, and family (see Comus 1877 folder, Carnival Collection, LaRC, Tulane University). Concerning the socially threatening role

of the suffragist, see Lisa Tickner, *The Spectacle of Women: Imagery of the Suffrage Campaign, 1907–14* (Chicago: University of Chicago Press, 1988), 192–205. For more about antisuffrage conservatism, see Kristy Maddux, "When Patriots Protest: The Anti-Suffrage Discursive Transformation of 1917," *Rhetoric & Public Affairs* 7, no. 3 (Fall 2004): 283–310.

17. Karen Trahan Leathem, "Queens and Kings of the New South," chap. 4 of "'A Carnival According to Their Own Desires': Gender and Mardi Gras in New Orleans, 1870–1941" (Ph.D. diss., University of Carolina at Chapel Hill, 1994), 101–61.

18. Box 1, Queens of Carnival Scrapbook Collection, 1953–1982, UC MSS 318, 83-21-L, Historic New Orleans Collection.

19. Charles L. Dufour and Leonard V. Huber, *If Ever I Cease to Love: One Hundred Years of Rex, 1872–1971* (New Orleans: School of Design, 1970), 39.

20. Herrick, Twelfth Night Reveler 1870 ball program, TNR box 22, Carnival Collection, LaRC, Tulane University Archives.

21. Perry Young, *The Mistick Krewe*, 115; Tallant, *Mardi Gras*, 143–44; Schindler *Mardi Gras*, 66.

22. "The First Queen of the New Orleans Carnival," *New Orleans Daily Picayune*, February 6, 1902, 3, cols. 3–4.

23. Dufour and Huber, *If Ever I Cease to Love*, 24.

24. This manly power falls in line with the idea of "manliness," argued by Gail Bederman, who asserts that manliness was the pervasive gender construct for Progressive Era manhood. It centered on "sexual self-restraint, a powerful will, and a strong character," as opposed to the concept of masculinity that evolved from there (which stressed aggression, both physical and sexual). Manliness, Bederman continues, constituted a "discourse of civilization," which ultimately advocated a social structure based on white male superiority (see Bederman, *Manliness and Civilization: A Cultural History of Gender and Race in the United States, 1880–1917* [Chicago: University of Chicago Press, 1996]).

25. Schindler, *Mardi Gras*, 102.

26. For a blog entry that discusses the relationship between American and European debutante practices during the Edwardian Age, see "The Edwardian Debutante," www .edwardianpromenade.com/society/the-edwardian-debutante/.

27. Mrs. Astor (Caroline Astor) claimed the name *The* Mrs. Astor despite being married to William Backhouse Astor, a second son and having a sister-in-law via her husband's older brother, John Jacob Astor III (thus making two Mrs. Astors). The Mrs. Astor ruled the "Old New York" social scene, inviting only families from her infamous list of "The 400" (families distinguished enough to mingle with her and each other). Her parties, hosted at her Fifth Avenue mansions, defined the social season. Supposedly, guests had to refrain from conversing about body parts (specifically, legs) or dancing the polka—it could reveal the indecent ankle—at her dances, which operated as an ultra-elite marriage market (see Rachel Torgerson, "What Was It Like to Attend Mrs. Astor's Gilded Age Parties," in *Gotham Magazine*, May 15, 2015, http://gotham-magazine.com/mrs-astor-gilded-age-parties; and "Mrs. Astor's Annual Ball," *New York Times*, January 30, 1900, 3).

28. See, for instance, "Society at Home and Abroad: Height of Mid-Winter Social Season," *New York Times*, January 14, 1912; and "To-Day's Coming-Out Teas: Eight Debutantes Will Formally Enter Society This Afternoon," *New York Times*, December 7, 1907, 9.

29. In nineteenth-century social dancing, balls often incorporated these three dances—the german, cotillion, and lancers—although the dances' names often referred to different evolutions and variations of the dances, depending on when in the century the dances were performed. The cotillion, for example, was a French *contredanse* that developed into the quadrille. "Cotillion," however, could also refer to a waltz cotillion or an early form of the german (which grew to include flirtatious party games). No matter the designation, however, cotillion, german, and lancers collectively referenced group dances whose dynamics were grounded in formality and stately tradition. For the interconnectedness of these dances, see Elizabeth Aldrich, "Nineteenth-Century Social Dance," Additionally, the lancers quadrille is spelled two ways: "lancers" and "lanciers." This spelling variance is seen throughout dance manuals and krewe dance cards, with "lancers" being the most popular choice.

30. Lewis Erenberg, *Steppin' Out: New York Nightlife and the Transformation of American Culture, 1890–1930* (Chicago: University of Chicago Press, 1981), 148–49.

31. Though other examples likely exist, outside of the Patriarch's Ball in New York City and the Artillery Club's Artillery Club Anniversary Ball in Galveston, Texas (and, of course, the old-line Carnival queen's formal entrance in New Orleans), debutante balls mentioned in historical news and current scholarship were predominantly organized by women. For debutante rituals of Gilded Age New York City, as well as a general description of the Patriarch's Ball, see Maureen E. Montgomery, "The Female World of Ritual and Etiquette," in *Displaying Women: Spectacles of Leisure in Edith Wharton's New York* (New York: Routledge, 1998), 39–61. For a brief description of the Artillery Club's ball, see Diana Kendall, *Members Only: Elite Clubs and the Process of Exclusion* (New York: Rowman and Littlefield, 2008), 13, 70.

32. According to Karal Ann Marling, old-line masked balls as a stage for debutantes influenced Kansas City and St. Louis debutante rituals, as well (see Marling, "The Veiled Prophet Chooses His Queen of Love and Beauty," in *Debutante: Rites and Regalia of American Debdom* [Lawrence: University Press of Kansas, 2004], 128–51).

33. Some old-line debutantes entered society through another Carnival ball ritual, the special call-out dances, which are further discussed in chapter 5.

34. Court participation for the ultra-elite families entails involvement in the main old-line krewes as well as the tableaux societies. Moreover, the dynasties are determined by female involvement in krewes, the only standard that exposes family names, since the men chosen as Comus, Momus, Proteus, and the King of Misrule were always masked (see tables 1 and 2 in the appendix).

35. Mary Orme Markle, *My Memories* (1972), 2–3, Markle Family Papers (371-C), LaRC, Tulane University.

36. "Maginnis, Arthur Ambrose," in *Louisiana: Comprising Sketches of Parishes, Towns, Events, Institutions, and Persons, Arranged in Cyclopedic Form*, vol. 3, ed. Alcée Fortier, (Century Historical Association, 1914), 544–45.

37. "Maginnis, Arthur Ambrose, Jr.," in *Louisiana: Comprising Sketches of Parishes, Towns, Events, Institutions, and Persons, Arranged in Cyclopedic Form,* vol. 3, ed. Alcée Fortier, Lit.D. (Century Historical Association, 1914), 545–47.

38. John Henry Maginnis had passed away by the time his daughter reigned. On July 4, 1888, while vacationing at his beachfront property in Ocean Springs, Mississippi, he was struck by lightning and died.

39. "J. B. Rose," *Printer's Ink: A Journal for Advertisers* 40, no. 5 (July 30, 1902): 6.

40. *Social Register, New York, 1917,* vol. 31, no. 1 (New York: Social Register Association, November 1916), 572.

41. The family was also closely intertwined with the Eustis family, prominent krewe members themselves. Between 1881 and 1914, six Eustis women served as maids across eight Carnival seasons. Most Eustis women, however, appeared on a single court, except for Kittie Eustis, maid of Twelfth Night Revelers, Momus, and Consus in 1898, who was rivaled only by Maud Eustis, 1909 Rex and Comus maid and queen of Atlanteans (see tables 1 and 2 in the appendix).

42. In addition to old-line courts, the Buckners also participated in four tableaux society courts: the Elves of Oberon, Atlanteans, Argonauts, and Nereus (see appendix table 1).

43. "Susan and Charles Zambito: 1410 Jackson Avenue," *Preservation in Print* 27, no. 10 (December 2000): 31–32. In today's dollars, $150,000 is roughly over $4 million.

44. "Death of James B. Eustis," *New York Times,* September 10, 1899.

45. "A. Baldwin & Co.: One Hundred Years in Business," *Mill Supplies: An Independent Monthly Journal Devoted to the Interest of the Jobbers and Manufacturers of Mill, Steam, Mine, and Machinery Supplies* 12, no. 1 (January 1922): 95.

46. Bertram Wyatt-Brown, *Southern Honor: Ethics and Behavior in the Old South* (New York: Oxford University Press, 1982), 221.

47. Leathem, "A Carnival According to Their Own Desires," 108, 110. Kinser's argument is located in Samuel Kinser, *Carnival, American Style: Mardi Gras at New Orleans and Mobile,* with photographs by Norman Magden (Chicago: University of Chicago Press, 1990), 119; see also Schindler, *Mardi Gras,* 102.

48. "Old Man of the Sea," *New Orleans Times-Democrat,* March 1, 1892, 10, cols. 1–2.

49. Thoinot Arbeau, *Orchesography,* trans. Mary Stewart Evans (New York: Dover, 1967), 59. For Renaissance royal entries, see Roy Strong, *Splendor at Court: Renaissance Spectacle and the Theater of Power* (Boston: Houghton Mifflin, 1973), 23–37.

50. Wendy Hilton, *Dance and Music of Court and Theater: Selected Writings of Wendy Hilton* (New York: Pendragon, 1997), 3. For more about Louis XIV as a dancer and how dancing was integral to France's unification politics, see Jennifer Homans, *Apollo's Angels: A History of Ballet* (New York: Random House, 2010).

51. Hilton, *Dance and Music of Court and Theater,* 9. See also Edmund Fairfax, *The Styles of Eighteenth-Century Ballet* (Lanham, Md.: Scarecrow, 2003).

52. Thomas Hillgrove, *A Complete Practical Guide to the Art of Dancing. Containing Descriptions of All Fashionable and Approved Dances, Full Directions for Calling the Figures, the Amount of Music Required . . .* (New York: Dick & Fitzgerald, 1863), 26.

53. Elizabeth Aldrich, "Nineteenth-Century Social Dance." See also clip 1, "Late Nineteenth-Century Dance: Grand March," as part of the American Ballroom Companion online collection, http://memory.loc.gov/ammem/dihtml/divideos.html#vc001.

54. At society balls, only the most affluent among the group were designated march leaders, and leading couples often maintained their role for years, even decades, as in cases of annual events such as charity balls in cosmopolitan cities (see, for instance, the *New York Times* articles: "Baltimore's Charity Ball," January 25, 1887; "Charity Ball Given for Sixtieth Time," February 2, 1917; and "Charity Ball Is Gayly Revived," February 8, 1919).

55. "The Proteus Ball," *New Orleans Times-Democrat,* February 14, 1893, 2.

56. For descriptions of the march, see "At the Ball," *New Orleans Daily Picayune,* February 11, 1902, 3, cols. 6–7.

57. For accounts that emphasize the double grand march's grandeur and awe, see Dorothy Spencer Collins, "Rambling through the Years to 1977" (1977), p. 28, box 10, Collins Papers, LaRC, Tulane University; and Young, *The Mistick Krewe,* 216–17. This double grand march is important, too, because Comus' ball unfolds during the most significant meeting time. It (like Rex's ball) is held on Mardi Gras night, whereas other balls occupy the time between the Epiphany (January 6) and the day before Mardi Gras.

58. Kinser, *Carnival, American Style,* 280.

59. Cynthia J. Novack, "Looking at Movement as Culture: Contact Improvisation to Disco," *TDR* 32, no. 4 (Winter 1988): 102–19.

60. Ramsay Burt, "Steve Paxton's 'Goldberg Variations' and the Angel of History," *TDR* 46, no. 4 (Winter 2002): 60.

61. See, for example, "The Brilliant Ball," *New Orleans Daily Picayune,* March 2, 1897, 6; and "Comus Ball in Keeping with Gorgeous Parade," *New Orleans Times-Democrat,* February 28, 1906, 12.

62. "Lessons for a Queen," newspaper article from Green Scrapbook, box 2, Queens of Carnival Scrapbook Collection, Historic New Orleans Collection.

63. Hilton, *Dance and Music of Court and Theater,* 269.

64. Frank Leslie Clendenen, *The Fashionable Quadrille Call Book and Guide to Etiquette* (Davenport, Ia.: F. L. Clendenen, 1895), 12.

65. Rudolph Radestock, *The Royal Ball-Room Guide and Etiquette of the Drawing-Room, Containing the Newest and Most Elegant Dances and a Short History of Dancing* (London: W. Walker and Sons, 1877), 23.

66. Alexander Strathy, *Elements of the Art of Dancing; with a Description of the Principal Figures in the Quadrille* (Edinburgh: Alexander Strathy, 1822), 13–14. The Library of Congress identifies this text as one of the most important manuals for early nineteenth-century dancing.

67. "Types of Fair Women," *Munsey's Magazine* 15 (April–September 1896): 428, 430. Nicholson wrote under the pseudonym "Pearl Rivers."

68. "The Krewe of Comus," *New Orleans Daily Picayune,* February 27, 1895, 1, 7.

69. Collins, "Rambling through the Years to 1977."

70. Mitchell, *All on a Mardi Gras Day,* 105.

71. Gary Hymel, "Queen in 1913 Here to Hail Carnival King," news clipping, Brown Scrapbook, box 2, Queens of Carnival Scrapbook Collection, Historic New Orleans Collection.

72. Leathem, "A Carnival According to Their Own Desires," 105, 124–26.

73. Edwards argues that wives had to support their southern men and their men's causes and economic and political positions. Edwards asserted that many southern women's "own place in the social hierarchy was also at issue, because these women's fortunes rose and fell with those of their menfolk" (Laura F. Edwards, *Scarlett Doesn't Live Here Anymore: Southern Women in the Civil War Era* [Urbana: University of Illinois Press, 2000], 84, 72).

74. Solomon, commenting on the streets crowded with Union officers, writes in her diary: "Oh! that we could strike them out as one man," continuing to say that she could foresee another civil war, believing that southerners could never be "united in the sacred ties of brotherhood with those for whom we entertain the most rancorous hatred" (Clara Solomon, *The Civil War Diary of Clara Solomon: Growing Up in New Orleans, 1861–1862*, ed. Elliott Ashkenazi [Baton Rouge: Louisiana State University Press, 1995], 374).

75. Other women's reactions: they glared and spit at soldiers, emptied their chamber pots over balconies onto soldiers' heads, and on one occasion, a woman flung herself into the gutter, proclaiming that she would prefer to lie in the street's filth rather than be helped by a Yankee (see Chester G. Hearn, *When the Devil Came Down to Dixie: Ben Butler in New Orleans* [Baton Rouge: Louisiana University Press, 1997], 97–104). Despite the breech in southern manners, many of these women were from the upper class. Mardi Gras historian Charles "Pie" Dufour recalled that his grandmother "told me how she used to chase Ben Butler's soldiers out of her yard, when they came there trying to scrounge around for things. My grandmother was every bit about five feet" (see Charles "Pie" Dufour interview, April 2, 1974, transcript, p. 14, side 1, Friends of the Cabildo Interview Transcripts, LaRC, Tulane University).

76. Hearn, *When the Devil Came Down to Dixie*, 103.

77. Drew Gilpin Faust, *Mothers of Invention: Women of the Slaveholding South in the American Civil War* (Chapel Hill: University of North Carolina Press, 1996), 210–12.

78. Ibid., 252–53.

79. In 1866 they reorganized as the Ladies' Confederate Memorial Association, changed to the Ladies Benevolent Society of Louisiana in 1867 and then to the Ladies' Confederate Memorial Association in 1894 (see Confederated Southern Memorial Association, *History of the Confederated Memorial Associations of the South* [New Orleans: Graham, 1904], 168–201).

80. Marilyn Mayer Culpepper, *All Things Altered: Women in the Wake of Civil War and Reconstruction* (Jefferson, N.C.: McFarland, 2002), 231.

81. Jane Turner Censer, *The Reconstruction of White Southern Womanhood, 1865–1895* (Baton Rouge: Louisiana State University Press, 2003), 9.

82. *History of the Confederated Memorial Associations of the South*, 191–96.

83. Censer, *The Reconstruction of White Southern Womanhood*, 50.

84. Louise Quentell von Meysenbug Autobiography, 86, Von Meysenbug-Lyons Papers, Historic New Orleans Collection.

85. 1923 Debutante Scrapbook Clippings, 59, Madeleine Villere Scoggin Papers, 1922–1923, MSS 407, LaRC, Tulane University.

86. Collins, "Rambling through the Years to 1977," 15; Leathem, "A Carnival According to Their Own Desires," 141–48.

87. "I. Louisiana," facts presented by Caroline E. Merrick (789–801), in *History of Woman Suffrage*, ed. Stanton, Anthony, and Gage, vol. 3, 1876–1885 (Rochester, N.Y.: Susan B. Anthony, 1886), 799nn. For histories of the woman's movement in Louisiana, see Marjorie Spruill Wheeler, *New Women of the New South: The Leaders of the Woman Suffrage Movement in the Southern States* (New York: Oxford University Press, 1993), esp. 20–40; Carmen Lindig, *The Path from the Parlor: Louisiana Women, 1879–1920* (Lafayette: Center for Louisiana Studies, University of Southwestern Louisiana, 1986); and Kenneth R. Johnson, "Kate Gordon and the Woman-Suffrage Movement in the South," *Journal of Southern History* 38, no. 3 (August 1972): 365–92.

88. Markle, "My Memories (1972)," 3.

89. Young, *The Mistick Krewe*, 195.

90. *New Orleans States,* January 12, 1896, 9, col. 2. See also *New Orleans Daily Picayune,* January 4, 1900, 3; and *New Orleans Times-Democrat,* January 4, 1900, 7.

91. Schindler, *Mardi Gras*, 161.

92. Arthur Hardy, *Mardi Gras in New Orleans: An Illustrated History,* 2nd ed. (Metairie, La.: Arthur Hardy Enterprises, 2003), 109; Schindler, *Mardi Gras,* 161.

93. After initially forming in 1922, the krewe disbanded in 1929, was temporarily revived, and then fully revived in 1938. In 1959, they added parading to their festivities (see Arthur Burton La Cour, *New Orleans Masquerade: Chronicles of a Carnival* [New Orleans: Pelican, 1952], 107–8; and Hardy, *Mardi Gras in New Orleans,* 92).

94. Hardy, *Mardi Gras in New Orleans,* 104. See Leathem, "A Carnival According to Their Own Desires," for Leathem's argument that Venus' 1941 parade was the event that signified the demise of old-line krewes' hold over Mardi Gras.

95. Suzanne Stouse, "Taking a Leap into Carnival Lore: Ladies' Krewe 'Quickened Pulse of Male Society,'" news clipping in Léda Hincks Plauché Papers, 89-35-L, Historic New Orleans Collection.

96. For the many meanings of poppies, see "The Poppy Flower: Its Symbol and Meaning," www.flowermeaning.com/poppy-flower-meaning/; "Poppy," in *New World Encyclopedia*, www.newworldencyclopedia.org/entry/Poppy; and "Flowers in Mythology," www.mythencyclopedia.com/Fi-Go/Flowers-in-Mythology.html#ixzz49VvSE2eq.

97. For the lineage of ballroom dance as elite power, from the Renaissance and into the court of Louis XIV, see Carol Lee, *Ballet in Western Culture: A History of its Origins and Evolution* (New York: Routledge, 2002).

98. Aldrich, "Nineteenth-Century Social Dance."

99. See, for instance, William B. De Garmo, *The Prompter: Containing Full Descriptions of all the Quadrilles, Figures of the German Cotillion, etc. Designed for the Assistance of the Pupils*

of Wm. B. De Garmo . . . (New York, Raymond & Caulon, Printers, 1865); and Professor C. Brooks, *The Ball-Room Monitor, or, Guide to the Learner; Containing the Most Complete Sets of Quadrilles Ever Published,* 3rd ed., with additions. (Philadelphia, J. H. Johnson, 1866).

100. Elizabeth Aldrich, *From the Ballroom to Hell: Grace and Folly in Nineteenth-Century Dance* (Evanston: Northwestern University Press, 1991), 16.

101. See J. A. French, ed., *The Prompter's Hand Book* (Boston: O. Ditson Co., 1893).

102. Hillgrove, *A Complete Practical Guide to the Art of Dancing,* 60.

103. "Manners and Tone of Good Society, by a Member of the Aristocracy" (London, 1879), 124–25, reprinted in Aldrich, *From the Ballroom to Hell,* 54.

104. Hillgrove, *A Complete Practical Guide to the Art of Dancing,* 62.

105. Clendenen, *Fashionable Quadrille Call Book and Guide to Etiquette,* 8.

106. *The Dancer's Guide and Ball-Room Companion* (New York: Frank M. Reed, 1875), 12.

107. Radestock, *The Royal Ball-Room Guide and Etiquette of the Drawing-Room,* 47.

108. *The Dance: Ancient and Modern,* trans. Arabella E. Moore (Philadelphia: A. Moore, 1900), 24.

109. Leathem, "A Carnival According to Their Own Desires," 140.

110. Wyatt-Brown, *Southern Honor,* 65–66.

111. Mitchell, *All on a Mardi Gras Day,* 106. Josie Halliday, queen of Carnival for 1904, used scraps from her Carnival queen dress as bridal veils for herself and friends (see Rose Kahn, "Carnival Queen of 1904 Returns Each [rest cut off]," box 1, Queens of Carnival Scrapbook Collection, Historic New Orleans Collection.

112. Leathem, "A Carnival According to Their Own Desires," 24–25.

113. Edwards, *Scarlett Doesn't Live Here Anymore,* 20.

114. This complicated entanglement continues to exist for the female family members who participate in old-line krewe rituals. See, for instance, Rebecca Snedeker's poignant documentary, *By Invitation Only,* which chronicles Snedeker's personal encounters of persistent racism and classism as she follows a friend's court debut and reveals her own recalcitrance about tableaux balls (*By Invitation Only,* dir. Rebecca Snedeker [New Orleans: New Day Films, 2006], DVD).

5. "THE VERY MADDEST WHIRLPOOL OF PLEASURE": BALLROOM DANCING IN THE PROGRESSIVE ERA

1. *New Orleans Daily Picayune,* February 20, 1906, 1–2.

2. Henri Schindler, *Mardi Gras: New Orleans* (New York: Flammarion, 1997), 107.

3. Leonard V. Huber, *A Pictorial History of Carnival in New Orleans* (Gretna, La.: Pelican, 2003), 53.

4. Schindler, *Mardi Gras,* 107.

5. Ibid.

6. Robert Tallant, *Mardi Gras . . . As It Was* (repr., Gretna, La.: Pelican, 1989), 13.

7. Schindler, *Mardi Gras*, 96–97.

8. Huber, *Pictorial History*, 53.

9. T. C. DeLeon, *Our Creole Carnivals: Their Origin, History, Progress and Results with Sketches of Outside Carnivals* (Mobile: Gossip Printing Co., 1890), 26, also points out that the reception committeemen and special invitations to the balls were further assurances of the men's reputable character.

10. *New Orleans Daily Picayune*, February 14, 1896, 6, col. 5.

11. *New Orleans Times-Democrat*, February 18, 1899, 8, cols. 6–7.

12. *New Orleans Times*, March 2, 1870, 2. The "quarried weight" phrase could also be a reference to the krewesmen, who had just depicted statues of great men in the "Great Men of Louisiana from 1539 to 1815" tableau performance. Naturally, the tableau participants wore white makeup to achieve the look of marbled statues.

13. *New Orleans Daily Picayune*, February 26, 1873, 6.

14. *New Orleans Times*, March 2, 1870, 2.

15. *New Orleans Times-Democrat*, February 8, 1907, 5.

16. "The King's Ball, Mardi Gras Night, 1879," from the *Weekly Budget*, 1974.25.19.377, Leonard V. Huber Collection within the Carnival Collection, Historic New Orleans Collection.

17. *The Dance: Ancient and Modern*, trans. Arabella E. Moore (Philadelphia: A. Moore, 1900), 27.

18. *The Dancer's Guide and Ball-Room Companion* reveals that the "country" dances (polkas, mazurkas and the like) were "thrown in as an occasional relief" from quadrilles and waltzes during modern balls in the nineteenth century (*The Dancer's Guide and Ball-Room Companion* [New York: Frank M. Reed, 1875], 9).

19. Arthur Burton La Cour, *New Orleans Masquerade: Chronicles of a Carnival* (New Orleans: Pelican, 1952), 218. To perform a racquet, dancers should "take two long galop slides with left foot on accent, and as right foot is brought up to left foot for second time, rest, and hold left foot in air. Repeat by sliding with right foot, etc." (Cartier, *Cartier's Practical Illustrated Waltz Instructor, Ball Room Guide, and Call Book. Giving Ample Directions for Dancing Every Kind of Square and Round Dances, Together with Cotillions—Including the Newest and Most Popular Figures of "The German"* [New York: De Witt, 1882], 45). For a description of the Saratoga, see "Saratoga Lanciers," in L. F. Segadlo, *Course of Instruction in Dancing and Aesthetic Development of the Body* (Newark, N.J., 1889).

20. Independent dance historian Susan de Guardiola has created an in-depth research blog where the differences between each dance listed here, as well as references to specific dancing manuals, can be found (see Capering & Kickery, www.kickery.com).

21. The author determined these shifts by looking at all of the old-line dance cards from 1870 to 1920 available at the Historic New Orleans Collection; the Carnival Collection housed in the Louisiana Research Collection at Tulane University; the Judge John Minor Wisdom Collection at the University of New Orleans Earl K. Long Library Special Collection; and the Carnival Collection within the Louisiana Division of the New Orleans Public Library.

22. *New Orleans Daily Picayune*, February 26, 1873, 2, cols. 1–3.

23. Rudolph Radestock, *The Royal Ball-Room Guide and Etiquette of the Drawing-Room, Containing the Newest and Most Elegant Dances and a Short History of Dancing* (London: W. Walker and Sons, 1877), 73.

24. *The Dancer's Guide and Ball-Room Companion*, 19.

25. Judson Sause, *The Art of Dancing, Embracing a Full Description of the Various Dances of the Present Day, Together with Chapters on Etiquette, the Benefits and History of Dancing*, 5th ed. (Chicago: Belford, Clarke & Co., 1889), 87–88.

26. Elizabeth Aldrich, "Nineteenth Century Social Dance," in "Western Social Dance: An Overview of the Collection," by Aldrich, part of the American Ballroom Companion Collection within the American Memory project of the Library of Congress, http://memory .loc.gov/ammem/dihtml/diessay6. For video clips of the Washington Two-Step, see clip 7, "Late Nineteenth-Century Dance: Washington Post Two Step"; and clip 8, "Late Nineteenth-Century Dance: The Washington Post Two Step," both part of the American Ballroom Companion: Dance Instruction Manuals, ca. 1490–1920 Video Directory, http://memory.loc.gov/ ammem/dihtml/divideos.html#vc007.

27. For the development of the waltz, see Ruth Katz, "The Egalitarian Waltz," *Comparative Studies in Society and History* 15, no. 3 (June 1973): 368–77.

28. Ibid., 368, 374–75.

29. For a visual example of the late nineteenth-century waltz, see video 62, "Late Nineteenth-Century Dance: Waltz," in the American Ballroom Companion Video Directory, http://memory.loc.gov/ammem/dihtml/divideos.html#vc062. For the standard early twentieth-century waltz, see clip 76, "Ragtime Dance: Standard Waltz," http://memory.loc .gov/ammem/dihtml/divideos.html#vc076.vlk.

30. Elizabeth Claire, "Women, Waltzing & Warfare: The Social Choreography of Revolution at the End of the Long 18th Century" (Ph.D. diss., New York University, 2004), 180.

31. Karen Trahan Leathem, "'A Carnival According to Their Own Desires': Gender and Mardi Gras in New Orleans, 1870–1941" (Ph.D. diss., University of Carolina at Chapel Hill, 1994), 178.

32. Thomas Hillgrove, A *Complete Practical Guide to the Art of Dancing. Containing Descriptions of All Fashionable and Approved Dances, Full Directions for Calling the Figures, the Amount of Music Required; Hints on Etiquette, the Toilet, etc.* (New York: Dick & Fitzgerald, 1863), 154.

33. W. G. Bowdoin, "The Mardi Gras Is On," news clipping from February 17, 1901, F 379. N5 B6, 73-408-L, Historic New Orleans Collection.

34. Edward Ferrero, *The Art of Dancing, Historically Illustrated. To Which Is Added a Few Hints on Etiquette; Also, the Figures, Music, and Necessary Instruction for the Performance of the Most Modern and Approved Dances . . .* (New York: Edward Ferrero, 1859), 142.

35. M. J. Koncen, *Prof. M. J. Koncen's Quadrille Call Book and Ball Room Guide; To Which Is Added a Sensible Guide to Etiquette and Deportment in the Ball and Assembly Room . . .* (St. Louis: Press of S. F. Brearley & Co., 1883), 9.

36. *New Orleans Daily Picayune*, February 14, 1877, 3.

37. See, for instance, *New Orleans Daily Picayune*, February 15, 1888, 8, cols. 1–2.

38. La Cour, *New Orleans Masquerade*, 213.

39. *New Orleans Times-Picayune,* February 17, 1915, 7.

40. *New Orleans Daily Picayune,* February 15, 1888, 8, cols. 1–2.

41. Perry Young, *The Mistick Krewe: Chronicles of Comus and His Kin* (New Orleans: Carnival, 1931), 194.

42. Ibid., 216.

43. *New Orleans Times-Democrat,* February 8, 1894, 10. See also Henri Schindler, *Mardi Gras Treasures: Jewelry of the Golden Age* (Gretna, La.: Pelican, 2006).

44. Dorothy Spencer Collins Papers, Memoirs, "Rambling through the Years to 1977," p. 1, Box 10, Dorothy Spencer Collins Papers, Louisiana Research Collection (LaRC), Tulane University.

45. Tallant, *Mardi Gras . . . As It Was,* 18.

46. Young, *The Mistick Krewe,* 220.

47. For more about social dance among the gentry in Georgian England (and about dance in Jane Austen's novels), see Nancy M. Lee-Riffe, "The Role of Country Dance in the Fiction of Jane Austen," *Women's Writing* 5, no. 1 (1998): 103–12; Joan Scanlon and Richard Kerridge, "Spontaneity and Control: The Uses of Dance in Late Romantic Literature," *Dance Research: Journal of the Society for Dance Research* 6, no. 1 (Spring 1988): 30–44; Nora Stovel, "'Every Savage Can Dance': Choreographing Courtship," *Persuasions* 23 (2001): 29–49; Allison Thompson, "The Felicities of Rapid Motion: Jane Austen in the Ballroom," *Persuasions: The Jane Austen Journal On-Line* 21, no. 1 (Winter 2000), www.jasna.org/persuasions/on-line/vol21no1/thompson.html; and Cheryl A. Wilson, "Dance, Physicality, and Social Mobility in Jane Austen's *Persuasion,*" *Persuasions* 25 (2003): 55–75.

48. See, for instance, *The Gentleman & Lady's Companion: Containing the Newest Cotillions and Country Dances, to Which Is Added, Instances of Ill Manners, to Be Carefully Avoided by Youth of Both Sexes* (Norwich: J. Trumbull, 1798).

49. For more about polite conversation, see Bharat Tandon, *Jane Austen and the Morality of Conversation* (London: Anthem, 2003).

50. See Stovel, "Every Savage Can Dance"; and Thompson "The Felicities of Rapid Motion."

51. Thompson, "The Felicities of Rapid Motion," 5.

52. Ferrero, *The Art of Dancing, Historically Illustrated,* 142.

53. See "Dancers Want Live, Not Canned Music," *New York Times,* July 5, 1914, 10.

54. The one-step, discussed in depth later in this chapter, was a ragged version of a tango-like dance. In newspapers and dancing manuals of the mid-1910s, the terms were often interchangeable.

55. The write-up states, for instance, that "there will be no snake-wriggling at the shoulders permitted" and that "as danced by some it is conducive to immorality" (*New Orleans Item,* January 14, 1914).

56. Thomas Griffin, "Lagniappe: Advice to Everyone: Let Yourself Go!," Green Scrapbook, box 2, Queens of Carnival Scrapbook Collection, 1953–1982, UC MSS 318, 83-21-L, Historic New Orleans Collection.

57. Tallant, *Mardi Gras . . . As It Was,* 207. By "lesser kings," Tallant means kings of krewes less prestigious than Rex and the other old-line organizations.

58. Schindler, *Mardi Gras*, 98.

59. *New Orleans Times-Democrat*, February 14, 1893, 2.

60. Bowdoin, "The Mardi Gras Is On."

61. Leathem, "A Carnival According to Their Own Desires," 30–31.

62. La Cour, *New Orleans Masquerade*, 214.

63. Ibid., 215.

64. Napier Bartlett, *Stories of the Crescent City* (New Orleans: Steel & Company's Times Job Print, 1869), 26, Historic New Orleans Collection.

65. Florence Dymond, "Life in New Orleans," p. 7, folder 6, Florence Dymond Papers, LaRC, Tulane University.

66. "Mistick Krewe of Comus," in *DeBow's Review* 6 (March 1869): 230.

67. John M. Parker Jr. and Mrs. Edith Parker, Friends of the Cabildo Interview Transcripts, p. 14, November 13, 1976, LaRC, Tulane University.

68. Young, *The Mistick Krewe*, 127.

69. Ibid., 206.

70. La Cour, *New Orleans Masquerade*, 218.

71. For leading documentation of early twentieth-century dance hall reform, see Louise De Koven Bowen, "Dance Halls," *Survey* 26 (June 3, 1911): 383–87; Mildred E. Chadsey, "The Influence of the Dance Hall," *Playground* 6, no. 9 (December 1912): 337–38; Committee of Fourteen, *The Social Evil in New York City: A Study of Law Enforcement* (New York: Kellogg, 1910); T. A. Faulkner, *From the Ball-Room to Hell* (Chicago: Henry Publishing Co., 1892); Belle Lindner Israels, "The Way of the Girl," *Survey* 22 (July 3, 1909): 486–97; Mrs. Charles H. Israels, "The Regulation of Dance Halls," *Playground* 6, no. 9 (December 1912): 339–40; Mrs. Charles H. Israels, "Social Dancing," *Playground* 5, no. 7 (October 1911): 231–36; Maria Ward Lambin, *Report of the Public Dance Hall Committee of the San Francisco Center of the California Civic League of Women Voters* (San Francisco: San Francisco Center of the California Civic League of Women Voters, 1924); Frederick Rex, "Municipal Dance Halls," *National Municipal Review* 4, no. 3 (July 1915): 413–19; and Julia Schoenfeld, "The Regulation of Dance Halls," *Playground* 6, no. 9 (December 1912): 340–42.

72. Linda Tomko, *Dancing Class: Gender, Ethnicity and Social Divides in American Dance, 1890–1920* (Bloomington: Indiana University Press, 1999), 43.

73. For an explanation of the African American dance aesthetic, see Robert Farris Thompson, "An Aesthetic of the Cool: West African Dance," *African Forum* 2 (Fall 1966): 85–102; and Robert Farris Thompson, "An Aesthetic of the Cool" *African Arts* 7, no. 1 (Autumn 1973): 40–43, 64, 67, 89–91.

74. Kathy Peiss, *Cheap Amusements: Working Women and Leisure in Turn-of-the-Century New York* (Philadelphia: Temple University Press, 1986), 102.

75. "Jazz Neighborhoods," National Park Service, www.nps.gov/jazz/learn/historyculture/jazz-map.htm. See Alecia P. Long, *The Great Southern Babylon: Sex, Race, and Respectability in New Orleans, 1865–1920* (Baton Rouge: Louisiana State University Press, 2004), 215.

76. "Women Tango Fiends Arrested by Police," *New Orleans Item*, December 10, 1914, 1.

77. "Reynolds, In Order, Puts Lid on Tango Belt: Closes Places," *New Orleans Item*, March 4, 1915, 1, 7. Close to fifty "entertainers"/"little daughters of joy" were arrested. Names of cabarets and clubs raided include: the Haymarket (the largest club in the area) and the Sans Souci, both operated by William Stock; the Pup; the Cadillac (operated by Joseph Crucia); the Black Cat (run by Jack Robertson); and the Turf (managed by Bush and Richard). After the March 4 raid, many establishments "closed for repairs" but the police returned the next day, this time arresting men "having no visible means of support" found in the remaining establishments, attempting to establish a dictum that "the Tango Belt must be operated on a highly respectable plan" (see "Tango Belt Tries to Be Good; Police Raid Again," *New Orleans Item*, March 5, 1915).

78. Randy McBee, *Dance Hall Days: Intimacy and Leisure among Working-Class Immigrants in the United States* (New York: New York University Press, 2000), 83.

79. Lewis Erenberg, *Stepping Out: New York Nightlife and the Transformation of American Culture, 1890–1930* (Chicago: University of Chicago Press, 1981), 154.

80. For more on the Castles' lives, see Irene Castle's *My Husband* (1919; repr., New York: Da Capo, 1979); and *Castles in the Air* (Garden City, N.Y.: Doubleday, 1958); as well as Eve Golden, *Vernon and Irene Castle's Ragtime Revolution* (Lexington: University Press of Kentucky, 2007).

81. Julie Malnig, *Dancing till Dawn: A Century of Exhibition Ballroom Dance* (New York: Greenwood, 1992), 39.

82. Vernon Castle and Irene Castle, *Modern Dancing* (New York: Harper and Brothers, 1914), 38–39.

83. Ibid., 32.

84. See, for instance, *New Orleans Times-Picayune*, January 10, 1915, 7; and February 7, 1915, 6.

85. *New Orleans Times-Picayune*, January 17, 1915, 2.

86. Charles "Pie" Dufour, Friends of the Cabildo Interview Transcripts, April 2, 1974, side 1, p. 3, LaRC, Tulane University.

87. 1923 Debutante Scrapbook, p. 62, Madeleine Villere Scoggin Papers, 1922–1923, MSS 407, LaRC, Tulane University. Maud Fox was a 1923 maid in the courts of Rex, Momus, and the tableaux society Atlanteans, while also serving as queen that year for the latest incarnation of the Twelfth Night Revelers.

88. "Newcomb Opens Tango Classes; Girls Teach Professors," *New Orleans Item*, January 15, 1914, 1.

89. Schindler, *Mardi Gras*, 94, 97.

90. "Program of Dances at the Grand Masked Ball," Southern Hardware Jobbers Association, April 22, 1915 at the St. Charles Hotel, New Orleans, call no. HNOC Pam GV 1750.S6 1915 Apr. 22.

91. For a movement clip of the one-step, see video 74, "Ragtime Dance: One Step Variations," in the American Ballroom Companion Video Directory, http://memory.loc.gov/ammem/dihtml/divideos.html#vc074.

92. According to their dance cards, Momus included the foxtrot and one-step in 1915, and TNR followed in 1916. For tableaux societies, the Falstaffians included a one-step in their 1914

program and added the foxtrot in 1916, accompanied by Nereus, who also added the foxtrot and one-step in 1916.

93. Though much later than the 1910s Carnival balls, the foxtrot scene from *Love in the Rough* (1930) shows the more genteel, or smooth, style of foxtrot, likely closer to what old-lines preferred (see "Foxtrot Scene from Love in the Rough," www.youtube.com/watch?v=xRsz TPEgNiE); see also a short, silent-film comedy, *Fox Trot Finesse* (1915), which shows the range that the foxtrot could assume, from genteel walking to a more ragging waltz: "1915— Fox Trot Finesse—MR. & MRS. SIDNEY DREW | Maurice Morris," www.youtube.com/ watch?v=HRyOtkUHbF4. For the promenading, rag version of the foxtrot (with hints at the smoother version), see the wedding scene from another silent film comedy, *The Oyster Princess* (1919): "Fox Trot Scene Oyster Princess Ernst Lubitsch Ossi Oswalda," www.youtube.com/ watch?v=2TSoffJ4sHk.

94. La Cour, *New Orleans Masquerade*, 218.

95. Young, *The Mistick Krewe*, 201; La Cour, *New Orleans Masquerade*, 93.

96. *New Orleans Times-Democrat*, March 2, 1892, 3, cols. 1–4.

CONCLUSION

1. Robert Tallant, *Mardi Gras . . . As It Was* (Gretna, La.: Pelican, 1989), 109; Karen Trahan Leathem, "'A Carnival According to Their Own Desires': Gender and Mardi Gras in New Orleans, 1870–1941" (Ph.D. diss., University of Carolina at Chapel Hill, 1994), 185–87; Al Rose, *Storyville, New Orleans: Being an Authentic, Illustrated Account of the Notorious Red-Light District* (Tuscaloosa: University of Alabama Press, 1974), 23.

2. Samuel Kinser, *Carnival, American Style: Mardi Gras at New Orleans and Mobile*, with photographs by Norman Magden (Chicago: University of Chicago Press, 1990), 128.

3. Qtd. in James Gill, *Lords of Misrule: Mardi Gras and the Politics of Race in New Orleans* (Jackson: University Press of Mississippi, 1997), 145.

4. For more about prostitution in New Orleans, see Alecia P. Long, *The Great Southern Babylon: Sex, Race, and Respectability in New Orleans, 1865–1920* (Baton Rouge: Louisiana State University Press, 2004).

5. Rose, *Storyville*, 62.

6. Ibid., 64. Though excluded from the upper-class French balls, tourists and middle-class men could still purchase tickets to other French ball parties via *Blue Book* advertisements.

7. Tallant, *Mardi Gras*, 174–75. For an explanation of elite women venturing into the prostitution district on Mardi Gras, see Tallant, *Mardi Gras*, 220–21; Rose, *Storyville*, 63–64; Leathem, "A Carnival According to Their Own Desires," 190; Kinser, *Carnival, American Style*, 130; and Gill, *Lords of Misrule*, 158.

8. For more about the *Blue Books*, see Pamela Arceneaux, "Guidebooks to Sin: The Blue Books of Storyville," *Louisiana History* 28 (Fall 1987): 397–405.

9. *Blue Book*, 10th ed., 1969.19.10, Historic New Orleans Collection.

10. *Blue Book* (no edition specified), Lyre & Lilies cover, Historic New Orleans Collection.

11. Leathem, "A Carnival According to Their Own Desires," 188.

12. Ibid., 189.

13. Rose, *Storyville*, 63.

14. Long, *The Great Southern Babylon*, 166.

15. Tallant, *Mardi Gras*, 173.

16. Schindler, *Mardi Gras: New Orleans* (New York: Flammarion, 1997), 160.

17. See Reid Mitchell, *All on a Mardi Gras Day: Episodes in the History of New Orleans Carnival* (Cambridge: Harvard University Press, 1995), 167–69.

18. See Lily Jackson, "French Opera House" *New Orleans Times Picayune*, February 5, 1984, sec. 4, p. 1.

19. Schindler, *Mardi Gras*, 150.

20. Ibid., 161. Krewe captains, always acknowledged as the real krewesmen of power, remained masked, even in the twentieth century.

21. Ibid., 201.

22. Kinser, *Carnival, American Style*, 125; Schindler, *Mardi Gras*, 161 (though this doesn't seem to be the general trend today).

23. Qtd. in "New Orleans' Black Society," by John E. Rousseau in the *Official Mardi Gras 1973 Special*, distributed by the Zulu Social Aid and Pleasure Club, Carnival Collection, New Orleans Public Library.

24. Interview with Mr. Boucre, from interviews conducted and compiled by Phoebe Ferguson, documentary filmmaker in residence at the Amistad Research Center. Ferguson's interviews were part of her research for *Member of the Club* (Bayou & Me Productions, 2008), a documentary about the Original Illinois Club. Ferguson also showed the author a video of a recent OIC ball, which included a performance of the Chicago Glide.

25. See Leathem, "A Carnival According to Their Own Desires," 192.

26. Marcus Christian Chapter 42: "Carnival Groups and Social, Aid, and Pleasure Clubs," in *The Black History of Louisiana*, 3; an unpublished manuscript written between 1938 and 1976 as part of the WPA Writers' Project, MSS11, Marcus Christian Collection, Earl K. Long Library, University of New Orleans.

27. Leathem, "A Carnival According to Their Own Desires," 228–29.

28. Schindler, *Mardi Gras*, 162.

29. Tallant, *Mardi Gras*, 190; Perry Young, *The Mistick Krewe: Chronicles of Comus and His Kin* (New Orleans: Carnival, 1931), 215.

30. See Schindler, *Mardi Gras*, chaps. 2–5, esp. p. 117.

31. Ibid., 102.

32. Victor Turner, *The Anthropology of Performance* (New York: PAJ, 1988), 22.

33. Kinser, *Carnival, American Style*, 91; Mitchell, *All on a Mardi Gras Day*, 14–15.

34. See Errol Laborde, *Krewe: The Early New Orleans Carnival, Comus to Zulu* (New Orleans: Carnival, 2007), 15–23, 51–55.

35. Mitchell, *All on a Mardi Gras Day*, 25–26.

36. Ibid., 23–27.

37. *One Hundred Years of Comus,* Comus ball booklet, p. 19, box 10, Dorothy Spencer Collins Papers, LaRC, Tulane University; Errol Laborde, *Marched the Day God: A History of the Rex Organization* (Metairie, La.: School of Design, 1999), 7.

38. Roy Strong, *Art and Power: Renaissance Festivals, 1450–1650* (Berkeley: University of California Press, 1973), 43.

BIBLIOGRAPHY

PRIMARY SOURCES

Archives and Manuscripts

Earl K. Long Library, Special Collections, University of New Orleans
Wisdom, Judge John Minor, Collection.
Christian, Marcus, Collection.

Historic New Orleans Collection
Blue Book. New Orleans, 1900–1901, 1903, 1905–9, and an undated edition with "Lyre
& Lilies" cover. Provided on microform to preserve originals.
Bright/Richardson Family Papers.
Carnival Collection (also comprising the Leonard V. Huber Collection).
Plauché, Léda Hincks, Papers.
Queens of Carnival Scrapbook Collection (1953–1982).
Von Meysenbug-Lyons Papers.
Vieux Carre Survey.
Walmsley Comus Collection.
Walmsley Family Papers.

Library of Congress, Music Division
An American Ballroom Companion: Dance Instruction Manuals, ca. 1490–1920.
Online collection in the American Memory Project: http://memory.loc.gov/
ammem/dihtml/dihome.html.

**Louisiana Research Collection, Howard-Tilton Memorial Library,
Tulane University**
Carnival Collection.

Collins, Dorothy Spencer, Papers.
Dymond, Florence, Papers.
Friends of the Cabildo Interview Transcripts.
Scoggin, Madeleine Villere, Papers, 1922–1923.
Markle Family Papers.
Rogers, William O., Collection, 1859–1900.
St. Martin Family Papers, 1732–1950.

New Orleans Public Library
Carnival Collection.
Durkee, Cornelius, Collection.
Teunisson, John N., Collection.

Books and Articles

"I. Louisiana." Facts presented by Caroline E. Merrick. In *History of Woman Suffrage*, vol. 3, *1876–1885*, edited by Stanton, Anthony and Gage, 789–801. Rochester, N.Y.: Susan B. Anthony, 1886.

"A. Baldwin & Co.: One Hundred Years in Business." *Mill Supplies: An Independent Monthly Journal Devoted to the Interest of the Jobbers and Manufacturers of Mill, Steam, Mine, and Machinery Supplies* 12, no. 1 (January 1922): 95.

Alexander, Sir James Edward. *Transatlantic Sketches: Comprising Visits to the Most Interesting Scenes in North and South American and the West Indies, with Notes on Negro Slavery and Canadian Emigration*. Philadelphia: Key and Biddle, 1833.

Arbeau, Thoinot. *Orchesography*. Translated by Mary Stewart Evans. New York: Dover, 1967.

The Ball-Room Guide. With Coloured Plates. London: F. Warne and Co., 1866.

Bartlett, Napier. *Stories of the Crescent City*. New Orleans: Steel & Company's Times Job Print, 1869.

Bowen, Louise De Koven. "Dance Halls." *Survey* 26 (June 3, 1911): 383–87.

Brooks, Professor C. *The Ball-Room Monitor, or, Guide to the Learner; Containing the Most Complete Sets of Quadrilles Ever Published*. 3rd ed., with additions. Philadelphia: J. H. Johnson, 1866.

Cartier. *Cartier's Practical Illustrated Waltz Instructor, Ball Room Guide, and Call Book. Giving Ample Directions for Dancing Every Kind of Square and Round Dances, Together with Cotillons—Including the Newest and Most Popular Figures of "The German."* New York: De Witt, 1882.

Castle, Irene. *Castles in the Air.* Garden City, N.Y.: Doubleday, 1958.

———. *My Husband.* 1919. Reprint, New York: Da Capo, 1979.

Castle, Vernon, and Irene Castle. *Modern Dancing.* New York: Harper and Brothers, 1914.

Chadsey, Mildred E. "The Influence of the Dance Hall." *Playground* 6, no. 9 (December 1912): 337–38.

Claiborne, W. C. C. *Official Letter Books of W. C. C. Claiborne (1801–1816).* Edited by Dunbar Rowland. Jackson, Miss.: Printed for the State Department of Archives and History, 1917.

Clendenen, Frank Leslie. *Prof Clendenen's Fashionable Quadrille Call Book and Guide to Etiquette.* Davenport, Ia.: F. L. Clendenen, 1895.

Committee of Fourteen. *The Social Evil in New York City: A Study of Law Enforcement.* New York: Kellogg, 1910.

Confederated Southern Memorial Association, *History of the Confederated Memorial Associations of the South.* New Orleans: Graham, 1904.

"Court and Fashionable Life." *Court Journal: Court Circular & Fashionable Gazette,* vol. 5, p. 788, col. 3. Alabaster, Pasemore & Sons, 1833.

The Dance: Ancient and Modern. Translated by Arabella E. Moore. Philadelphia: A. Moore, 1900.

The Dancer's Guide and Ball-Room Companion. New York: Frank M. Reed, 1875.

De Garmo, William B. *The Prompter: Containing Full Descriptions of all the Quadrilles, Figures of the German Cotillon, etc. Designed for the Assistance of the Pupils of Wm. B. De Garmo....* New York: Raymond & Caulon, Printers, 1865.

Faulkner, T. A. *From the Ball-Room to Hell.* Chicago: Henry Publishing Co., 1892.

Ferrero, Edward. *The Art of Dancing, Historically Illustrated. To Which Is Added a Few Hints on Etiquette; Also, the Figures, Music, and Necessary Instruction for the Performance of the Most Modern and Approved Dances....* New York: Edward Ferrero, 1859.

French, J. A., ed., *The Prompter's Hand Book.* Boston: O. Ditson Co., 1893.

The Gentleman & Lady's Companion: Containing the Newest Cotillions and Country Dances, to Which Is Added, Instances of Ill Manners, to be Carefully Avoided by Youth of Both Sexes. Norwich: J. Trumbull, 1798.

Grant, Professor N. *How to Become Successful Teachers of the Art of Dancing, in Conjunction with How to Manage a Favor-German.* Buffalo, N.Y.: Kraft and Stern, Printers, 1893.

Greene, William E. *The Terpsichorean Monitor.* Providence, R.I.: E.A. Johnson & Co., 1889.

Gumbo Ya-Ya: A Collection of Louisiana Folk Tales. Compiled by Lyle Saxon, Edward Dreyer, and Robert Tallant. 1987; rpr. Gretna, La.: Pelican, 1998.

Hearn, Lafcadio. *Creole Sketches.* Boston: Houghton Mifflin, 1924.

———. *Leaves from the Diary of an Impressionist; Creole Sketches; and Some Ghosts.* Boston: Houghton Mifflin, 1911.

Hillgrove, Thomas. *A Complete Practical Guide to the Art of Dancing. Containing Descriptions of All Fashionable and Approved Dances, Full Directions for Calling the Figures, the Amount of Music Required. . . .* New York: Dick & Fitzgerald, 1863.

A History of the Knights of Momus. N.p. Published on the Occasion of the Annual Banquet, March 18, 1922.

Hone, Philip. *The Diary of Philip Hone, 1828–1851.* Vol. 2, edited by Bayard Tuckerman. New York: Dodd, Mead, 1889.

Howe, Elias. *American Dancing Master, and Ball-Room Prompter: Containing about Five Hundred Dances Including all the Latest and Most Fashionable. . . .* Boston: E. Howe, 1862.

Israels, Belle Lindner. "The Way of the Girl." *Survey* 22 (July 3, 1909): 486–97.

Israels, Mrs. Charles H. "The Regulation of Dance Halls." *Playground* 6, no. 9 (December 1912): 339–40.

———. "Social Dancing." *Playground* 5, no. 7 (October 1911): 231–36.

"J. B. Rose." *Printer's Ink: A Journal for Advertisers* 40, no. 5 (July 30, 1902): 6.

Koncen. M. J. *Prof. M. J. Koncen's Quadrille Call Book and Ball Room Guide; To Which Is Added a Sensible Guide to Etiquette and Deportment in the Ball and Assembly Room. . .* St. Louis: Press of S. F. Brearley & Co., 1883.

Kopp, E. H. *The American Prompter and Guide to Etiquette.* Cincinnati: J. Church Co., 1896.

Lambin, Maria Ward. *Report of the Public Dance Hall Committee of the San Francisco Center of the California Civic League of Women Voters.* San Francisco: San Francisco Center of the California Civic League of Women Voters, 1924.

Latrobe, John H. B. *Impressions Respecting New Orleans: Diary & Sketches, 1818–1820.* Edited by Samuel Wilson Jr. New York: Columbia University Press, 1951.

———. *Southern Travels: Journal of H. B. Latrobe, 1834.* Edited by Samuel Wilson Jr. New Orleans: Historic New Orleans Collection, 1986.

Mather, Increase. *An Arrow against Profane and Promiscuous Dancing Drawn out of the Quiver of the Scriptures; By the Ministers of Christ at Boston in New England.* Boston: Printed by Samuel Green, 1684.

Moreau de St. Mery, Mederic Louis Ellie. *Moreau de St. Mery's American Journey (1793–1798).* Translated and edited by Kenneth Roberts and Anna M. Roberts. New York: Doubleday, 1947.

New York Social Register, 1917. Vol. 31, no. 1. New York: Social Register Association, November 1916.

Radestock, Rudolph. *The Royal Ball-Room Guide and Etiquette of the Drawing-Room, Containing the Newest and Most Elegant Dances and a Short History of Dancing.* London: W. Walker and Sons, 1877.

Rameau, Pierre. *The Dancing Master.* Translated by Cyril W. Beaumont from the original 1725 Paris edition. Alton, Hampshire, Eng.: Dance, 2003.

Rex, Frederick. "Municipal Dance Halls." *National Municipal Review* 4, no. 3 (July 1915): 413–19.

Robin, C. C. *Voyage to Louisiana, 1803–1806.* Translated by Stuart O. Landry Jr. New Orleans: Pelican, 1966.

Sala, George Augustus. *America Revisited: From the Bay of New York to the Gulf of Mexico, and from Lake Michigan to the Pacific.* 4th ed. London: Viztelly & Co., 1883.

Sause, Judson. *The Art of Dancing, Embracing a Full Description of the Various Dances of the Present Day, Together with Chapters on Etiquette, the Benefits and History of Dancing.* 5th ed. Chicago: Belford, Clarke & Co., 1889.

Schoenfeld, Julia. "The Regulation of Dance Halls." *Playground* 6, no. 9 (December 1912): 340–42.

Segadlo, L. F., trans. *Course of Instruction in Dancing and Aesthetic Development of the Body.* Newark, N.J., 1889.

Solomon, Clara. *The Civil War Diary of Clara Solomon: Growing up in New Orleans, 1861–1862.* Edited by Elliott Ashkenazi. Baton Rouge: Louisiana State University Press, 1995.

Stebbins, Genevieve. *Delsarte System of Expression.* New York: Edgar S. Werner, 1902.

Strathy, Alexander. *Elements of the Art of Dancing; with a Description of the Principal Figures in the Quadrille.* Edinburgh: Alexander Strathy, 1822.

Tableaux, Charades and Pantomimes: Adapted Alike to Parlor Entertainments, School and Church Exhibitions and for Use on the Amateur Stage. 1889. Reprint, Freeport, N.Y.: Books for Libraries Press, 1971.

"Types of Fair Women." *Munsey's Magazine,* April–September 1896, 428–30.

Waitz, Julia LeGrand. *The Journal of Julia Le Grand, New Orleans, 1862–1863.* Edited by Kate Mason Rowland and Mrs. Morris L. Croxall. Richmond: Everett Waddey, 1911.

Watkins, Joel H. *Cotillion Figures.* New York: Neale, 1911.

Newspapers and Magazines

DeBow's Review
Harper's New Monthly Magazine
New Orleans Daily Picayune

New Orleans Democrat
New Orleans Item
New Orleans States
New Orleans Times
New Orleans Times-Democrat
New Orleans Times-Picayune
New York Times

SECONDARY SOURCES

Akins, Ann Severance. "Dancing in Dixie's Land: Theatrical Dance in New Orleans, 1860–1870." Ph.D. diss., Texas Woman's University, 1991.

Aldrich, Elizabeth. *From the Ballroom to Hell: Grace and Folly in Nineteenth-Century Dance.* Evanston: Northwestern University Press, 1991.

———. "Nineteenth Century Social Dance." In "Western Social Dance: An Overview of the Collection," part of the American Ballroom Companion Collection within the American Memory project of the Library of Congress. Http://memory .loc.gov/ammem/dihtml/diessay6.html.

Alonso, Ana Maria, "Men in 'Rags' and the Devil on the Throne: A Study of Protest and Inversion in the Carnival of Post-Emancipation Trinidad." *Plantation Society in the Americas* 3, no. 1 (1990): 73–120.

Arceneaux, Pamela. "Guidebooks to Sin: The Blue Books of Storyville." *Louisiana History* 28 (Fall 1987): 397–405.

Arthur, Stanley Clisby. *Old New Orleans: A History of the Vieux Carre, Its Ancient and Historical Buildings.* New Orleans: Harmanson, 1936.

Auerbach, Nina. *Private Theatricals: The Lives of the Victorians.* Cambridge: Harvard University Press, 1990.

Baltzell, E. Digby. *The Protestant Establishment: Aristocracy and Caste in America.* New York: Random House, 1964.

Banes, Sally. *Dancing Women: Female Bodies on Stage.* New York: Routledge, 1998.

Bartlett, Larry. "Rex—A Century of Merriment." *Dixie Roto* 21 (February 1971): 8–11.

Bederman, Gail. *Manliness and Civilization: A Cultural History of Gender and Race in the United States, 1880–1917.* Chicago: University of Chicago Press, 1995.

Bergeron, Arthur W., Jr. *Guide to Louisiana Confederate Military Units, 1861–1865.* Baton Rouge: Louisiana State University Press, 1989.

Bisland, Mary. "King Carnival in New Orleans." *Cosmopolitan,* February 1890, 469–78.

Blassingame, John. *Black New Orleans, 1860–1880.* Chicago: University of Chicago Press, 1973.

Brown, Kathleen M. *Good Wives, Nasty Wenches, and Anxious Patriarchs: Gender, Race, and Power in Colonial Virginia.* Chapel Hill: University of North Carolina Press, 1996.

Bull, Cynthia Jean Cohen. "Sense, Meaning, and Perception in Three Dance Cultures." In *Meaning in Motion: New Cultural Studies in Dance,* edited by Jane C. Desmond, 269–87. Durham, N.C.: Duke University Press, 1997.

Burt, Ramsay. *The Male Dancer: Bodies, Spectacle, Sexualities.* 2nd ed. New York: Routledge, 2007.

———. "Steve Paxton's 'Goldberg Variations' and the Angel of History." *TDR* 46, no. 4 (Winter 2002): 46–64.

Bushman, Richard L. *The Refinement of America: Persons, Houses, Cities.* New York: Knopf, 1992.

By Invitation Only. DVD. Directed by Rebecca Snedeker. New Orleans: Palmetto Pictures: 2006.

Bynum, Victoria E. *Unruly Women: The Politics of Social and Sexual Control in the Old South.* Chapel Hill: University of North Carolina Press, 1992.

Carnes, Mark C. *Secret Ritual and Manhood in Victorian America.* New Haven: Yale University Press, 1989.

Carter, Hodding, William Ransom Hogan, John W. Lawrence, and Betty Werlien Carter, eds. *The Past as Prelude: New Orleans, 1718–1968.* New Orleans: Tulane University, 1968.

Castle, Terry. *Masquerade and Civilization: The Carnivalesque in Eighteenth-Century English Culture and Fiction.* Stanford: Stanford University Press, 1986.

Celestin, Denise A. "Being Called Out: Ritual and Experience in the Mardi Gras Balls of New and Old New Orleans." In *Speaking of History: Dance Scholarship in the 90s,* 187–94. Riverside, Calif.: Society of Dance History Scholars, 1996.

Censer, Jane Turner. *The Reconstruction of White Southern Womanhood, 1865–1895.* Baton Rouge: Louisiana State University Press, 2003.

Chapman, Mary. "'Living Pictures': Women and *Tableaux Vivants* in Nineteenth-Century American Fiction and Culture." *Wide Angle* 18, no. 3 (1996): 22–52.

Cheung, Floyd D. "*Les Cenelles* and Quadroon Balls: 'Hidden Transcripts' of Resistance and Domination in New Orleans, 1803–1845." *Southern Literary Journal* 29 (1995): 5–16.

Claire, Elizabeth. "Women, Waltzing & Warfare: The Social Choreography of Revolution at the End of the Long 18th Century." Ph.D. diss., New York University, 2004.

Clark, Maribeth. "Understanding French Grand Opera through Dance." *Publicly Accessible Penn Dissertations.* Paper 955: 1998. http://repository.upenn.edu/cgi/viewcontent.cgi?article=2114&context=edissertations.

Clawson, Mary Ann. *Constructing Brotherhood: Class, Gender, and Fraternalism.* Princeton, N.J.: Princeton University Press, 1989.

Clinton, Catherine. "Scepter and Masque: Debutante Rituals in Mardi Gras New Orleans." In *Manners and Southern History,* edited by Ted Ownby, 76–96. Jackson: University Press of Mississippi, 2007.

Clinton, Catherine, and Nina Sibler, eds. *Battle Scars: Gender and Sexuality in the American Civil War.* New York: Oxford University Press, 2006.

Confederate Southern Memorial Association. *History of the Confederate Memorial Associations of the South.* New Orleans: Graham, 1904.

Connelly, Thomas L. *The Marble Man: Robert E. Lee and His Image in American Society.* Baton Rouge: Louisiana State University Press, 1977.

Cook, Cita. "Women's Role in the Transformation of Winnie Davis into the Daughter of the Confederacy." In *Searching for Their Places: Women in the South across Four Centuries,* edited by Thomas H. Appleton Jr. and Angela Boswell, 144–60. Columbia: University of Missouri Press, 2003.

Cott, Nancy F. *The Bonds of Womanhood: "Woman's Sphere" in New England, 1780–1835.* New Haven: Yale University Press, 1977.

Couch, R. Randall. "The Public Masked Balls of Antebellum New Orleans: A Custom of Masque outside the Mardi Gras Tradition." *Louisiana History* 35, no. 4 (1994): 403–31.

Culpepper, Marilyn Mayer. *All Things Altered: Women in the Wake of the Civil War and Reconstruction.* Jefferson, N.C.: McFarland, 2002.

Davis, Susan G. *Parades and Power: Street Theatre in Nineteenth-Century Philadelphia.* Berkeley: University of California Press, 1986.

de Caro, Frank, and Tom Ireland. "Every Man a King: Worldview, Social Tension, and Carnival in New Orleans." In *Mardi Gras, Gumbo, and Zydeco,* edited by Marcia Gaudet and James C. McDonald, 26–41. Jackson: University Press of Mississippi, 2003.

DeLeon, T. C. *Our Creole Carnivals: Their Origin, History, Progress and Results.* Mobile: Gossip Printing, 1890.

DeMetz, Kaye. "Theatrical Dancing in Nineteenth-Century New Orleans." *Louisiana History* 21, no. 1 (Winter 1980): 23–42.

Desmond, Jane C. "Embodying Differences: Issues in Dance and Cultural Studies." In *Meaning in Motion: New Cultural Studies of Dance,* edited by Desmond, 29–54. Durham, N.C.: Duke University Press, 1997.

———. "Making the Invisible Visible: Staging Sexualities through Dance." Introduction to *Dancing Desires: Choreographing Sexualities On and Off the Stage*. Madison: University of Wisconsin Press, 2001.

Dodge, M. R. "Recollections of Mardi Gras." *Outing*, February 1886, 570–74.

Dow, Marguerite. "The Carnival in New Orleans." *Signet*, May 1923, 29–31.

Dufour, Charles L. *Krewe of Proteus: The First Hundred Years*. New Orleans: Krewe of Proteus, 1981.

Dufour, Charles L., and Leonard V. Huber. *If Ever I Cease to Love: One Hundred Years of Rex, 1872–1971*. New Orleans: School of Design, 1970.

Edmonson, Muro S. "Carnival in New Orleans." *Caribbean Quarterly* 4 (March–June 1956): 233–45.

Edwards, Laura. *Gendered Strife and Confusion: The Political Culture of Reconstruction*. Chicago: University of Illinois Press, 1997.

———. *Scarlett Doesn't Live Here Anymore: Southern Women in the Civil War Era*. Urbana: University of Illinois Press, 2000.

Elbert, Monika M. "Striking a Historical Pose: Antebellum Tableaux Vivants, 'Godey's' Illustrations, and Margaret Fuller's Heroines." *New England Quarterly* 75, no. 2 (June 2002): 235–75.

Emery, Lynne Fauley. *Black Dance: From 1619 to Today*. 2nd ed. Hightstown, N.J.: Princeton Book Company, 1988.

Enstad, Nan. *Ladies of Labor, Girls of Adventure: Working Women, Popular Culture, and Labor Politics at the Turn of the Twentieth Century*. New York: Columbia University Press, 1999.

Erenberg, Lewis. *Stepping Out: New York Nightlife and the Transformation of American Culture, 1890–1930*. Chicago: University of Chicago Press, 1981.

Fairfax, Edmund. *The Styles of Eighteenth-Century Ballet*. Lanham, Md.: Scarecrow, 2003.

Faust, Drew Gilpin. *Mothers of Invention: Women of the Slaveholding South in the American Civil War*. Chapel Hill: University of North Carolina Press, 1996.

Ferrari, Michelle. "American Experience: New Orleans." Transcript. Webpage created on December 1, 2006. www.pbs.org/wgbh/amex/neworleans/filmmore/pt.html.

Finnegan, Margaret. *Selling Suffrage: Consumer Culture and Votes for Women*. New York: Columbia University Press, 1999.

Flaherty, Peter. "Reading Carnival: Towards a Semiotics of History." *Clio* 15 (Summer 1986): 411–28.

Ford, Linda G. *Iron-Jawed Angels: The Suffrage Militancy of the National Woman's Party, 1912–1920*. New York: University Press of America, 1990.

Forman, William H., Jr. "William P. Harper and the Early New Orleans Carnival." *Louisiana History*, 14, no. 1 (1973): 40–47.

Fossier, Albert E. *New Orleans: The Glamour Period, 1800–1840.* New Orleans: Pelican, 1957.

Foster, Craig L. "Tarnished Angels: Prostitution in Storyville, New Orleans, 1900–1910." *Louisiana History* 31 (Winter 1990): 387–97.

Friend, Craig Thompson. "From Southern Manhood to Southern Masculinities: An Introduction." In *Southern Masculinities: Perspectives on Manhood in the South since Reconstruction,* edited by Friend and Lorri Glover. Athens: University of Georgia Press, 2009.

Gehman, Mary. *Women and New Orleans: A History.* New Orleans: Margaret Media, 1988.

Gehman, Mary, and Nancy Ries. *A History of Women in New Orleans.* New Orleans: Margaret Media, 1988.

Gill, James. *Lords of Misrule: Mardi Gras and the Politics of Race in New Orleans.* Jackson: University Press of Mississippi, 1997.

Gilmore, David D. *Carnival and Culture: Sex, Symbol, and Status in Spain.* New Haven: Yale University Press, 1998.

Glassberg, David. *American Historical Pageantry: The Uses of Tradition in the Early Twentieth Century.* Chapel Hill: University of North Carolina Press, 1990.

Golden, Eve. *Vernon and Irene Castle's Ragtime Revolution.* Lexington: University Press of Kentucky, 2007.

Guillory, Monique. "Some Enchanted Evening on the Auction Block: The Cultural Legacy of the New Orleans Quadroon Balls." Ph.D. diss., New York University, 1999.

Guillotte, Joseph V., III. "Every Man a King: Reflections on the Aesthetics of Ritual Rebellion in Mardi Gras." *Plantation Society in the Americas* 3, no. 1 (1990): 33–46.

Guren, Jay, and Richard Ugan. *Carnival Panorama: New Orleans Mardi Gras Medals and Krewes, 1884–1965.* New Orleans: Anderson, 1966.

Halttunen, Karen. *Confidence Men and Painted Women: A Study of Middle-Class Culture in America, 1830–1870.* New Haven: Yale University Press, 1982.

Hanna, Judith Lynne. *To Dance Is Human: A Theory of Nonverbal Communication.* Chicago: University of Chicago Press, 1987.

Hardy, Arthur. *Mardi Gras in New Orleans: An Illustrated History.* 2nd ed. Metairie, La.: Arthur Hardy, 2003.

Harris-Warrick, Rebecca, and Carol G. Marsh. *Musical Theatre at the Court of Louis XIV: Le Mariage de la Grosse Cathos.* New York: Cambridge University Press, 1994.

Hart, W. O. "Rights of Women in Louisiana." *Louisiana Historical Quarterly* 4 (1921): 437–58.

Hearn, Chester G. *When the Devil Came Down to Dixie: Ben Butler in New Orleans.* Baton Rouge: Louisiana University Press, 1997.

Hilkey, Judy. *Character Is Capital: Success Manuals and Manhood in Gilded Age America.* Chapel Hill: University of North Carolina Press, 1997.

Hilton, Wendy. *Dance and Music of Court and Theater: Selected Writings of Wendy Hilton.* New York: Pendragon, 1997.

Hirsch, Arnold R., and Joseph Logsdon, eds. *Creole New Orleans: Race and Americanization.* Baton Rouge: Louisiana State University Press, 1992.

Hogue, James K. *Uncivil War: Five New Orleans Street Battles and the Rise and Fall of Radical Reconstruction.* Baton Rouge: Louisiana State University Press, 2006.

Holmström, Kirsten Gram. *Monodrama, Attitudes, Tableaux Vivants: Studies on Some Trends of Theatrical Fashion, 1770–1815.* Stockholm: Almqvist and Wiksell, 1967.

Homans, Jennifer. *Apollo's Angels: A History of Ballet.* New York: Random House, 2010.

Hovet, Grace Ann, and Theodore R. Hovet. "*Tableaux Vivants:* Masculine Vision and Feminine Reflections in Novels by Warner, Alcott, Stowe, and Wharton." *American Transcendental Quarterly* 7, no. 4 (December 1993): 336–56.

Huber, Leonard V. "I Remember Mardi Gras." *New Orleans Magazine,* February 1972.

———. *Mardi Gras: A Pictorial History of Carnival in New Orleans.* Gretna, La.: Pelican, 2003.

———. "Mardi Gras: The Golden Age." *American Heritage* 16, no. 2 (1965): 16–23.

———. *Mardi Gras Invitations of the Gilded Age.* New Orleans: Upton Creative Printing, 1970.

———. *New Orleans: A Pictorial History.* New York: Crown, 1971.

Humphrey, Chris. *The Politics of Carnival: Festive Misrule in Medieval England.* Manchester: Manchester University Press, 2001.

Jabour, Anya. *Scarlett's Sisters: Young Women in the Old South.* Chapel Hill: University of North Carolina Press, 2007.

Jackson, Joy J. *New Orleans in the Gilded Age: Politics and Urban Progress, 1880–1896.* Baton Rouge: Louisiana State University Press, 1969.

Jewell, Edwin L., ed. *Jewell's Crescent City Illustrated: The Commercial, Social, Political, and General History of New Orleans, Including Biographical Sketches of Its Distinguished Citizens.* N.p., 1873.

Johnson, Kenneth R. "Kate Gordon and the Woman-Suffrage Movement in the South." *Journal of Southern History* 38, no. 3 (August 1972): 365–92.

Jonas, Gerald. *Dancing: The Pleasure, Power, and Art of Movement.* New York: Abrams, 1998.

Jones, Steven Swann. *The Fairy Tale: The Magic Mirror of Imagination.* New York: Twayne, 1995.

Kasson, John F. *Rudeness and Civility: Manners in Nineteenth-Century Urban America.* New York: Hill and Wang, 1990.

Katz, Ruth. "The Egalitarian Waltz." *Comparative Studies in Society and History* 15, no. 3 (June 1973): 368–77.

Kendall, Diana. *Members Only: Elite Clubs and the Process of Exclusion.* Lanham, Md.: Rowman and Littlefield, 2008.

Kendall, John. "The Carnival, Opera and the Drama." Chapter 45 of *History of New Orleans.* Chicago: Lewis, 1922. Reproduced online at: http://penelope.uchicago.edu/Thayer/E/Gazeteer/Places/America/United_States/Louisiana/New_Orleans/_Texts/KENHNO/45*.html.

———. *The Golden Age of the New Orleans Theater.* Baton Rouge: Louisiana State University Press, 1952.

Kernodle, George R. "Renaissance Artists in Service of the People: Political Tableaux and Street Theaters in France, Flanders, and England." *Art Bulletin* 25, no. 1 (March 1943): 59–64.

King, Grace. *New Orleans.* New York: Macmillan, 1895.

———. *New Orleans: The Place and the People.* Reprint, New York: Macmillan, 1907.

Kinser, Samuel. *Carnival, American Style: Mardi Gras at New Orleans and Mobile.* Photographs by Norman Magden. Chicago: University of Chicago Press, 1990.

Kmen, Henry. *Music in New Orleans: The Formative Years, 1791–1841.* Baton Rouge: Louisiana State Press, 1966.

———. "Singing and Dancing in New Orleans: A Social History of the Birth and Growth of Balls and Opera, 1791–1841." Ph.D. diss., Tulane University, 1961.

Komis, Benton Jay. "A Reading of Cultural Diversity: The Island New Orleans." Ph.D. diss., Harvard University, 1998.

Koolsbergen, William John. "A Study in Popular Culture—the New Orleans Mardi Gras: Formation of the Mistick Krewe of Comus and the Krewe of Rex." Ph.D. diss., City University of New York, 1989.

La Cour, Arthur Burton. *New Orleans Masquerade: Chronicles of a Carnival.* New Orleans: Pelican, 1952.

Laborde, Errol. "Behind the Mask of Mardi Gras: A Socio-Political Analysis of the Impact of a Large-Scale Festival on a Major Metropolitan Area." Master's thesis, Louisiana State University–New Orleans, 1971.

———. *Krewe: The Early New Orleans Carnival, Comus to Zulu.* New Orleans: Carnival, 2007.

———. *Marched the Day God: A History of the Rex Organization.* Metairie, La.: School of Design, 1999.

Lafargue, Andre. "Opera in New Orleans in Days of Yore." *Louisiana Historical Quarterly* 29 (1946): 660–78.

Leathem, Karen Trahan. "'A Carnival According to Their Own Desires': Gender and Mardi Gras in New Orleans, 1870–1941." Ph.D. diss., University of North Carolina at Chapel Hill, 1994.

———. "Women on Display: The Gendered Meanings of Carnival in New Orleans, 1870–1900." *Locus* 5, no. 1 (Fall 1992): 1–18.

Lee, Carol. *Ballet in Western Culture: A History of its Origins and Evolution.* New York: Routledge, 2002.

Lee-Riffe, Nancy M. "The Role of Country Dance in the Fiction of Jane Austen." *Women's Writing* 5, no. 1 (1998): 103–12.

Letellier, Robert, ed. *The Ballets of Daniel-Francois-Esprit Auber.* Newcastle upon Tyne: Cambridge Scholars, 2011.

Levy, Russell. "Of Bards and Bawds: New Orleans Sporting Life before and during the Storyville Era, 1897–1917." Master's thesis, Tulane University, 1967.

Lewis, Robert. "Domestic Theater: Parlor Entertainments as Spectacle, 1840–1880." In *Ceremonies and Spectacles: Performing American Culture,* edited by Teresa Alves, Teresa Cid, and Heinz Ickstadt, 48–62. Amsterdam: VU University Press, 2000.

———. "Tableaux Vivants: Parlor Theatricals in Victorian America." *Revue Française d'Études Américaines* 36 (April 1988): 280–91.

Lindig, Carmen. *The Path from the Parlor: Louisiana Women, 1879–1920.* Lafayette: Center for Louisiana Studies, 1986.

Long, Alecia P. *The Great Southern Babylon: Sex, Race, and Respectability in New Orleans, 1865–1920.* Baton Rouge: Louisiana State University, 2005.

Loomis, Frank L. *A History of the Carnival and New Orleans Illustrated.* New Orleans: American Printing, 1905.

MacAloon, John J. Introduction to *Rite, Drama, Festival, Spectacle: Rehearsals toward a Theory of Cultural Performance,* edited by MacAloon. Philadelphia: Institute for the Study of Human Issues, 1984.

Maddux, Kristy. "When Patriots Protest: The Anti-Suffrage Discursive Transformation of 1917." *Rhetoric & Public Affairs* 7, no. 3 (Fall 2004): 283–310.

Magill, John. "The Dance Craze." *Historic New Orleans Collection Quarterly* 10 (Fall 1992): 8–9.

"Maginnis, Arthur Ambrose, Jr." In *Louisiana: Comprising Sketches of Parishes, Towns, Events, Institutions, and Persons, Arranged in Cyclopedic Form.* Vol. 3, edited by Alcée Fortier, 545–47. Century Historical Association, 1914.

Malnig, Julie. *Dancing till Dawn: A Century of Exhibition Ballroom Dance.* New York: Greenwood, 1992.

Malone, Bobbie. "New Orleans Uptown Jewish Immigrants: The Community of Congregation Gates of Prayer, 1850–1860." *Louisiana History* 32 (Summer 1991): 239–78.

Mancoff, Debra N., ed. *King Arthur's Modern Return.* New York: Garland, 1998.

Marks, Joseph E., III. *America Learns to Dance: A Historical Study of Dance Education in America before 1900.* New York: Exposition, 1957.

Marling, Karal Ann. *Debutante: Rites and Regalia of American Debdom.* CultureAmerica Series. Edited by Marling and Erika Doss. Lawrence: University Press of Kansas, 2004.

Mason, Peter. *Bacchanal! The Carnival Culture of Trinidad.* Philadelphia: Temple University Press, 1998.

McBee, Randy. *Dance Hall Days: Intimacy and Leisure among Working-Class Immigrants in the United States.* New York: New York University Press, 2000.

McCullough, Jack W. *Living Pictures on the New York Stage.* Ann Arbor: UMI Research Press, 1983.

McGowan, Philip. *American Carnival: Seeing and Reading American Culture.* Contributions to the Study of American Literature, No. 10. Westport, Ct.: Greenwood, 2001.

Miceli, Augusto P. *The Pickwick Club of New* Orleans. 2nd ed. New Orleans: Pickwick, 1964.

"Mistick Krewe of Comus." *DeBow's Review,* March/April 1870, 253–62.

Mitchell, Reid. *All on a Mardi Gras Day: Episodes in the History of New Orleans Carnival.* Cambridge: Harvard University Press, 1995.

Montgomery, Maureen E. *Displaying Women: Spectacles of Leisure in Edith Wharton's New York.* New York: Routledge, 1998.

Morazan, Ronald R. "'Quadroon' Balls in the Spanish Period." *Louisiana History* 14 (1973): 310–15.

Morton, Alice Elizabeth. "Three Mardi Gras Rex Queen Gowns: An Evolution from 1930–1960." Master's thesis, Louisiana State University Agricultural and Mechanical College, 1985.

Mulvey, Laura. "Visual Pleasure and Narrative Cinema." *Screen* 16, no. 3 (Autumn 1975): 6–18.

Nevile, Jennifer. *The Eloquent Body: Dance and Humanist Culture in Fifteenth-Century Italy.* Bloomington: Indiana University Press, 2004.

Novack, Cynthia J. "Looking at Movement as Culture: Contact Improvisation to Disco." *TDR* 32, no. 4 (Winter 1988): 102–19.

O'Brien. Rosary Hartel. "The New Orleans Carnival Organizations: Theatre of Prestige." Ph.D. diss., University of California, Los Angeles, 1973.

Ott, Victoria E. *Confederate Daughters: Coming of Age during the Civil War.* Carbondale: Southern University Illinois Press, 2008.

Peiss, Kathy. *Cheap Amusements: Working Women and Leisure in Turn-of-the-Century New York.* Philadelphia: Temple University Press, 1986.

Perry, Elisabeth Israels. "'The General Motherhood of the Commonwealth': Dance Hall Reform in the Progressive Era." *American Quarterly* 37, no. 5 (Winter 1985): 719–33.

Prevots, Naima. *American Pageantry: A Movement for Art & Democracy.* Theatre and Dramatic Studies Series 61. Ann Arbor: UMI Research Press, 1990.

Pugh, Tison. *Queer Chivalry: Medievalism and the Myth of White Masculinity in Southern Literature.* Baton Rouge: Louisiana State University Press, 2013.

Raabe, Phyllis Hutton. "Status and Impact: New Orleans' Carnival, the Social Upper Class and Upper-Class Power." Ph.D. diss., Pennsylvania State University, 1973.

Reinders, Robert C. *End of an Era: New Orleans, 1850–1860.* New Orleans: American Printing, 1964.

———. "Slavery in New Orleans in the Decade before the Civil War." In *Plantation Town and Country: Essays on the Local History of American Slave Society,* edited by Elinor Miller and Eugene Genovese, 365–76. Chicago: University of Illinois Press, 1974.

Remedi, Gustavo. *Carnival Theater: Uruguay's Popular Performers and National Culture.* Translated by Amy Ferlazzo. Cultural Studies of the Americas, vol. 15. Minneapolis: University of Minnesota Press, 2004.

Ribeiro, Aileen. "The Old and New Worlds of Mardi Gras." *History Today* [Great Britain] 36 (February 1986): 30–35.

Rightor, Henry, ed. *The Standard History of New Orleans.* Chicago: Lewis, 1900.

Robbins, Peggy. "Where Carnival Is King." *American History Illustrated* 13, no. 10 (1979): 4–11, 46–49.

Robinson, Lura. *It's an Old New Orleans Custom.* New York: Vanguard, 1948.

Rose, Al. *Storyville, New Orleans, Being an Authentic, Illustrated Account of the Notorious Red-Light District.* Tuscaloosa: University of Alabama Press, 1974.

Russo, Mary. *The Female Grotesque: Risk, Excess and Modernity.* New York: Routledge, 1995.

———. "Female Grotesques: Carnival and Theory." In *Feminist Studies/Critical Studies,* edited by Teresa de Laurentis, 213–29. Bloomington: Indiana University Press, 1986.

Ruvoldt, Maria. *The Italian Renaissance Imagery of Inspiration: Metaphors of Sex, Sleep, and Dreams.* Cambridge: Cambridge University Press, 2004.

Ruyter, Nancy Lee Chalfa. "Antique Longings: Genevieve Stebbins and American Delsartean Performance." In *Corporealities: Dancing Knowledge, Culture and Power,* edited by Susan Leigh Foster, 72–91. New York: Routledge, 1995.

———. *The Cultivation of Body and Mind in Nineteenth-Century American Delsartism.* Westport, Ct.: Greenwood, 1999.

———. "The Genteel Transition: American Delsartism." In *Reformers and Visionaries: The Americanization of the Art of Dance,* 16–30. New York: Dance Horizons, 1979.

Ryan, Mary P. "The American Parade: Representations of the Nineteenth-Century Social Order." In *The New Cultural History,* edited by Lynn Hunt, 131–53. Berkeley: University of California Press, 1990.

Saxon, Lyle. *Fabulous New Orleans.* New York: Century, 1928.

Scanlon, Joan, and Richard Kerridge. "Spontaneity and Control: The Uses of Dance in Late Romantic Literature." *Dance Research: The Journal of the Society for Dance Research 6,* no. 1 (Spring 1988): 30–44.

Schindler, Henri. *Mardi Gras: New Orleans.* New York: Flammarion, 1997.

———. *Mardi Gras Treasures: Costume Designs of the Golden Age.* Gretna, La.: Pelican, 2002.

———. *Mardi Gras Treasures: Invitations of the Golden Age.* Gretna, La.: Pelican, 2000.

———. *Mardi Gras Treasures: Jewelry of the Golden Age.* Gretna, La.: Pelican, 2006.

Schneider, Gretchen. "Using Nineteenth-Century American Social Dance Manuals. *Dance Research Journal 14,* no. 1 & 2 (1981–82): 39–42.

Schott, Matthew J. "Death of Class Struggle: End of Louisiana History?" *Louisiana History 31* (Winter 1990): 349–71.

Schuler, Kathryn Reinhart. "Women in Public Affairs in Louisiana during Reconstruction." *Louisiana Historical Quarterly 19* (July 1936): 668–750.

Scott, Anne Firor. *The Southern Lady: From Pedestal to Politics, 1830–1930.* Chicago: University of Chicago Press, 1970.

Sibler, Nina. "When Charles Francis Adams Met Robert E. Lee: A Southern Gentleman in History and Memory." In *Inside the Confederate Nation: Essays in Honor of Emory M. Thomas,* edited by Lesley J. Gordon and John C. Inscoe, 349–60. Baton Rouge: Louisiana State University Press, 2005.

Sklar, Deidre. "Five Premises for a Culturally Sensitive Approach to Dance." In *Moving History/Dancing Cultures: A Dance History Reader,* edited by Ann Dils and Ann Cooper Albright, 30–32. Middletown, Ct.: Wesleyan University Press, 2001.

Smith, Karen Manners. "Half My Heart in Dixie: Southern Identity and the Civil War in the Writings of Mary Virginia Terhune." In *Beyond Image and Convention: Explorations in Southern Women's History,* edited by Janet L. Coryell et al., 119–37. Columbia: University of Missouri Press, 1998.

Smith, Michael P. "New Orleans' Carnival Culture from the Underside." *Plantation Society in the Americas* 3, no. 1 (1990): 11–32.

Smith, Thomas Ruys. "'Oh, weep for New Orleans!': Civil War and Reconstruction." Chap. 4 of *Southern Queen: New Orleans in the Nineteenth Century*. London: Continuum, 2011.

Smith-Rosenberg, Carroll. *Disorderly Conduct: Visions of Gender in Victorian America*. New York: Knopf, 1985.

Snitow, Ann, Christine Stansell, and Sharon Thompson, eds. *Powers of Desire: The Politics of Sexuality*. New York: Monthly Review Press, 1983.

Somers, Dale A. "Black and White in New Orleans: A Study in Urban Race Relations, 1865–1900." *Journal of Southern History* 40 (February 1974): 19–42.

Souther, Jonathan Mark. *New Orleans on Parade: Tourism and the Transformation of the Crescent City*. Baton Rouge: Louisiana State University Press, 2006.

Sponsler, Claire. *Ritual Imports: Performing Medieval Drama in America*. Ithaca, N.Y.: Cornell University Press, 2004.

Stearns, Marshall, and Jean Stearns. *Jazz Dance: The Story of American Vernacular Dance*. Updated ed. New York: DaCapo, 1994.

Steele, Valerie. *Fashion and Eroticism: Ideals of Feminine Beauty from the Victorian Era to the Jazz Age*. New York: Oxford University Press, 1985.

Stovel, Nora. "'Every Savage Can Dance': Choreographing Courtship." *Persuasions* 23 (2001): 29–49.

Strong, Roy. *Art and Power: Renaissance Festivals, 1450–1650*. Berkeley: University of California Press, 1973.

———. *Splendor at Court: Renaissance Spectacle and the Theater of Power*. Boston: Houghton Mifflin, 1973.

"Susan and Charles Zambito: 1410 Jackson Avenue." *Preservation in Print* 27, no. 10 (December 2000): 31–32.

Swerdlow, Amy. *Women Strike for Peace: Traditional Motherhood and Radical Politics in the 1960s*. Chicago: University of Chicago Press, 1993.

Tallant, Robert. *The Romantic New Orleanians*. New York: Dutton, 1950.

———. *Mardi Gras . . . As It Was*. Reprint, Gretna, La.: Pelican, 1989.

Tandon, Bharat. *Jane Austen and the Morality of Conversation*. London: Anthem, 2003.

Taplin, Oliver. "Tableaux, Noises, and Silences." In *Greek Tragedy in Action*, by Taplin. New York: Routledge, 2003.

Thesander, Marianne. *The Feminine Ideal*. Translated by Nicholas Hill. London: Reaktion, 1997.

Thomas, Emory M. *Robert E. Lee: A Biography*. New York: Random House, 2000.

Thomas, Helen. *The Body, Dance and Cultural Theory.* New York: Palgrave Macmillan, 2003.

Thompson, Allison. "The Felicities of Rapid Motion: Jane Austen in the Ballroom." *Persuasions: The Jane Austen Journal On-Line* 21, no. 1 (Winter 2000). www.jasna .org/persuasions/on-line/vo121no1/thompson.html.

Thompson, Robert Farris. "An Aesthetic of the Cool." *African Arts* 7, no. 1 (Autumn 1973): 40–43, 64, 67, 89–91.

———. "An Aesthetic of the Cool: West African Dance." *African Forum* 2 (Fall 1966): 85–102.

Tickner, Lisa. *The Spectacle of Women: Imagery of the Suffrage Campaign, 1907–14.* Chicago: University of Chicago Press, 1988.

Tinker, Frances, and Edward Larocque Tinker. *Old New Orleans: Mardi Gras Masks (The Nineties).* New York: D. Appleton, 1931.

Tomko, Linda. *Dancing Class: Gender, Ethnicity, and Social Divides in American Dance, 1890–1920.* Bloomington: Indiana University Press, 1999.

Tregle, Joseph G., Jr. "Creoles and Americans." In *Creole New Orleans: Race and Americanization,* edited by Arnold R. Hirsch and Joseph Logsdon, 131–85. Baton Rouge: Louisiana State University Press, 1992.

———. "Early New Orleans Society: A Reappraisal." *Journal of Southern History* 18 (February 1952): 20–36.

Turner, Victor. *The Anthropology of Performance.* New York: PAJ, 1988.

———. *From Ritual to Theatre: The Human Seriousness of Play.* New York: PAJ, 1982.

Tyler, Pamela. *Silk Stockings and Ballot Boxes: Women and Politics in New Orleans, 1920–1963.* Athens: University of Georgia Press, 1996.

Van Hook, Bailey. *Angels of Art: Women and Art in American Society, 1876–1914.* University Park: Pennsylvania State University Press, 1996.

Veblen, Thorstein. *The Theory of the Leisure Class.* Boston: Houghton Mifflin, 1973.

Vennman, Barbara. "Boundary Face-Off: New Orleans Civil Rights Law and Carnival Tradition." *TDR* 37, no. 3 (Autumn 1993): 76–109.

Waldo, J. Curtis. *History of the Carnival in New Orleans from 1857 to 1882.* New Orleans: L. Graham & Son, 1882.

Warner, Marina. *Monuments & Maidens: The Allegory of Female Form.* London: Weidenfeld and Nicholson, 1985.

Watts, Trent, ed. *White Masculinity in the Recent South.* Baton Rouge: Louisiana State University Press, 2008.

Wheeler, Marjorie Spruill. *New Women of the New South: The Leaders of the Woman Suffrage Movement in the Southern States.* New York: Oxford University Press, 1993.

Whites, LeeAnn. *The Civil War as a Crisis in Gender: Augusta, Georgia, 1860–1890.* Athens: University of Georgia Press, 1995.

———. "'Stand by Your Man': The Ladies Memorial Association and the Reconstruction of Southern White Manhood." In *Women of the American South: A Multicultural Reader,* edited by Christie Anne Farnham, 133–49. New York: New York University Press, 1997.

Wickiser, Ralph, Caroline Durieux, and John McCrady. *Mardi Gras Day.* New York: Henry Holt, 1948.

Williams, Karen Luanne. "Images of Uneasy Hybrids: Carnival and New Orleans." Ph.D. diss., Emory University, 1992.

Wilson, Cheryl A. "Dance, Physicality, and Social Mobility in Jane Austen's *Persuasion.*" *Persuasions* 25 (2003): 55–75.

Winter, Marian Hannah. "Juba and American Minstrelsy." In *Chronicles of the American Dance: From the Shakers to Martha Graham,* edited by Paul Magriel, 39–63. New York: Henry Holt, 1948.

Wolff, Janet. "Reinstating Corporeality: Feminism and Body Politics." In *Meaning in Motion: New Cultural Studies of Dance,* edited by Jane C. Desmond, 81–99. Durham, N.C.: Duke University Press, 1997.

Wyatt-Brown, Bertram. *Southern Honor: Ethics and Behavior in the Old South.* New York: Oxford University Press, 1982.

Young, Perry. *Carnival and Mardi-Gras in New Orleans.* New Orleans: Harmanson's, 1939.

———. *The Mistick Krewe: Chronicles of Comus and His Kin.* New Orleans: Carnival, 1931.

INDEX

Addison, Lloyd Dulaney, 22

admit cards, 31, 33, 36, 45, 187

animal dances, 142–46; and class tensions, 149; and open exploration of sexuality, 143, 145; and racial tensions, 72–73, 145; and reform, 143–44, 150; turkey trot, 142–43, 146

Athenaeum, 41

Baby Dolls, 156

Ball of the Two Well-Known Gentlemen, 153

balls: *bals de bouquet,* 17; *bals de roi,* 17, 23; charity, 58, 112, 203; and class distinctions, 14, 47; debutante coming out, 97–98; French, 8, 153–55; in Georgian England, 137; private, 1–2, 4, 12, 14, 17, 19, 21, 26, 56, 137, 155, 159; public, 12–13, 16, 53; society/subscription, 17; as stabilizing agent, 6, 13

Battle of Liberty Place, 66

Behan, Bessie, 36–37, 50

"black coats," 49, 135

blue books, 154, 212

bonds of brotherhood, 65, 104

Buckner family, 98, 100–101, 163–64, 171

call-outs, 29, 35, 42, 46, 115, 121, 134–36, 140–41, 159

captain, 3–4, 23–24, 31–38, 42–43, 60–62, 91, 102–4, 140

Castle, Irene, 146–50

Castle, Vernon, 146–50

Chicago Glide, 157, 213

chivalry, 16, 55–56, 65–66, 82, 89

Churchill, Charles H., 22

Civil War, 2, 8, 20–23, 26–27, 64–65, 72, 95, 101, 111, 150, 153, 159

Collins, Dorothy Spencer, 37–39, 109

Comus, Mistick Krewe of (MKC): "The Aryan Race" (1877), 74–75, 172, 199; "The Demon Actors in Milton's *Paradise Lost*" (1857), 59, 172; "Dreams of Homer" (1872), 1, 78, 172, 179; "The English Holidays" (1859), 60, 172; "The History of Louisiana from 1539 to 1815" (1870), 79, 172; "Illustrated Ireland" (1884), 91, 172; "The Missing Links to Darwin's Origin of Species" (1873), 68–71, 141, 172; "Nippon: The Land of the Rising Sun" (1892), 61–62, 92, 99, 171, 172; "Salammbo" (1893), 88, 172; "Scenes from the *Metamorphoses* of Ovid" (1878), 83, 172; "Statues of the Great Men of Our Country" (1860), 60, 66, 79, 172; "The Visit of Envoys from the Old World and New to the Court of Comus" (1874), 86, 172 costumes, 10–11, 24, 29, 31–32, 35–36, 43, 49–50, 54, 104, 120, 124, 134–35, 140–41, 159, 187

cotillion, 12, 97, 119, 201

Cotton Exchange, 24, 67, 100, 109

Cowbellian de Rankin Society, 21

Creoles, 17–21, 41, 76, 114, 120, 153, 183–85; and gossip, 45; and intermarriage, 19, 158, 185, 195; and racism, 14, 19

cup bearer, 36

dance cards, 33, 128, *129, 130,* 151, 160, 201, 207, 211

dance halls, 143–45, 149–50

dance manuals, 7, 106, 128, 136, 138, 146, 207, 209

Davis, Jefferson, 91–92, 99

Davis, Varina "Winnie," 91–93, 96

debutantes: coming-out balls, 97–98; empowerment through dance, 75, 111, 123, 160, 199; and marriage market, 94, 105, 114, 200; New Orleans, 96; New York City, 14, 46–47, 57, 97–100, 146, 148; as reflection of father's reputation, 40, 98, 122; selection as queen, 28, 38, 55, 96; social season of, 3–8, 12, 97, 200; training for krewe court, 39–40, 106, 148

decorations, 32, 42, 60

Delsartism, 7, 57–58, 181

Downman, Sadie, 37, 58

Dufour, Charles "Pie," 148

Dufour, Willie, 37–38

duke, 1, 27, 36, 56, 92, 95, 116, 139, 155, 160

Duncan, Isadora, 58, 105

Ellison, Joseph, 22–23

Ellison, William, 22–23

etiquette, 3–5, 14, 39–41, 45, 140, 146, 160; manuals, 3, 107

Eustis, Gladys, 149, 164

Exposition Hall, 41, 44, 96

Fairchild, Lydia, 139

favors, 33, 135

Fearn, Mrs. Walker, 96

Finley, Lydia, 51

floor committee, 135

Flower, Walter C., 67

Fox, Maud, 148

foxtrot, 150–51, 211–12

French balls, 8, 153–55

French Opera House, 3, 41–46, 55, 89, 91, 124, 139, 143, 155

Gaiety Theatre, 10

"gas light rule," 138

gâteau des roi, 17, 188

general dancing, 8, 125–39, 162; and courtship, 15, 28, 126, 132, 136–39; and emergence of tableaux societies, 125; and generational shifts, 142, 145; and old-line marriages, 142

german (dance), 97, 201

glide, 129–31, 150

Golden, Bertha, 154

grand march (polonaise), 7–9, 18, 29, 42–45, 60, 62, 78, 88, 91–123, 141, 155–60; curtsies, 3, 7, 41, 104, 106, 109–10, 121, 123; double grand march, 4, 104; emphasis on courtliness, 104, 159; in nineteenth-century balls, 3, 7, 129, 132; and polished pedestrian, 94, 105–7, 110, 123, 160, 199; and subservience, 109–10

Grand Opera House, 3, 41

Grand Shadow Dance, 155

guests: arrival, 44–45; *costume de rigueur,* 49; and fashion, 44, 47–48, 53; gossiping, 45–47, 53, 127, 136; seating, 29, 46, 134–35, 189

Gustave III (Le bal masqué), 18

Halliday, Josie, 39, 50

Hayne, Franklin B., 109

heel and toes (dance), 129
Hennessy, David, 153; investigation, 67, 194n42
Hill, D. H., 91–92
Hill, Nannie, 91, 96
Howard, Frank T., 139

invitation, 27, 30–36, 43, 48, 157, 159, 187, 207; committee, 33, 35

Jackson, Julia, 91, 96
Jackson, Stonewall, 91
Janvier, Charles, 67
Janvier, George, 38, 187
Jefferson City Buzzards, 157

king, 1, 36–37, 49–50, 62–65, 90–98, 101–4, 115–16, 139–41, 155, 160–61; of Carnival (Rex), 7, 24, 36, 109, 139; crowned, 17; marrying queen, 139; reigning, 4, 24, 28, 50, 92, 95, 110; self-proclaimed, 26–27
Knight, Wiley, 156
Krewe of Proteus: "E Pluribus Unum" (1899), 86, 177; "Sherwood" (1916), 89, 178
Krewe of Venus, 115
krewesmen, 2, 8, 11, 20, 24–29, 30–54, 55–90, 92–95, 102–23, 124–27, 134–37, 140–52, 153–62, 188, 207, 213

Ladies Memorial Association (LMA), 112
La Salle Conde, 16
Leathem, Karen Trahan, 26, 63, 83, 101, 110–11, 122, 132, 154, 157
Lee, Mary, 91, 96
Lee, Mildred, 91–92, 96
Lee, Robert E., 81, 91
Les Mysterieuses, 114–16
Lord High Chamberlain, 56
Lost Cause movement, 64–65, 92, 112, 160
Louis XIV, 86, 103, 106, 120

Maginnis, Josephine, 99–100, 167
maid, 1, 28, 36–42, 53, 56, 89, 92–100, 107–16, 121–25, 134–39, 149, 160, 170, 185, 188, 189, 202, 211
Markle, Mary Orme, 99, 114
masking, 1, 19, 26, 140–41, 153–58, 161, 189; ban, 12–13, 182
mazurka, 12, 128–29, 207
McStea, Elise, 96
Merriam, A. W., 22–23
minstrelsy, 72, 196
minuet, 12, 15, 132
Mitchell, Reid, 12, 68, 69, 92, 110, 183, 186
Mittens, the, 115
Momus, Knights of, 1, 23, 37, 55, 179; "The Coming Races (Entwicklungsgeschichte)" (1873), 68–69, 72, 175; "A Dream of Fair Women" (1880), 76–77, 176; "Hades: A Dream of Momus" (1877), 73, 176, 196; "Legends from the Court of King Arthur" (1900), 89, 176; "Palmer Cox's Brownies" (1891), 60, 176; "The Passions" (1884), 139, 176
Municipal Reform League, 67, 194
Mystic Maids, the, 115

Newport (waltz), 129

octoroon, 154
Odd Fellows Hall, 154
one-step, 7, 138–39, 149–51
Order No. 76, 111
Original Illinois Club, 156, 213

page, 36, 95
pageants:
    "The Aryan Race" (Comus, 1877), 74–75, 172, 199
    "The Coming Races (Entwicklungsgeschichte)" (Momus, 1873), 68–69, 72, 175

pageants (*continued*):
  "The Demon Actors in Milton's *Paradise Lost*" (Comus, 1857), 59, 172
  "A Dream of Fair Women" (Momus, 1880), 76–77, 176
  "Dreams of Homer" (Comus, 1872), 1, 78, 172, 179
  "The English Holidays" (Comus, 1859), 60, 172
  "E Pluribus Unum" (Proteus, 1899), 86, 177
  "Hades: A Dream of Momus" (Momus, 1877), 73, 176, 196
  "The History of Louisiana from 1539 to 1815" (Comus, 1870), 79, 172
  "Illustrated Ireland" (Comus, 1884), 91, 172
  "The Kingdom of Flowers" (TNR, 1884), 139, 173
  "The Land of Frontinback and Upondown" (Consus, 1906), 124, 141
  "Legends from the Court of King Arthur" (Momus, 1900), 89, 176
  "The Missing Links to Darwin's Origin of Species" (Comus, 1873), 68–71, 141, 172
  "Nippon: The Land of the Rising Sun" (Comus, 1892), 61–62, 92, 99, 171, 172
  "Palmer Cox's Brownies" (Momus, 1891), 60, 176
  "The Passions" (Momus, 1884), 139, 176
  "Salammbo" (Comus, 1893), 88, 172
  "Scenes from the *Metamorphoses* of Ovid" (Comus, 1878), 83, 172
  "Sherwood" (Proteus, 1916), 89, 178
  "Statues of the Great Men of Our Country" (Comus, 1860), 60, 66, 79, 172
  "The Visit of Envoys from the Old World and New to the Court of Comus" (1874), 86, 172

"The World of Audubon" (TNR, 1873), 1, 68, 72, 173
pavan, 102
Pickwick Club, 23, 99, 180, 185
Poitevent, Emily, 107–9
polonaise. *See* grand march
Pope, J. H., 22–23

quadrille, 2, 7–9, 12, 17–18, 29, 91–123, 126–36, 145, 156, 160, 181, 184; formal movement style, 120; lancers, 103, 120–21, 129, 201; Saratoga, 129; as status symbol, 118
queen, 3–4, 25, 36–45, 50–58, 82, 88–90, 92–116, 121–25, 134, 139–40, 160–61, 170, 185; as afterthought, 101; of Carnival, 24, 36–38, 50, 58, 92, 94–95, 110, 121, 156, 206; of Comus, 37–39, 45, 51, 52, 92–93, 98–99, 104, 107–9, 110, 114; crowned, 17, 56, 153; jewels of, 32, 50, 53; of Proteus, 88, *113*; reigning, 4, 24, 28, 50, 92, 95, 110; selection of, 17, 28, 36–38, 55–56, 88

racquet, 129, 207
ragtime, 7–8, 126, 149–52, 161; animal dances, 142–46, 149; Argentine tango, 142–45; and the Castles, 146–50; and class tensions, 149; and dance halls, 143–45, 149–50; foxtrot, 150–51, 211–12; hesitation waltz, 143; maxixe, 143; one-step, 7, 138–39, 149–51; and open exploration of sexuality, 143, 145; and racial tensions, 72–73, 145; and reform, 143–44, 150; and Tango Belt, 144–45, 153; turkey trot, 142–43, 146
reception committee, 45, 207
Reconstruction, 8, 23–28, 55–90, 160–61; dance choices during, 126; end of, 25, 30, 65, 68; healing of, 24; krewes formed during, 23, 57; in Louisiana, 2
reel, 12, 129

rehearsals, 42–43

Rex, 4–8, 21, 32–39, 44, 48–50, 56, 67–68, 95–99, 104–9, 114, 125, 163–75; as King of Carnival, 7, 24, 36, 109, 139; semi-civic nature of, 1, 7, 23–25, 36, 191; as unique balls, 7–8, 24–25

Reynolds, Police Superintendent James W., 138–39, 144–45

Richardson, Susan "Susie," 92, 96, 168

royal maskers' dances, 94, 96, 116, 120, 127, 128, 134

Sander, Flora Ascott, 148

Schmidt, May, 51–53

schottisches, 129

Semmes, Myra, 139

Shakespeare, Joseph, 153, 194

Shaw, Franklin, Jr., 22–23

Spectacle de la rue St. Pierre, 13

Storyville, 8, 144, 153–55

tableau program, 47

tableaux societies, 125, 179; Atlanteans, 50, 149, 163–71; Consus, 124–25, 141, 149, 164–71; Elves of Oberon, 37, 114, 149, 163–71; High Priests of Mithras, 149, 171; Nereus, 149, 163–71

tableaux vivants, 7, 25, 42, 54, 125, 142, 153, 159; Armed Maiden in, 83–86; and Comus ball of 1857, 11, 28; and costumes, 55–90; and grotesque female characters, 73, 82; and marble men, 82–83, 90; and masculinity, 8, 65, 77, 89, 93, 150; neoclassical, 57, 60, 77, 87; and Reconstruction, 55–90; romantic, 77; stylized poses in, 9; and sublime goddesses, 82; and whiteness, 81; and women's rights, 71, 75, 90, 160

Tango Belt, 144–45, 153

Todd, S. M., 22

turkey trot, 142–43, 146

Twelfth Night Revelers (TNR), 7, 23, 28, 37–38, 61, 68–69, 88, 95–96, 149, 163–71, 179; "The Kingdom of Flowers" (1884), 139, 173; "The World of Audubon" (1873), 1, 68, 72, 173

two-step, 130–31, 150

ultra-elite Carnival families, 97–100, 121, 200, 201

von Meysenbug, Corinne, 114

Walker, Rita, 154

Walmsley, S. P. "Buzz," 37, 139

waltz, 5–8, 27, 29, 71, 126–38, 143–52, 157, 160–61; and democratic freedom, 132; deux-temps, 130–31; and exploration of desire, 133; galopade (gallop/galop), 12, 18, 128, 184; and patriarchal control, 132; polka, 128–31, 135; and trancelike abandon, 131, 138; two-step, 130–31, 150

Washington, George, 14, 15, 17, 66

Washington Artillery Hall, 41

White, Elizabeth, 114

"Woman Order" (General Orders No. 28), 111

World War I, 21, 32–33, 143, 146, 151, 155–58, 162

yorke, 129–30

Young, Perry, 10, 36, 115, 135–36, 142–43, 170–71, 175, 178, 180

Zulu Social Aid & Pleasure Club, 156